"Reith distills the literature on consumption and addiction into a biting, Laschian commentary on a system that encourages collective excess while celebrating the neoliberal ideal of individual responsibility. The result is a meticulous dissection of the cultural contradictions of a supercharged consumer capitalism that sorts, labels and blames failed managers of hedonism – the bingers, the obese, the machine gamblers – even as it empties their pockets."

David T. Courtwright, *author of*
Dark Paradise *and* Forces of Habit

"In an analysis informed by classic works of the sociological canon and some of the most important social theorists of the twentieth and twenty-first centuries, Reith masterfully excavates the complex social relations concealed by the various discourses of addiction, demonstrating how the meaning and expanding scope of addiction reflect the contradictions of our hyper-consumption society. Although this is a scholarly work, it is a must-read for any thoughtful person who feels a sense of disquiet about our modern preoccupation with consumer goods and the growing problems of addiction in contemporary society."

Stephen Lyng, *Professor of Sociology,*
Carthage College, USA

"Skilfully charting the intersection of longstanding debates about the cultural ambivalences surrounding modern consumerism with the more specialised debates concerning the medicalisation of addiction, Reith brilliantly demonstrates their profound and enduring relationships to one another. *Addictive Consumption* is a fascinating and important study. Indeed, a tour de force!"

Darin Weinberg, *Reader in Sociology, King's College,*
University of Cambridge, UK

"This book is a banquet of provocative ideas. Reading it, you'll find yourself wanting to underline every third sentence, better to remember what the author said and how she said it. Here's one thought to munch on: capitalism sets us the incompatible goals of being both champion producers and champion consumers. People who over-achieve as consumers (perhaps at the expense of their productivity) risk being accused of having an "addiction" – to eating, shopping, drinking, gambling, sex, and so on – variously explained and treated by pathology experts. The personal manifestations may vary, but they are all symptoms of a deeper social disorder: late capitalism. After reading this book, the notion of 'responsible gambling' will make about as much sense as the notion of 'responsible cannibalism'."

Lorne Tepperman, *Professor of Sociology,*
University of Toronto, Canada

"The publication of *Addictive Consumption* is a crucial and important development for social scientists involved in the field of addiction research. Professor Reith examines the 'shifting trajectories' of those commodities implicated in 'discourses of addiction' within a historical, socio-economic and political perspective. In so doing, she provides us with an essential understanding of the contradictory nature of contemporary health and public policy interventions directed at the individual, which stigmatize those in the most marginalized groups, while allowing the wider societal environment to continue encouraging excessive consumption."

Geoffrey Hunt, *Professor, Centre for Alcohol and Drug Research (CRF), School of Business and Social Sciences, University of Aarhus, Denmark*

"This book tells a fascinating story of excess and necessity, the inseparable extremities of consumption in capitalism, from colonial exploitation to neoliberalism. It describes how control theory has developed from repression to brain-based addiction. Commercial capitalism dematerializes consumption, fuels desires but individualizes responsibility. An indispensable gateway to key issues in contemporary society."

Pekka Sulkunen, *Professor Emeritus of Sociology, University of Helsinki, Finland, Past President, European Sociological Association*

ADDICTIVE CONSUMPTION

In this engaging new book, Gerda Reith explores key theoretical concepts in the sociology of consumption. Drawing on the ideas of Foucault, Marx and Bataille, amongst others, she investigates the ways in which understandings of 'the problems of consumption' change over time, and asks what these changes can tell us about their wider social and political contexts. Through this, she uses ideas about both consumption and addiction to explore issues around identity and desire, excess and control, reason and disorder. She also assesses how our concept of 'normal' consumption has grown out of efforts to regulate behaviour historically considered as disruptive or deviant, and how in the contemporary world the 'dark side' of consumption has been medicalised in terms of addiction, pathology and irrationality. By drawing on case studies of drugs, food and gambling, the volume demonstrates the ways in which modern practices of consumption are rooted in historical processes and embedded in geopolitical structures of power. It not only asks how modern consumer culture came to be in the form it is today, but also questions what its various manifestations can tell us about wider issues in capitalist modernity.

Addictive Consumption offers a compelling new perspective on the origins, development and problems of consumption in modern society. The volume's interdisciplinary profile will appeal to scholars and students in sociology, psychology, history, philosophy and anthropology.

Gerda Reith is Professor of Social Science in the School of Social and Political Sciences at the University of Glasgow, UK. Her research interests lie in the intersections of sociology, political economy, public health and psychology, with a particular focus on the substantive areas of consumption, risk and addiction. She has written and lectured extensively on the empirical and theoretical issues around these topics, and her work has been translated into a number of languages, including Korean, Chinese, Spanish and Hungarian. Her book, *The Age of Chance: Gambling in Western Culture* (Routledge) won the Philip Abrams Prize for the best book in sociology for 2000.

ADDICTIVE CONSUMPTION

Capitalism, Modernity and Excess

Gerda Reith

LONDON AND NEW YORK

First published 2019
by Routledge
2 Park Square, Milton Park, Abingdon, Oxon OX14 4RN

and by Routledge
711 Third Avenue, New York, NY 10017

Routledge is an imprint of the Taylor & Francis Group, an informa business

© 2019 Gerda Reith

The right of Gerda Reith to be identified as author of this work has been asserted in accordance with sections 77 and 78 of the Copyright, Designs and Patents Act 1988.

All rights reserved. No part of this book may be reprinted or reproduced or utilised in any form or by any electronic, mechanical, or other means, now known or hereafter invented, including photocopying and recording, or in any information storage or retrieval system, without permission in writing from the publishers.

Trademark notice: Product or corporate names may be trademarks or registered trademarks, and are used only for identification and explanation without intent to infringe.

British Library Cataloguing-in-Publication Data
A catalogue record for this book is available from the British Library

Library of Congress Cataloging-in-Publication Data
Names: Reith, Gerda, 1969- author.
Title: Addictive consumption : capitalism, modernity and excess / Gerda Reith.
Description: Abingdon, Oxon ; New York, NY : Routledge, 2018. | Includes bibliographical references and index.
Identifiers: LCCN 2018015260| ISBN 9780415268264 (hardcover) | ISBN 9780415268271 (pbk.) | ISBN 9780429464447 (ebook)
Subjects: LCSH: Consumption (Economics)—Social aspects. | Consumption (Economics)—Psychological aspects. | Consumer behavior. | Compulsive behavior.
Classification: LCC HC79.C6 R445 2018 | DDC 339.4/7—dc23
LC record available at https://lccn.loc.gov/2018015260

ISBN: 978-0-415-26826-4 (hbk)
ISBN: 978-0-415-26827-1 (pbk)
ISBN: 978-0-429-46444-7 (ebk)

Typeset in Bembo
by Apex CoVantage, LLC

*This book is dedicated to the memory of Andy,
and to our children, Alina, Harvey and Aidan,
who remember him with me*

The life of the dead is placed in the memory of the living
Cicero

CONTENTS

List of images xii
Acknowledgements xiii

Introduction: consumer capitalism and addiction 1
Consumer capitalism: identity, desire and excess 2
  Consumption and its discontents 3
Addiction and the commodity 6
Outline of the book 7

PART I
The shifting problem of consumption 11

1 Luxurious excess: the emergence of commodity culture 13
Introduction 13
The emergence of commodity culture 14
  'Psychoactive revolutions': colonialism, drug foods and power 14
  Mercantilism and slavery 15
  The trickle down of 'infinite desire' 16
The dualism of consumption: respectability and luxury 18
  Consumption, luxury and excess 19
    'A Chinese drug called tea' 22
    Coffee and tobacco: a 'eunuch's drink' and a 'filthie noveltie' 24
    From aqua vitae *to Gin Lane 26*
  Luxury, contagion and addiction 27
  Stimulating commodities and the spirit of capitalism 28
  Productive consumption: sugar 30
'Private vices, publick benefits': the transformation of luxury 31
End points 33

2 Industrial modernity: the birth of the addict — 35

Introduction 35
The nineteenth century: 'addictive modernity' 36
Addiction: disease of the will 38
'The great technology of power' 42
 The habits of the population: opium and the addicted 'others' 43
 Ethnicity: 'racialised others' 46
The disciplining of the will 48
The birth of the addict 50
End points 51

3 Intensified consumption and the expansion of addiction — 53

Introduction 53
The spread of consumerism: desire and excess 54
 Intensification, identity and desire 55
Freedom and governance 60
The expanding landscape of addiction 63
 From diseased wills to diseased brains: the rise of addiction neuroscience 64
 Diagnosing desire 67
 Making up addictions 67
 Addiction as metaphor 70
 Disordered identities and the proliferation of addictions 71
 Risky subjects 73
End points 74

PART II
Addictive consumptions: drugs, food, gambling — 77

4 Drugs: intoxicating consumption — 79

Introduction 79
Intoxication and governance 80
 Discipline and punish 82
Commodification, normalisation and the spread of intoxicating environments 83
 Commodifying Ecstasy 84
 Cannabis: from the counterculture to the mainstream 87
 Drugs 2.0: legal highs 88
 Alcohol and the night-time economy 89
Denormalisation and new forms of governance 91
 The governance of space and the mobilisation of morality 93
  The 'blacke stinking fumes' of smoking (and vaping) 93
  The binge drinkers of Gin Lane 97
End points 100

5 Food: embodied consumption   103

   Introduction 103
   'Big Food': overabundance, excess and waste 104
     Producing excess 104
     The manufacture of desire: craving and bliss 105
     Marketing junk 106
   Obesity, addiction, risk 108
     Addiction and mental disorder: food and neurochemical selfhood 109
     Food addiction: this is your brain on sugar 110
   The governance of consuming bodies 113
     Bodies in culture 113
     Bodies and brains 114
     The normalising logic of public health 116
     Technologies of the self: 'discipline is liberation' 117
     The hidden despotism of food 118
   Metaphorical bodies 119
     Obesity: excessive bodies 120
     Anorexia: regulated bodies 121
     Bulimia: wasteful bodies 122
   End points 123

6 Gambling: dematerialised consumption   125

   Introduction 125
   The gambling state 126
   Intensified consumption and the spread of aleatory environments 129
     Mobile and social: the new gambling landscape 131
     Poor gamblers 134
   The neurobiology of chance: risky technologies and addiction 135
     Neuroscience: the ghost in the (gambling) machine 136
     DSM-5 and the risky subject 137
     Governing risk 138
     Rage against the machine 140
   Dematerialised consumption and the disorders of chance 141
   End points 144

Afterword   146

   The shifting problem of consumption 146
   The contradictions of consumer capitalism 149
   Trajectories of excess 151
   Problematic pleasures 153

Bibliography   156
Index   173

IMAGES

I.1 View of Barbara Kruger's 'Untitled (I Shop Therefore I Am)', on display during the Whitney Biennial, New York, New York, 9 April 1987.   4
1.1 *Beware of Luxury* ('In Weelde Siet Toe') Painting by Jan Steen (1626–1679) 1663 Dim. 105 × 145 cm Kunsthistorisches Museum Vienna.   21
3.1 *Barbara Kruger, 'You want it, You buy it, You forget it' (2006).*   59
4.1 Ecstasy tablets.   85
4.2 Jennifer Lawrence for Dior Addict lipstick.   86

ACKNOWLEDGEMENTS

This book began as a series of lectures to my undergraduate class of students, and evolved, over many years, through invited talks and journal articles, into the form that it is in now. During its long gestation, thanks are due to a number of people, especially all those students whose enthusiastic engagement with the material encouraged me to keep working on the project, and to colleagues, who gave me space at the end to finish it.

I am also grateful for invitations to present some of the ideas in the book at various workshops and gatherings around the world, particularly Cornelius Torp, at the Munk School of Global Affairs, University of Toronto, Charles Livingstone, at the Centre for Social Inquiry at the University of La Trobe, Melbourne; Charles Picket at the Sydney Writers' Festival, Ceridwen Roberts from the *Myths and Realities* debates at the British Library, Phil Withington at the University of Sheffield and Sylvia Kairouz at Concordia, Montreal: feedback and discussion were always stimulating and helpful for refining my arguments.

Thanks to the *British Journal of Sociology* for parts of my articles: 'Consumption and its discontents: Addiction, identity and the problems of freedom' 2004, 55(2): 283–300, in Chapter 2 and Chapter 4, and for parts of 'Techno economic systems and excessive consumption: a political economy of "pathological" gambling' 2013, 64(4), 717–738, in Chapter 6.

Parts of 'Gambling and the contradictions of consumption: a genealogy of the pathological subject' were originally published in *American Behavioral Scientist* 2007, 51(1): 33–56.

Thanks also to friends and colleagues for ongoing discussion and distraction, as well as support; in particular to Heather Wardle, Fiona Dobbie, and Emma Casey. And to Andy, for everything.

INTRODUCTION

Consumer capitalism and addiction

On 10 January 2017, *The Birmingham Mail* reported on the case of Denise Clifford, a worker at a Coventry firm who had stolen £370,000 from her employers to fund a television shopping addiction. While her barrister noted that she had no 'need' for her purchases, which were either given away or hoarded in her spare bedroom, the judge who sentenced her appeared bemused by the 'worthless, useless items' that she bought, concluding, 'The benefit to you out of all this seems to be negligible; you've just got a lot of stuff'. Denise was given a suspended prison sentence and ordered to participate in unpaid work and therapy.

The previous year, the *Daily Mail* carried the story of Kathy O'Sullivan, whose six litre a day Coca-Cola habit cost her £2,000 a year, destroyed her health and led her to require blood transfusions. Speaking of her failed attempts to stop, she confessed to being 'terrified my Coke addiction will eventually kill me', and warned others to be aware just 'how quickly this sort of habit can ruin your life' (*The Daily Mail*, 24 January 2016).

In another narrative in Ohio, married father of three and respected businessman Scott Stevens was addicted to gambling. He played the same slot machine at his local casino every day for over a year, embezzling $7 million from his employer, emptying his families' saving account and his children's college fund. On 13 August 2012, when the money ran out, Scott drove to a local park, where he shot himself. His widow is now suing the casino for exploiting his addiction (*The State Journal*, 8 August 2014).

Over the same period of time as these reports, the supposedly 'addictive' aspects an ever-expanding roll call of commodities was being announced, with lurid stories about the dangers of caffeine and sugar, smartphones and video games. The provocative suggestion by scientists from the University of Michigan that cheese stimulates the same part of the brain as hard drugs launched a wave of tabloid headlines, and placed cheese in the same 'toxic' category as sugar. At the same time, the governments of Korea and China were busy creating 'boot camps' for young people addicted to smartphones and the Internet, with reports that some had been 'busted' for smuggling phones inside, and others attempting to 'break out' of the camps in search of an Internet café (Fifield 2016).

How have so many everyday forms of consumption become caught up in cautionary tales of addiction, suicide and ill health? What can these seemingly disparate stories about addiction tell us about consumption and, conversely, what do these images of consumption 'gone wrong' say about cultural ideas of addiction? This book sets out to explore these questions, asking why these kinds of narratives have become so resonant today, and what the relationships they express might tell us about wider social issues. As its starting point, it is based on the premise that consumption and addiction are powerful narratives of modernity. They each tell a story about the relationship we have with ourselves and with others, as well as about the way we interact with commodities. The stories they tell are very different, however. And, although the commodities and practices involved in both are interlinked, discourses of consumption seldom engage with those of addiction, and vice versa.

Over the following pages, this book attempts to bring them together. In doing so, it aims to explore how ideas about addiction and consumption evolve in relation to each other within the shifting socio-economic climates in which they are embedded. The argument put forward, broadly, is that ideas about addiction articulate long-running tensions around consumption, and particularly those relating to control: whether of individuals, populations, commodities or markets. Historically, consumption has been regarded as a potential threat to the individual as well as to the body politic, and as such, struggles around consumption can be said to articulate wider concerns around issues of desire and excess and impulse and reason as well as freedom and responsibility.

To begin, this introductory section sets out to locate some of the general themes of the book. It briefly outlines ideas about identity, desire and excess in modern consumer capitalism before moving on to look at the contradictory meanings of consumption itself, followed by their interaction with ideas about addiction.

Consumer capitalism: identity, desire and excess

Today, consumption is a global force as well as a site for new forms of social pathology. Driven by intersections between the neoliberal state and powerful transnational corporations, it plays a central role in the everyday lives of millions of individuals. In recent years, innovations in technological and financial systems, together with new styles of marketing, have generated a system of 'turbo' (Schor 2008) or 'hyper' (Ritzer 1999) consumption that is increasingly intense and pervasive. As a result, the reach of twenty-first century consumer culture is vast in scale: global yet intimate. The logos of corporate giants such as Facebook and Apple brand social space in their own image while apps and social media deliver personalised shopping tips direct to individuals' smartphones. This is the landscape of one-click buying and instant downloads, where the marketing of multinational corporations extends to the furthest parts of the world as well as the smartphone in your hand.

However, in a culture of super-sized foods and mobile gambling, the tropes of addiction are also expanding to encompass ever more types of consumption. The personal problems of people like Denise, Kathy and Scott are supplemented by reports of disordered consumption on a larger scale, with, for example, the rise of eating disorders in the Far East (Tsai 2000), Internet addiction ('wang yin') in China (Cao and Su 2006) and smartphone dependence in India (Davey and Davey 2014). As commodity culture spreads around the globe, ideas about addiction follow, like a comet dragging a tail of pathologies behind it.

In *The Romantic Ethic and the Spirit of Modern Consumerism* Colin Campbell (1987) described the key role played by consumption in driving the development of capitalism as well as forming particular types of subjectivity based around the quest for self-fulfilment, authenticity and pleasure. His approach can be described loosely as the 'Romantic tradition', in which the manipulation of commodities is conceived as a creative practice with a crucial role in the realisation of selfhood. This perspective is particularly relevant in terms of the historical shift to neoliberalism, in which sovereign individuals use consumption to create what Anthony Giddens (1991) describes as 'a narrative of the self'. In this perspective, with an increasing number of commodities and lifestyles on offer, and with almost limitless freedom to indulge in the temptations of consumer capitalism, the formation of identity can appear to be almost a matter of personal choice. As Ewen and Ewen (1982, 249) put it: 'There are no rules only choices . . . Everyone can be anyone'. Today, it seems as though a kind of liberating materialism has turned Cartesian dualism on its head, so that, as Barbara Kruger's iconic aphorism declares: 'I shop therefore I am' (see Image I.1).

The ideal of self-realisation through commodity exchange is a powerful cultural narrative, running through both the manipulations of marketing and the literary imagination alike. Don de Lillo captured the dynamic in his description of a shopping trip in *White Noise*, in which the protagonist, Jack Gladney, recalled:

> I shopped with reckless abandon. I shopped for its own sake, looking and touching, inspecting merchandise I had no intention of buying, then buying it. I began to grow in value and self-regard. I filled myself out, found new aspects of myself, located a person I'd forgotten existed.
>
> *(de Lillo 1985, 84)*

Gladney's stature filled out and expanded in the course of his impulsive spree, in a kind of symbolic extension of his selfhood that Russell Belk (1988) has described as the 'extended self'. This is an almost literal expression of the idea of material self-fulfilment, in the sense used by Melanie Klein to refer to a 'taking in' or 'filling up' of the self with 'good objects' (in Falk 1994, 130). In the case of Denise from Coventry, it is the taking in of 'just a lot of stuff'.[1]

Gladney's shopping trip was propelled by desire rather than need. However, it is a very particular concept of desire that is central to capitalism, and is one which, Campbell argues, does not actually aim to satisfy. Rather, its goal is to maintain a continual state of longing that is projected onto an ever-changing stream of new commodities and experiences and so, is, essentially, infinite. In this sense, modern consumers are characterised by what he describes as 'an insatiability which arises out of a basic inexhaustibility of wants themselves' (Campbell 1987, 104). In such accounts of consumerism, the modern self is fuelled by both endless desire and continual dissatisfaction: a dynamic that drives consumer capitalism to ever new heights and also produces, as its corollary, large amounts of waste. As Zygmunt Bauman (2007, 48), puts it, amongst other things, consumerism is 'an economics of waste and excess', where the discarded goods that fail to meet expectations fill up garbage bins just as quickly as novelties to replace them fill the shelves.

Consumption and its discontents

The dynamic of consumption is an ambivalent one, however. As well as a source of self-realisation, authenticity and desire, it can also be regarded as a site of danger and conflict, and this is especially so when its pleasures are associated with marginalised social groups. Some of this is historical, as we will see throughout the book, and the legacy of old ideas about

IMAGE I.1 View of Barbara Kruger's 'Untitled (I Shop Therefore I Am)', on display during the Whitney Biennial, New York, New York, 9 April 1987.

Source: Photo by Fred W. McDarrah/Getty Images.

excess, 'luxury', willpower and disorder. But some of it is new and represents uniquely modern responses to global commodity culture.

To explore this ambiguity further, we can note that the very notion of consumption is founded on a contradiction that stems from the etymology of the term itself. One root, from the Latin *consummare* has positive connotations: 'to make the sum' or 'sum up', as in to carry to completion, to perfect. This is related to the English *consummate*, and suggests an end point, a final achievement (in Williams 1982, 6). However, the other root, *consumere* means 'to make away with, to devour, waste, destroy' (OED 2003) and is associated with destruction and decay – whether of things, as in being consumed by fire, or bodies, as in the disease of tuberculosis, also known as consumption. The historian Phil Withington has noted that the etymology of the word consumption in English is complex, with the Anglo-Norman medical term *(consumpcion)* referring to an internal wasting of the body, alongside the Latin implications of wearing away, destruction and death, and quotes Samuel Johnson's definition of it as an 'act of consuming; waste; destruction' (in Withington 2017, 6). Withington also draws attention to the fact that consumption was a term of medical pathology long before it became an economic descriptor, but that its negative, medicalised meanings nevertheless persisted into the early seventeenth century, when it came to be have specialised meanings in political economy within an expanding capitalist system of production (2017, 8). According to Rosalind Williams, it is only since the beginning of the twentieth century that consumption has come to be associated with notions of enrichment and improvement (1982, 68).

The argument being made here, however, is that these contradictory meanings remain and, furthermore, that they reflect long-standing tensions in Western thought. Historically, these tensions have been concerned with the subjugation of excess and desire to the civilising effects of society and the taming of the unruly appetites of the body to the rational force of the mind. Within the classical Western canon, the exploration of such issues in writers from Aristotle and J. S. Mill to Freud and Weber have produced a privileging of the values of productivity, reason and control and have elevated ideals of the rational management of the self and the restraint of excess to universal ethical virtues. For example, in his essay *Civilization and Its Discontents* (1985 [1930]), Freud articulated the contradictory forces at work when he wrote that civilisation was created through restraint – was 'built up upon a renunciation of instinct' – a dynamic which was at the same time the source of tension, its discontents.

The issue of excess has been framed as especially problematic when linked with the poor, who have long been associated with the material side of Cartesian dualism: with embodied and, particularly, 'disorderly' habits (Bourdieu 1984). Although what George Bataille (1985) describes as the 'unproductive expenditures' of wasteful consumption has historically been regarded as a legitimate expression of status when carried out by elite groups, similar ostentation amongst the 'lower orders' has persistently been a source of fear and criticism. As Nietzsche put it, 'Excess is a reproach only against those who have no right to it' (1987, 124). And so, the consumption practices of the poor, rendered visible through their appearance, their diet and their everyday pleasures, have been consistently criticised for their dangerous or risky potential, their threats to health, their excess and poor taste (Skeggs 1997).

More recently, Daniel Bell has investigated the tensions within consumption in his analysis of *The Cultural Contradictions of Capitalism*. Bell's quote that 'one is to be a straight by day and a swinger by night' (1976, 92) expressed what he called the fundamental contradiction of capitalism: in essence, the conflict between a production-centred ethic and a consumption-based one. The former originated in the puritan work ethic of the bourgeoisie, based on calculative rationality, discipline and control, and the latter a consumerist hedonism based on the pursuit of instant gratification, self-expression and pleasure.[2]

It is suggested here that these tensions are embodied in consumption, which presents individuals with a paradox. On the one hand, they are encouraged to consume, to give in and abandon themselves to the pleasures of self-fulfilment; on the other, to exercise self-control and restraint. Surrounded by a dizzying display of commodities and experiences, they must steer a careful path: giving in to consumption, but not *too* much – never quite losing control. They must keep their consumer selves and their producer selves balanced in order to function in society – something that becomes increasingly difficult as the temptations and inducements of consumer culture increase on a global scale and as self-realisation increasingly becomes elevated to the status of individual 'right'. Such contradictory demands are articulated around ideas about addiction. In particular, the argument here is that ideas about 'addictive consumption' are actually cyphers for wider concerns about issues of governance and control – whether of individuals, commodities, markets or larger social groups – that are shifting and historically variable. Such claims will be explored both historically and through a series of case studies throughout the book. But first we turn to look in more detail at the concept of addiction itself.

Addiction and the commodity

The negative associations of consumption, *consumere*, as a force that can destroy the individual, have some resonance with the original meaning of 'addiction'. The latter derives from the Latin *addictus*, where it designated a kind of enslavement: 'To devote, make over; to surrender, to enslave' (Oxford Latin Dictionary 2012), or devotion 'bound or devoted (to someone)' (OED 2003). In Roman Law between the fifth and the third century BCE, those unable to repay their debts could be turned over to their creditors to be killed or sold as slaves, meaning an *addictus* was someone enslaved for debt or theft. The passive use of *addico* thus denoted subjection and enslavement as well as disgrace and loss of identity (Rosenthal and Faris 2016). However, by the first century BC, the sense of addiction had expanded to include the idea of excessive or inappropriate devotion to something – a meaning that was carried over into the early modern period, as in, for example, Thomas Hearne's (1698) description of Plato's early education as one in which he 'addicted himself to poetry' (Rosenthal and Faris 2016). We can see from these early, dualistic meanings that there is some convergence between the idea of consumption as a force that can destroy the individual with this framing of addiction as something that can enslave them.

From its origins in Roman Law, the concept of addiction has had a long and somewhat fragmented journey, with ideas from medicine and law, as well as religious beliefs about free will and autonomy, leaving their mark in different ways. In medicine, for example, the term denotes physiological dependence; in psychiatry, a mental disorder; legally, it tends to be discussed in terms of responsibility or culpability, whereas popular beliefs and media representations are made up of a range of moral, medical and mythical configurations in which addicts are sometimes regarded as victims, sometimes as criminals or simply as distinct 'types' of person. Furthermore, ideas, experiences and practices of addiction are changing and culturally specific, so much so that commentators have described the very concept of addiction as a 'shifting kaleidoscope' (Room 1998) or a 'shifting landscape' (Netherland 2012) that is characterised by 'conceptual acrobatics' (Reinarman 2005). However, it is also this very malleability that makes ideas about addiction a lens through which to view broader issues of social life – about pleasure, consumption and risk, and about control and free will – in modern capitalist societies.

Although notions of addiction are context specific and variable, I would argue that they also embody features that are intimately associated with capitalism. In this vein, Robin Room (1969) has written of the 'cultural framing of addiction' as an idea that is entwined with modern capitalist systems of globalisation, commodification and control, and whose meanings are subject to constant revision by political, medical and juridical forces. Although his analysis focused exclusively on drugs and alcohol, I would suggest that this kind of 'cultural framing' could be extended to encompass a wider range of commodities and experiences as well as ideas about addiction themselves, in ways that tell us something about consumer capitalism more generally.

In particular, the general idea of addiction brings us back to ideas about the commodity. In them, a substance or experience tends to be attributed with influential powers – no less than the ability to overwhelm the susceptible individual and transform them into something else entirely: an addict. As the bearer of these 'addictive' properties, the commodity appears to take on a life of its own and swallows up everything – reason, volition and autonomy – it comes into contact with. A useful point of departure here can be found in Marx's deconstruction of the commodity. In Volume One of *Capital*, he explains how its fetishisation as an inherently valuable natural object actually conceals the social relations that create it. He begins his analysis of capitalism with an analysis of the commodity form which, he writes, is a mysterious thing 'abounding in metaphysical subtleties and theological niceties' and surrounded by 'magic and necromancy' (Marx 1976 [1867], 163, 169). Although commodities embody only the objectified labour of workers, value is actually ascribed to them as things, and it is this that 'transforms every product of labour into a social hieroglyphic' (Marx 1976 [1867], 167). Marx describes this transformation as 'fetishism' – the process whereby the social relations concealed within the commodity form appear as a relation between things. The transformative power is taken a step further when commodities actually appear to assume an autonomous power and come to dominate the workers themselves. We can recognise a similarly transformative power ascribed to the commodities involved in discourses of addiction, and in fact, Derrida (1981a) has already argued that the 'fetishism of [drug] addiction' exists only in a rhetorical sense: not as a 'real' feature of the world, but rather as a part of a complex of cultural norms and structural relations. In a similar vein, it is being suggested here that, just as the general commodity form mystifies human relations, so the specific commodities that are caught up in discourses of addiction also conceal wider social relations.

In this sense, one of the arguments of this book is that ideas about addictive consumption act as a discursive device that articulates concerns about loss of control and are tied up in relations of socio-economic and political power. The aim here is to try to untangle some of the complex social forms that such ideas about addictive commodities conceal and to explore the ways they evolve in relation to each other.

Outline of the book

As was noted at the beginning of this chapter, ideas about consumption and addiction rarely come together, although they are intimately entwined. The aim here is to explore their inter-relations by taking a dual approach. The historical focus of the first part of the book is intended to provide a broad, synoptic overview of the relations between shifting epistemological understandings of 'the problems of consumption', broadly conceived, and the wider political–economic and social climates they are embedded in. This wide-ranging perspective gives way to a closer 'zooming in' on specific instances of consumption in three case studies on drugs, food and gambling in the second part. This closer analysis allows for a more detailed focus on particular themes and the ways that they are played out in specific contexts of consumption.

So to begin the story, we must first go back. The first part of the book is historical and traces the development of modernity through one of its most distinguishing features: consumption. It focuses on three particular moments: roughly, the end of the mercantile period, around the late seventeenth and early eighteenth centuries; the period of industrial capitalism in the nineteenth century, and the neoliberal era of the late twentieth and early twenty-first centuries. Each one demarcates a period when consumption underwent a change in scale and character, with each change accompanied by a critical response that reflected its prevailing epistemological climate.

The starting point of Chapter 1 is the emergence of a dualistic conception of consumption in the eighteenth century. During this period of mercantile capitalism, increasing quantities of colonial commodities – particularly the so-called drug foods of coffee, tea, sugar and tobacco – trickled down the social hierarchy to be transformed from the luxury goods of the aristocracy into necessities of everyday life. Responses to the new colonial commodities were ambivalent from the outset. On the one hand, they were regarded as indices of respectability amongst the emergent middle classes, who used them to display their new-found status. On the other hand, however, as they became consumed by increasing numbers of the 'lower orders', they were also viewed as agents of social and economic disorder, and subject to a range of quasi-medical and religious criticisms expressed in the 'critique of luxury'. This articulated a range of concerns around shifting socio-economic relations, particularly mercantile concerns over the balance of trade. In a climate in which the mass uptake of imported goods was seen to threaten national productivity, criticisms of 'luxurious excess' were expressed in exogenous ideas about the threat of foreign commodities invading the nation and undermining national productivity.

The second chapter moves on to the nineteenth-century period of industrial modernity, when the notion of addiction as a 'disease of the will' first appeared. In this period of classical liberalism, shifting social relations elicited heightened concerns around productivity and labour discipline and lent new importance to self-control as both personal and political virtues. At this time, a 'democratisation of luxury' saw increased levels of consumption throughout the population – a situation that again elicited a critical response in which the excesses of consumption were portrayed as a threat to the moral and political order of industrial society. This new political-economic and social climate produced a shift in the location of understandings of problematic consumption. Although mercantilist fears over luxurious excess had been couched in terms of dangerous, usually foreign, commodities, the period of industrial capitalism saw the locus of the problem move deeper into the individual and, in particular, into the moral-medical hybrid of 'the will'. Central to the idea of addiction as a 'disease of the will' was loss of control, and in this, it acted as a culturally expedient idea that linked ideas about vulnerable wills and physical pathology with the irresistible temptations of commodity culture. Such moral-medical ideas introduced new ways of conceiving the consumption of particular commodities, and it introduced the idea of the flawed consumer as a distinct type of person: an addict, who was, furthermore, also a rightful object of governance.

The historical focus of the first two chapters brings together a large body of diverse work on the place of various commodities, from tea and coffee to sugar and opium, as well as practices of consumption, in the geopolitical development of capitalist modernity.

As the historian Phil Withington (2011) has noted in the context of his study of intoxication, it is unusual for so many commodities and approaches to be treated together, with the result that the study of that topic tends to be fractured in ways that obscure its overall importance. One of the aims of this book, then, is to bring together what is a similarly fragmented understanding of the inter-relations between addiction and consumption in an assemblage of diverse work. Such a project does not aim to provide a detailed analysis of the vast amount of scholarship that exists on these areas, but is rather intended to provide breadth to a more general argument about the inter-relations between consumption and addiction.

The narrative changes direction in Chapter 3, when we turn to explore the modern consumer landscape and the development of biomedical ideas about addiction within it. Here, the argument is that as consumerism becomes more intense and prolific, explanations for addiction go deeper into the individual. Away from the dangerous commodities or weak wills of the mercantile and liberal eras, the shift to neoliberalism sees understandings of addiction move into the interior space of the consumer: specifically, their brains and subjective states. Along with the development of new techniques of governance associated with the shift to neoliberal societies, new epistemological orientations have radically transformed the ways we understand addiction. The rise of neuroscience has shifted the focus of the 'problem' of excessive consumption from a disease of the will to a disease of the brain. Ironically, as its focus has narrowed, the potential field of addiction itself has expanded to include an increasingly large range of commodities and experiences, from sugar and caffeine to gambling and shopping, that greater numbers of people fear undermines their personal agency and threatens their very freedom as consumers. This 'pathologising' of consumption and the corresponding proliferation of 'addict identities' that has occurred during the last few decades is also a focus of this chapter.

The book changes direction again in Part Two. Here, the discussion of broad general themes and historical shifts gives way to a focus on three specific case studies as a means of 'zooming in' more closely on particular areas. This approach is designed to explore different issues and to show that 'addictive consumption' is not a singular category, but rather a relationship that varies across different practices and forms of consumption. The idea of addiction is, if nothing else, a versatile concept, continually adapting itself to different contexts. So chapters on drugs, food and gambling are designed to illustrate central themes of the previous chapters while also highlighting unique aspects of consumption, drawing out the ways that practices of consumption can be, variously, intoxicating, embodied and dematerialised.

Chapter 4 argues that, as a form of intoxicating consumption, drugs are a problematic, as well as a central and highly profitable, feature of consumer capitalism. Although often presented as a paradigmatic form of addiction, the trajectories of intoxicating commodities are fluid and boundaries between licit and illicit forms of consumption are becoming increasingly blurred. In particular circumstances, the consumption of some substances, such as Ecstasy and cannabis, has been subject to processes of commodification and normalisation, whereas others, such as cigarettes and 'binge drinking', are currently moving in the opposite direction in processes of denormalisation. The argument here is that the drivers of intensified consumption that we saw in Chapter 3 have produced an expansion of the spaces and opportunities to consume drugs in the spread of what can be described as entire environments of 'intoxicating consumption'. Such an expansion also produces the requirement for more pervasive forms of governance in ideas about responsible consumption, which are also backed up by more disciplinary forms of control. These processes highlight the shifting and fluid nature of ideas about drugs and concepts of addiction and, in doing so, exemplify wider tensions within the cultural values of sobriety and productivity in consumer capitalism.

Chapter 5 argues that food is a form of consumption which is quite literally embodied and, as such, reveals the contradictions of consumption in very visible as well as symbolic ways. It depicts a climate in which the excesses of 'Big Food' – the (over) production and marketing of cheap, energy-dense 'junk' foods – is matched by an increasing medicalisation of certain foods as sources of obesity, addiction and risk, and of entire 'obesogenic environments' of ill health. In such a situation, the contradictions of neoliberal consumer culture are thrown into sharp relief. Just as ever more individual self-control is required to resist temptation, we see the growth of the diet industry in tandem with the expansion of the food industry itself. The chapter argues that, in this climate, pathologies of food and eating such as obesity, anorexia and bulimia have wider metaphorical significance as cultural conditions in which the tensions between hedonism and discipline that are produced by a system of overabundance and excess are played out within the individual body of the consumer. The argument here is also concerned with the ways in which such processes work to make ideas about food a form of biomedical governance, whose gaze is particularly directed towards women, the poor and ethnic minorities.

The final chapter considers gambling which, as a dematerialised form of consumption, stands in contrast to the embodied aspects of food. It explores the transformation of gambling over the course of the late twentieth and early twenty-first centuries, from a small-scale, stigmatised activity into a massive global industry with deep ties to state power. Driven by innovative forms of technology and marketing, games of chance are becoming increasingly intensified in ways that have both a social and geographical gradient. They are also increasingly dispersed throughout what are described as 'aleatory environments', in which gambling is more ubiquitous and normalised than ever before. Alongside its commercial expansion, however, neuroscientific and psychological forms of knowledge have also positioned it as a new form of pathology: a behavioural addiction based on impulsive and irrational cognitions. The chapter suggests that their focus on the apparent economic irrationality of gambling in terms of its waste of time and money actually works to highlight some of the contradictions of gambling as a form of dematerialised consumption, whose logic, in turn, reflects features of the wider system of financial capitalism itself.

Together, the historical dimension of the study, along with the examples of the case studies, works to highlight the ways in which changing understandings of 'the problems of consumption', broadly conceived, are driven by political and economic processes, and situated within specific social and historic contexts. They suggest that notions of 'addictive consumption' are caught up in discourses of disorder and identity, distinctions between normal and pathological, excess and desire, as well as concerns about health, risk and responsibility. Underlying all this is the enduring historical concern about how to steer a path through the temptations and the dangers of commodity culture.

And so, although the problems that people like Denise, Kathy and Scott have with consumption are distinctive, they also share common themes. It is these commonalities and distinctions that are our focus in this book as we explore the ebb and flow of ideas about addictive consumption, both over time and across their changing social contexts.

Notes

1 By definition, such 'filling up' also implies the exclusion or refusal of 'bad' objects, and so consumption involves both a rejection of 'bad things' and a 'filling up' with good ones.
2 See also Pasi Falk (1994) on what he calls the 'bivalance' of the term consumption.

PART I
The shifting problem of consumption

In this first section of the book, we trace shifting ideas about 'the problem of consumption' as they emerged in the eighteenth century and were gradually transformed, in relation to changing socio-economic and political conditions, over the course of the next two centuries, into current understandings in the present day.

1

LUXURIOUS EXCESS

The emergence of commodity culture

Capitalism is 'the illicit child of luxury'.

– *Werner Sombart (1913)*

Introduction

This chapter argues that the system of Western consumerism was built on what could be called 'addictive consumption': the trade in psychoactive commodities as well as the relationships of power and domination that produced them. To illustrate this, it explores the emergence of a dualistic conception of consumption in the eighteenth century, tracing the cultural biographies of some of the goods that shaped the modern world as well as the discourses and cultures of consumption that formed around them. Doing this reveals how what were called 'drug foods' – alcohol, coffee, tea, sugar and tobacco – were transformed over the centuries from the rarified, luxury goods of the aristocracy into necessities of everyday life.

From the outset, responses to the new colonial commodities were deeply ambivalent. On the one hand, they were regarded as a means for the emerging middle class to demonstrate status and respectability. But at the same time, they were also subject to a range of critical discourses, largely expressed though the 'critique of luxury'. Such criticisms articulated long-standing tensions between autonomy and dependence and expressed deeper anxieties around shifting political, economic and social relations, particularly mercantile concerns over the balance of trade. In a climate in which the mass uptake of imported goods was seen to threaten national productivity, criticisms of 'luxurious excess' were expressed in terms of the disruptive potential of foreign commodities to undermine or weaken the individual as well as the social body, especially when consumed by the 'lower orders'.

In this chapter, following the trajectories of some of these commodities highlights the geopolitics of consumption, and it links large-scale processes of capitalist development with the everyday practices of individual consumers. The chapter begins by considering the unequal economic relations of dependence and slavery that the colonial project was founded on and considers the place of 'drug foods' as sources of both profit and subjugation within such a system. It moves on to outline the consumer revolution of the eighteenth century, noting the economic impact of the colonial commodities as well as their role in generating new ideas about the self and about desire. The next section discusses the dualistic response to consumption, looking first at the ways that the critique of luxury expressed mercantile concerns over the balance of trade, as well as about social mobility, in both religious and quasi-medical discourses. It argues that, in this, it acted as a normative project that attempted to govern the consumption of the population, particularly women and the poor. The section moves on to consider an oppositional set of discourses in which the new forms of consumption were also entwined with ideas about productivity and respectability in ways that both highlighted the increasing power of the bourgeoisie and also underlined the gendered division of public and private space. Finally, the chapter briefly notes the transformation of ideas about luxury as the mercantile period gave way to an era of classical liberalism, paving the way for a recognition of the benefits of consumption for economic growth and an understanding of capitalism as 'the illicit child of luxury'.

The emergence of commodity culture

Between the fifteenth and eighteenth centuries, the spectre of consumption haunted the West. Claims over its first sightings are disputed: some have argued for fifteenth-century England (Mukerij 1983) and others for seventeenth-century Dutch culture (Schama 1987), whereas some saw it in pre-industrial eighteenth-century Britain (McKendrick et al. 1982; Smith 1992). By the eighteenth century, there appeared to be little doubt of its presence, however, with a number of scholars pointing to the emergence of a large-scale desire for consumer goods stimulating trade and acting as a motor of economic growth (McCracken 1988; McKendrick et al. 1982; Smith 1992).[1] During this period, shifting political, economic and social relations were turning the world upside down and bringing new ways of being into existence. The development of global trading networks based on colonial exploitation and oceangoing commerce, the increasing influence of the merchant bourgeoisie and the rise of modern state bureaucracies generated new structures of power. A new, speculative spirit of commerce was encouraging the growth of new kinds of financial institutions and abstract entities, such as 'the market' (Reith 1999). Meanwhile, the shift of large numbers of the agrarian, rural population into urban centres created new forms of social organisation, expressed in the shifting boundaries between the public and private spheres, as the middle classes became increasingly powerful, and women became more visible in public life (Matthee 1995, 25). Consumption was at the vanguard of these changes, both driving, and driven by, developments in the world around it. It played an integral part in the development of capitalism in the early modern period, as we shall see in this chapter.

'Psychoactive revolutions': colonialism, drug foods and power

From around the sixteenth century, exotic new commodities had trickled into the West from the distant lands of the 'New World' of the Americas, the Middle East and Asia. Spices and sugar, tea, coffee and chocolate, distilled spirits and tobacco as well as textiles and fabrics made their way into the homes of the ruling elites of Europe.

Their rarity and expense initially limited these commodities to the aristocracy, where their conspicuous consumption acted as both material and symbolic means of displaying wealth and status. At the same time, their stimulant, psychoactive properties encouraged consumption for medicinal purposes, earning them the label 'drug foods' (Mintz 1985). They were panaceas for a range of ailments, with tea used for colds and scurvy, coffee taken to reduce tiredness and chocolate lauded for its restorative benefits. Tobacco was considered to possess divine properties and was known as the 'holy herb' for its abilities cure a wide range of illnesses, from toothache to chest ailments and cancer. Sugar was renowned for its soothing properties and its ability to clear the blood, calm the stomach and strengthen the body and mind. Distilled spirits – *aqua vitae*, or 'water of life' – were consumed for a variety of ailments, such as plague and gout, and sold in apothecaries. For a long time, the line between drug, food and medicine was not clearly drawn, lending these commodities an indeterminate status as they circulated around the courts of the European aristocracy.

The consumption of these new goods also had political significance. These were the commodities of colonial exploitation, whose circulation linked the globe in trade and supplied the raw materials for the development of capitalism. For Fernand Braudel, these relationships were responsible for creating the modern world system as well as the Western diet. As he put it in his sweeping three-volume analysis of *Civilization and Capitalism* (1979), the foods that we eat today are a direct result of the dominance of the food preferences of powerful nations, and as such, 'the success of a food is the success of a culture'. And indeed, their legacy remains today as the forerunners of some of the world's largest and most powerful industries, such as 'Big Tobacco' and 'Big Sugar'. The fact that many of these commodities were, from the outset, regarded as drugs, and are today still regarded as problematic and sometimes even 'drug-like' is key for this study of addictive consumption.

An alternative reading of history describes this period, in the phrase of David Courtwright (2001), as one of 'psychoactive revolution'. A number of writers have noted the correspondence between the development of capitalism and the emergence of global trading empires based on the production, exchange and consumption of psychoactive or intoxicating commodities (Withington 2011; Bancroft 2009). In his study of the political economy of opium, for example, Carl Trocki states that 'the entire rise of the West from 1500–1900 depended on a series of drug trades' (1999, xii). It was a trade that had more than mere commercial significance, because it also served as a 'means to control manual labourers and exploit indigenes', as Courtwright (2001, 3) puts it, and as we will see in the following sections.

Mercantilism and slavery

The new colonial commodities were produced through a system of mercantilism that was founded on slavery and various forms of unfree labour. Mercantilist policies attempted to make trade favourable to nation states – an aim that from the sixteenth century onwards was increasingly bound up with imperial geopolitical relations. Aware of their position in the world economy, Western states attempted to gain political power and economic influence by limiting imports from weaker, peripheral states to raw materials and food supplies, and increasing their own industrial production and output to compete with strong, core states. In this way, they used policies of economic protectionism to attempt to establish their dominance and sustain their autonomy by restricting the flow of bullion out of the country as well as by subsidising exports and by imposing tariffs and quotas on imports. They also relied heavily on slavery, and in this, the colonies played a particularly important role. As well as supplying labour, these peripheral settlements also provided raw materials and markets in an unequal relationship that allowed the core states to avoid the worst excesses of dependency upon each other. The system operated on a triangular route linking the western European powers with the West coast of Africa and the West Indies in the Atlantic Slave Trade. European dealers traded goods for African slaves, who were sold and transported to the sugar, tobacco and coffee plantations.[2] These supplied raw materials to the core states, who then turned them into finished – profitable – commodities through manufacture (Braudel 1979). Meanwhile, to the east, the British East India Company acted as a proxy government and presided over unfree labour in the tea plantations in India. A vast, global system of dependence – namely, slavery and various forms of unfree labour – thus underpinned the mercantile system, and over a four hundred-year period, more than eleven million slaves were transported within it, with almost half as many again dying in the process.

Distilled spirits are entwined with the history of slavery, both as products of that system and as agents for the control of individuals within it. In the seventeenth and eighteenth centuries, however, the production and consumption of potent alcohol increased substantially, as spirits found a new role as the currency of slavery itself. European traders used a variety of products in exchange for slaves, such as textiles and metals, but the most popular amongst African slaves were spirits, in particular, brandy and rum. The latter was made from molasses, a by-product of sugar production itself, and came to be used not only to purchase slaves but also to control them. Regular rations were given to slaves, upon which they were encouraged to become dependent to help them to blot out the intolerable conditions of enslavement, and to make them docile and controllable. The production and consumption of rum was thus integral to the system of slavery in the foundation of commodity capitalism, and it is in this role, Tom Standage writes, that 'rum was the liquid embodiment of both the triumph and the oppression of the first era of globalisation' (2007, 205). Other spirits were used in similar ways on indigenous peoples. Whereas British colonists used rum, the French spirit of subjugation was brandy, and the Spanish one mescal. The Spanish conquistadors also exploited South American Indians' consumption of coca leaf when they realised that chewing the plant enabled their slaves to work longer with less food, so turning a native form of consumption against them. British colonists involved in the tea trade regularly gave opium to plantation workers to allow their undernourished bodies to better tolerate hardship, with one official admitting 'this country [India] could not have been opened up without the opium pipe' (in Griffiths 2011, 97). Such a blunt statement articulates the more general role of intoxicating commodities in the imperial venture, which were deliberately used as a means of both alleviating hardships the colonists themselves had imposed and creating a state of dependence that made the labour force more controllable.

The trickle down of 'infinite desire'

Between the seventeenth and eighteenth centuries, the expansion of a world system of trade dramatically increased the supply of these psychoactive commodities, as well as other new goods such as fabrics, ceramics and homewares, while the development of mass production lowered their costs. Calico and porcelain, muslin and cotton, spices and silks now entered the homes and brightened the everyday lives of larger sections of the population, creating enduring relationships with material culture as they did so. This movement eventually reached critical mass in the eighteenth century when, for McKendrick et al. (1982), an 'orgy of spending' ushered in the 'consumer revolution', and for Braudel (1982), an influx of foodstuffs oversaw the 'dietary revolutions' of the West. In particular, tea, coffee, sugar and tobacco soon became western Europe's 'licit drugs' of choice: mildly psychoactive substances that became integral to the culture of everyday life (Goodman 1993). Their stimulant properties ensured their speedy popularisation, both as pleasurable substances in themselves and, especially amongst the working poor, as palliatives that would relieve hunger and tiredness, provide an energy boost and generally ease the harshness of everyday life. In this, they went some small way to alleviating the austerity and monotony of the pre-modern diet and easing the conditions of working life for many. In Sidney Mintz's (1985) neo-Marxist interpretation, these were 'the people's opiates', linking the consumption habits of the poor with the colonial enterprise. Their pleasurable stimulations increased workers' productivity, meaning that they 'figured importantly in balancing the accounts of capitalism' (1985, 148).

The economic impact of the global commodities was enormous. Between the start of the seventeenth and the mid-eighteenth centuries, annual per capita consumption of tobacco increased from 0.01lb to 1.94lbs (Goodman 1993, 60). At the end of the eighteenth century, per capita sugar consumption had risen by a staggering 2,500 per cent over the previous one hundred and fifty years (Mintz 1985, 73). In a similar period, consumption of the stimulant drinks and sugar products comprised ten per cent of the British population's total expenditure on foods (Shammas 1990, 137), and by 1885, taxation from alcohol, tea and tobacco made up almost half of the gross income of the British government (Courtwright 2001, 5). The psychoactive consumption habits of Western consumers fuelled the new global economy, meaning that, as Courtwright puts it, 'Drug taxation was the fiscal cornerstone of the modern state, and the chief financial prop of European colonial empires' (2001, 5).

Just as important as their economic impact was the role of the new commodities in the generation of new mindsets amongst European consumers. Mintz describes the colonial transfer of 'shiploads of stimulants, drugs and sweeteners for the growing urban populations of Europe' as a process that generated 'a critical connection between the will to work and the will to consume' (1985, 64, 5). In this, they generated desires for new forms of consumption in sections of the population that had previously never experienced such things and reoriented them towards a culture that was based on 'commodity gratification' (Goodman 1993, 135).

This period of modernity heralded new relations between the individual and material culture based on ideas about autonomy, freedom and selfhood (McCracken 1988; Campbell 1987). Material goods had broken free of their roles as reflectors of fixed status and became more fluid vessels for individual self-realisation. The emergent concept of 'the self' was the medium of these new ideas, whereas the notion of fashion represented an ideal in which identity was constructed – not ascribed – through the consumption of goods. Indeed, McCracken argues that 'with the growth of fashion grew an entirely new habit of mind and pattern of behaviour' (McCracken 1988, 19). These habits and patterns were lived out through consumption, where the fashionable quest for 'the new' was nothing less than the quest for self-creation through material culture. The consumption of the new colonial goods brought enjoyment into the lives of many, and it introduced the population to the pleasures of commodity gratification and self-expression for the first time (Courtwright 2001). Perhaps most of all, they brought expression to the modern notion of desire as that which was potentially infinite. Up until now, the concept of desire had been of something that was limited, after Aristotle's teleological concept of *eudaimonia* (desire), which he described in *Nicomachean Ethics* as the goal of the good life, and which was regarded as an end in itself. (*Nich Eth* 1097). Those who attained it existed in an ideal, 'desire-less' state (Berry 1994, 113). Now, however, a new conception of desire as something potentially unending, and open to fleeting satisfaction through continual engagement in commodity culture, developed. It was also within this emergent worldview that ideas about desire as a driving force of consumption, as well as the concept of consumption as both a reward and an incentive for industrial labour, so widespread in contemporary Western societies, were forged.

The dualism of consumption: respectability and luxury

From the outset, responses to the new colonial commodities were deeply ambivalent. As the luxuries once restricted to an elite minority trickled down the social hierarchy to increasingly mass consumption, their meanings changed, and they became highly charged symbols of wider social concerns. In their downwards movement, we can see what the anthropologist Igor Kopytoff (1986) describes as 'the cultural biography of things'. Commodities, he argues, are not just inert objects, but have trajectories that are transformed through social relations as they move through time. They move through different phases, going in and out of fashion as they are consumed by different social groups, with different values, in different contexts. Exploring these cultural biographies, or what Arpan Appadurai (1986) calls the 'social lives of things', reveals how their meanings and values change over time. As we shall see, many of the commodities of the early modern period, particularly the drug foods of tea, coffee, tobacco and alcohol, had active social lives that symbolised wider socio-economic and political tensions.

As their consumption fanned out from elite circles into wealthy households and gradually to the bulk of the population, they became caught up in a process of what Goodman (1993) calls 'Europeanisation', in which their meanings were continually revised within a political, social and symbolic economy. Mintz's notions of extensification and intensification describe similar processes, with the former referring to the expansion of consumption throughout the population in ways that change its meanings, and the latter referring to the retention of older meanings and associations from the past within that expansion (Mintz 1985, 264). His history of sugar, for example, encapsulates both processes in his description of the commodity as, variously, a precious substance, a spice, a medicine, a luxury, and, eventually, as a kind of fuel, powering the engine of the British empire by providing its workers with sweet, cheap calories. For Mintz, the declining symbolic importance of sugar was matched by a rise in its economic importance: a relationship that also applied to the other drug foods as they became more widely consumed throughout the population.

This movement returns us to Marx's observations on the commodity which, he noted, goes beyond the material and, in its embodiment of social relations and values, acts as a 'social hieroglyphic', surrounded by 'magic and necromancy' (1976, 163). It is argued here that these goods were similarly 'magical', embodying shifting social relations and ideas in a range of complex ways. On the one hand, they were regarded as sources of pleasure and of new ideas about the self as well as repositories for the creation of new relations with material culture. Some commodities – in particular, tea, coffee, sugar and tobacco – became important symbols of the increasing power of the bourgeoisie. They were incorporated into both public and private rituals of consumption, which allowed the emergent middle classes to demonstrate their status and respectability and underlined gendered divisions of pubic space. On the other hand, however, the new goods were also the source of widespread fears and often fierce criticism. In a mercantile system, the mass consumption of foreign goods threatened the balance of trade, and they also gave visible expression to shifting class and gender relations. As such, as Mattee puts it, psychoactive substances were alternately 'denounced as emblems of moral rot and social degeneracy, or celebrated as the embodiment of sobriety and vigilance' (1995, 24).

A number of writers have argued for a kind of 'commodity dualism', with coffee and tea associated with the qualities of bourgeois respectability and the work ethic and counterposed to the excesses of alcohol (e.g. Courtwright 2001; Schivelbusch 1992). Nicholls, for example, argues that coffee and gin formed a 'cultural dialectic', with each negating, and yet defined by, the other (2006, 133). However, I would argue that it is not a case of a simple distinction between 'disorderly alcohol' on the one hand and the 'sober' commodities on the other. Rather, many of the psychoactive commodities of the colonial era had a dual nature and were regarded as emblematic of both excess *and* control – albeit in different contexts.

It is to these complex meanings that we now turn, looking first at critical ideas about luxury and excess, followed by those of sobriety and respectability, as they were embodied in the new commodities themselves.

Consumption, luxury and excess

The idea of consumption as a fearful, disruptive force with the power to enslave the individual and the nation emerged with birth of consumer society itself. From the outset, the new commodities were subject to a range of critical discourses, expressed in terms of the disruptive effects of inherently dangerous commodities, which came from abroad and threatened productivity by undermining morality, encouraging idleness, and so enervating the strength of both the individual and the nation. Criticisms were persistently articulated in metaphors of enslavement and dependence of the economic as well as the individual body.

These discourses were largely expressed though the 'critique of luxury': a trope in eighteenth-century civil discourse that marshalled a number of concerns into a generalised critique of the new landscape of consumption, in particular, mercantilist concerns over the balance of trade as well as around increased social mobility (Berg and Eger 2003). It incorporated such concerns into religious and quasi-medical critiques that focused on the threat posed by mass consumption, particularly when carried out by women, the poor and the emergent middle classes.

These discourses filled the regulatory space left by the demise of sumptuary law: an institution whose importance had always lain more in its symbolic affirmation of the social hierarchy than its actual governance of consumption (Hunt 1996). It had attempted to prevent the downwards diffusion of consumption throughout the population and so reinforce social distinctions by setting down in law every detail of an individual's consumption habits: from what they could eat and wear to how they might spend their leisure time. Sumptuary regulations meant that physical marks of status were inscribed onto the body and visibly displayed in the homes and the appearance of the estates (Hunt 1996; Braudel 1979). However, from the end of the seventeenth century, the influx of cheap new commodities and fashions and the increasing wealth and mobility of the 'middling ranks' created a situation in which social distinctions became blurred, boundaries volatile. In this climate, the regulations that had once 'fixed' physical markers of status were breaking down and failing to 'fix' status in a way that was clear and unambiguous. Conspicuous displays of consumption that had once been the prerogative of the aristocracy were now seeping throughout the social fabric: servants could wear the same patterns, and take the same tea and sugar, as their employers (McCracken 1988).

Although sumptuary legislation was unable to regulate these new consumption practices, its demise did not imply the end of attempts to regulate consumption. Its spirit lived on, albeit in a different form, continued in a complex of critical, moralistic discourses and economic projects.

20 The shifting problem of consumption

In his *Governance of the Consuming Passions,* Alan Hunt describes this as a process in which 'sumptuary law diminishes if not disappears, while moral and economic regulation march on as central arenas of governmental activity down to the present' (Hunt 1996, 41). One of the most striking forms of such governance was to be found in critical discourses of luxury, which attempted to direct the consumption of the population, particularly of the lower orders and women. The historian of luxury, John Sekora, is unequivocal about the significance of what he calls this protean concept, describing it as 'the oldest, most pervasive negative principle for organising society western history has ever known' (1977, 2). From its Old Testament associations with Original Sin, concerns about luxury were consistently couched in terms of materialism and desire: of the overwhelming of the individual and the surrender of autonomy to a dependency on things. For centuries, luxury had played a central role in the social hierarchy. The aristocracy used the conspicuous consumption of enormous amounts of material goods as symbolic markers of status and prestige. Such expenditures – which George Bataille (1985) described as 'unproductive expenditures' – were based on a 'principle of excess', whose aim was to waste or use up wealth, and in which those who were able to throw the most ostentatious parties or give the most elaborate gifts, transferred material wealth into symbolic capital, so displaying their owners' position as the most powerful in the social hierarchy. The historical practice of making 'sugar sculptures' is one such example. At a time when it was a precious commodity more expensive than silver, sugar would be sculpted into a clay then baked and hardened to make into sculptures of the castles and lands of the ruling elite, known as 'subtleties', displayed to guests at banquets and then, having been suitably admired, broken up and eaten. Such displays were part of a symbolic economy in which sugar embodied its hosts' power and status. The quite literal conspicuous consumption of such a precious commodity was a form of excess and a way of very visibly marking the power of the sovereign (see Mintz 1985, 88–95). Such 'unproductive expenditures' were central to the rituals and obligations of the ruling elite and were regarded as legitimate displays of an individual's place in the social hierarchy. As such, criticisms of luxury were tempered by recognition of the role of the aristocracy in maintaining the order of the social hierarchy, with legislation distinguishing between those who were entitled to it and those who were not, between, as Sekora puts it, the 'immoral and illegal lust for false wealth' and the natural and admirable expression of position and self-interest' (Sekora 1977, 52).

In the eighteenth century, however, the notion of luxury underwent a change of focus. The expansion of consumption throughout the population saw the subject of luxury shift from the excesses of the nobility onto what was perceived as the disorder of society in general – and especially amongst the lower and middling orders and women. Unlike the excessive but legitimate excesses of the wealthy, amongst these groups, indulgence in 'luxury' was regarded as an insolent attempt to consume 'above their station' – as Nietzsche's aphorism put it: 'Excess is a reproach only against those who have no right to it' (1987, 124). It is in this sense that the critique of luxury can be seen as a normative project that attempted to govern the consumption of the population.

In Jan Steen's 1663 painting, *Beware of Luxury* ('In Weelde Siet Toe'), we see the disorderly chaos of an ordinary household cluttered with the new goods: tobacco pipes, fashionable ornaments and alcohol, as social relations run amok (see Image 1.1).

This re-focusing of the luxury debates was a direct response to shifting political, economic and social relations, in which the bourgeoisie were overtaking the power of the landed aristocracy, and women were becoming increasingly visible in public life. These stratified concerns

IMAGE 1.1 *Beware of Luxury* ('In Weelde Siet Toe') by Jan Steen. *Beware of Luxury* – Allegorical representation of the defects affecting men and women.

Painting by Jan Steen (1626–1679) 1663 Dim. 105 × 145 cm Kunsthistorisches Museum Vienna.

Source: Photo by Leemage/Corbis via Getty Images.

had a very specific focus on the consumption of foreign goods, and mercantilist fears about the balance of trade run as a leitmotif throughout these critical discourses. In short, demands for self-control in the face of 'mass' consumption were especially strident when the origin of the commodities in question was overseas. Luxury had always been associated with 'foreignness' (Berg and Eger 2003), but now the concern was with the danger of foreign manufacture to British trade interests. As we have seen, the imperial project was all about creating dependency: both in individuals, through slavery, and in colonised nations, through political domination and protectionist trade arrangements. In many ways, the overriding concern of nations who pursued mercantile policies was to maintain autonomy and avoid dependency in trade – although, of course, they were not averse to creating dependency in others. However, the fact was that no state could avoid some degree of dependence on another for at least some of their trading exchanges. In this, dependence became an economic and political issue (Hunt 1996). It was also expressed in criticisms of consumption: not so much in terms of consumption *per se*, but insofar as consumption of foreign or 'luxury' goods were increasing, and so upsetting the balance of trade that mercantilism rested on. Thomas Mun, a director of the East India Company and pamphleteer, articulated this approach, and spelled out the route to increased national wealth in his 1664 tract, *England's Treasure by Forreign Trade*, referring to 'Silks, Sugars and Spices' as 'unnecessary wants', and stating simply that 'the ordinary means . . . to increase our wealth and treasures is by Forreign Trade wherein we must . . . . sell more to strangers yearly than we consume of theirs in value' (in Berry 1994, 103).

'A Chinese drug called tea'

Tea was a very clear case of trade imbalance, in which England did not 'sell more to strangers than we consume of theirs in value'. In fact, the British imported vast quantities of the commodity from China: in 1789, annual outlay on tea was £3 million, out of a total state revenue of only £16 million (Kohn 1987, 27). However, they exported little to China in return, leaving them with an uneasy dependence on the nation. This situation produced virulent criticism against the 'debauchery' of tea drinking. In such critiques, tea is consistently referred to as a drug, and its disorderly effects on the individual and the national body emphasised. The theologian and jurist Duncan Forbes, for example, made such connections explicit when he outlined the deleterious effects of the increasing trade in tea, even lamenting its overtaking the consumption of national drinks such as beer:

> When the opening [of] a Trade with the East Indies brought the price of tea so low, that the *meanest* labouring Man could compass the Purchase of it [and] introduced the Common Use of that Drug among the lowest of the People; – when *Sugar*, the inseparable Companion of Tea, came to be in the possession of the very poorest Housewife, when formerly it had been a great rarity . . . . and when Tea and Punch became thus the *Diet* and *Debauch* of all the Beer and Ale drinkers, the effects were very suddenly and severely felt.
>
> *(Forbes 1744, in Mintz 1985, 114)*

Such criticisms continued long-standing associations of luxury with women. From its inception in the Old Testament, the concept of luxury was gendered in the figure of Eve who was the conduit for materialism and forbidden desire (Sekora 1977), into the eighteenth century, when the entire realm of consumption was aligned with the negative, feminised characteristics of luxury and unpredictability, and opposed to the 'masculine' realm of production, which was affiliated with the values of strength and stability. Central to the discourse of luxury was a set of dualisms, Hunt (1996) claims, that played on the negative connotations of 'effeminate', in ideas about the power of female sexuality to weaken the strength of the male. The imagery and language of consumption was consistently feminised in notions of 'soft' living and indulgence as opposed to the 'hard' life of frugality and discipline. Mandeville summed up the common perception that

> luxury is as destructive to the wealth of the whole Body Politic, as it is to that of every individual who is guilty of it . . . it effeminates and enervates the People, by which the Nations become easy Prey to the first Invaders.
>
> *(in Sekora 1977, 67)*

This convergence of gender with national, economic interests meant that indulging in luxury was much worse when those luxuries were foreign.

Even more stridently, in his *Essay on Tea*, the eighteenth-century social reformer Jonas Hanway wrote of what he called 'a Chinese drug called tea' as the epitome of irrationality, and of tea drinking itself a frivolous activity that undermined the morals of the individual, especially if that individual was female and poor. Tea was persistently gendered as a fashionable vanity that encouraged idleness and gossip, with John Wesley, for example, condemning it for its 'effeminate aura' and the indolence to which it was supposed to lead (in Matthee 1995, 35), whereas others criticised the amount of money that the working classes spent on it, and on the sugar they put in it. The language Hanway used to describe the 'enervating nature' of tea is significant, as it links feminised critiques of consumption with fears of the decline of nation, expressed in quasi-medical metaphors of disease. In his *Essay* (1756, 276), he railed against:

A Chinese drug called
TEA
The infusion of which had been for many years
Drank in these realms and dominions,
Injuring the health
Wasting the fortunes,
And exporting the riches,
Of his majesty's liege subjects

He went on to bemoan that tea was responsible for 'exporting the riches of His Majesty's subjects', 'pernicious to HEALTH, obstructing INDUSTRY, and impoverishing the NATION'. It was also an inherently dangerous substance that should be consumed only by elites rather than 'common mortals'. But, as he put it, 'it is the cursse of this nation that the labourer and mechanic will ape the lord. . . . It is an epidemical disease; if any seeds of it remain, it will engender a universal infection' (in Kohn 1987, 20).

These kinds of criticisms were about far more than poor people drinking tea. Rather, they articulated some of the wider geopolitical tensions involved in the trade in psychoactive commodities, as a slight diversion at this point in our story will illuminate. As we have seen, British consumption of tea upset its balance of trade, and into this situation, opium emerged as a contender to redress the balance. The British East India Company had obtained a monopoly over the production of opium in its colonies in India and now used this, instead of silver, to trade with China. So began a hugely profitable, and illegal, trade in which opium was foisted upon China, and its profits used to finance payments for tea. At a time when fears were being voiced over the dangerous effects of the drug in Britain, it was effectively forced upon China in an illegal and highly unethical trade war. It has been estimated that between 1767 and 1850, there was a seventy-fold increase in Chinese opium consumption, and that eight million Chinese addicts existed by the end of the nineteenth century (Schivelbusch 1992; Conrad and Schneider 1992). When the Chinese outlawed this highly lucrative commodity, its beneficiaries – the East India company, the British government and the Indian administration – circumvented the law through a complex network of smuggling to protect their interests. Continued Chinese resistance was met with the full might of the Empire: two Opium Wars, in which China was defeated and the British increased their illegal distribution of opium. They gained Hong Kong through the peace treaty of Nanking but lost their international reputation in the episode. The eventual political 'victory' of Britain over China was the symbolic victory of tea over opium, an outcome that underscored the power of the British Empire. Schivelbusch summarised the relationship succinctly, writing: 'Tea, the beverage that was to keep English society fit to carry out its great global undertakings, was paid for with opium, which made Chinese society indolent, dreamy, inactive, uncompetitive – manageable' (1992, 223). In opium and tea, then, we can see commodities that symbolised, at the same time that they produced, the geopolitics of addictive consumption. They embody the opposing values of economic and cultural dependence versus autonomy: a relationship that represented the nature of the imperial powers' broader engagement with the rest of the world. Tea, then, not only served as a means of profit, but also was, in Mintz's words, a signifier 'of the power to rule' (Mintz 1985, 114).

Although it is a stark example, opium was not the only drug trade upon which the imperial powers' profits were built. As both Bancroft (2009) and Courtwright (2001) have pointed out, the political economies of tea itself, as well as those of coffee, tobacco and sugar, have had equally significant impacts on geopolitical relations, and their legacies, because licit, are more entrenched. The profits of all these commodities shaped global processes of trade and underscored the political and economic dominance of the West for centuries.

Coffee and tobacco: a 'eunuch's drink' and a 'filthie noveltie'

Criticisms of coffee and tobacco were frequently articulated in gendered ways that also highlighted shifting social relations as well as the public spaces that they were developing in. From their Islamic origins in the Middle East, coffee houses developed in urban centres in Europe from the end of the seventeenth century and became a focal point for business exchanges as well as a popular space for a predominantly male clientele to meet to discuss politics, science and public affairs. These new spaces were viewed with suspicion by a range of voices, however, who regarded their Muslim associations as un-Christian and their platform for airing political opinions as potentially seditious. In addition, a vocal body of women drew on medical criticisms of coffee as an anti-aphrodisiac and a 'eunuch's drink' (Braudel 1979, 257) to complain that coffee houses encouraged men to waste money and spend time away from the home and that the coffee itself made them sexually inactive, so endangering the reproduction of the race (Matthee 1995, 36). Some of their public proclamations left readers in no doubt as to the emasculating nature of the problem, as with the 1674 broadsheet, 'Women's Petition Against Coffee', which was quite explicit in its message. Invoking its Islamic origins, it claimed that coffee 'made men as unfruitful as the deserts whence that unhappy berry is said to be brought', and went on to complain that

> never did Men wear *greater Breeches*, or carry *less* in them of any *Mettle* whatsoever.... They come from it [the coffee house] with nothing *moist* but their snotty Noses, nothing *stiffe* but their joints, nor *standing* but their Ears.
>
> *(in Wild 2005, 91)*

This linking of consumption with degenerist national concerns mirrored gendered criticisms that were more usually directed against women's consumption, particularly of alcohol, as we will see later. It also converged with political and economic concerns: conservative commentators regarded coffee houses as dens of political sedition, with Charles II even going so far, in 1675, as to issue 'A proclamation for the suppression of coffee houses', in light of their 'very evil and dangerous effects' (Charles 1675),[3] which, although quickly revoked, highlights the perceived political threat created by these new spaces of consumption. Elsewhere, economic issues were foremost. In Germany, for example, criticisms of 'fashionable' French coffee were driven by concerns over the effect of imports on domestic production of other beverages, particularly wine and beer, whose producers feared for their livelihoods. As a result, policy was disciplinary and aimed at stopping widespread consumption by banning consumption amongst the rural and urban poor throughout the eighteenth century (Matthee 1995, 37).

Similar criticisms were levelled against tobacco, which, at various times, was subject to widespread disapproval from both church and state over its disruptive effects among the working classes, and its perceived damaging effect on the brain and reproductive system. In gendered language similar to that directed against coffee, it was argued that smoking 'withereth our unctuous and radical moisture', so that 'the sperm and seed of man [is] greatly altered and decayed' (in Goodman 1993, 77). So at the same time that it was lauded for its medicinal properties as a 'holy herb', tobacco was also being criticised as a 'devlish' substance or, as one critic suggested, 'herba insana' for its destructive ones (in Goodman 1993, 77). Medical and religious discourses combined in attacks on its pagan origins in the New World, with a number of theologians warning that its use in traditional spiritual or 'heathen' belief systems made it unfit for Christian consumption. Its overseas origin was the focus of perhaps the first anti-tobacco publication, King James I's *Counterblaste to Tobacco*, whose rhetoric appears surprisingly modern in terms of the current position of tobacco. In it, he railed against the 'blacke stinking fumes' of 'this filthie noveltie' which was 'a customse loathsome to the eye, hateful to the Nose, harmefull to the braine, dangerous to the Lungs' and in the 'blacke stinking fumes thereof, neerest resembling the horrible Stigian smoke of the pit that is bottomelesse'. He addressed his subjects directly, telling them that this 'vain', shameful custom 'thereof making your selves to be wondered at by all forraine civil Nations, and by all strangers that come among you, to be scorned and condemned' (James 1604). Other monarchs were more disciplinary, with a number of European states banning tobacco consumption, especially amongst the poor, throughout the seventeenth and eighteenth centuries on the grounds it harmed human reproduction (Courtwright 2001; Matthee 1995).[4]

Criticisms of widespread 'luxury' also re-invigorated Protestant critiques of idleness – its most visible aspects a very obvious disregard for the values of labour and the utilisation of time – and lent renewed urgency to ideas about self-control and discipline. In the eighteenth century, a puritanical emphasis on self-control found resonance with a secular focus on the regulation of labour – a growing concern at a time when economic stability and productivity were coming to be regarded as dependent on labour discipline. In such a discursive climate, idleness came increasingly to be seen as a disruptive force that could lead to all kinds of social unrest and crime and was to be countered by strict legislation (Hunt 1996). In the midst of all this, the temptations and pleasures of consumerism – particularly working class activities such as feasting, drinking and gambling – were framed as particularly unproductive and sinful and, in the case of gambling, an activity that divorced effort from reward and so undermined the Protestant work ethic and destabilised the social hierarchy (Hunt 1996, 274–275). Indeed, a stratified system of governance attempted to prohibit gambling among the poor while allowing it to go on in its most extravagant forms amongst the wealthy. So whereas cards and dice were taxed at a level that made them prohibitively expensive for the bulk of the population, specific games were outlawed and the owners of public gaming houses penalised, the gambling of the upper classes carried on, conducted in private clubs and court circles, in displays of excess and status in which whole estates were lost on the turn of a card (Reith 1999).

From aqua vitae to Gin Lane

The consumption of alcohol was widespread throughout the early modern period, and often excessive. Beer, ale and wine were cheap, easily available and, at a time when water quality was poor, often served as the drink of choice as well as a source of calories for many. Beer and wine drinking were part of the rituals of the elites as well as the lower orders, and daily life for both was frequently spent in a mild haze of inebriation. In the seventeenth century, ritualised heavy drinking was common, and affluent young gentlemen were actively expected to consume large quantities of alcohol to excess, but also to retain control of their reason, and be able to display wit and banter (Withington 2011); a dualistic imperative that remains today, with the expectation of controlled or 'responsible' drinking. Distilled alcohol, however – *aqua vitae* – was generally confined to medicinal use and dispersed by chemists for ailments such as gout and colds, rather than sold in taverns (Courtwright 2001, 73).

However, in the eighteenth century, new techniques of distilling introduced an intensification of consumption in the form of strong spirits. Rum, brandy, whiskey and gin were ten times stronger than beer and were drunk more quickly to produce an acceleration of intoxication that was attuned to the general speeding up of the early modern era itself or, in Schivelbusch's words, was 'intrinsically related to other processes of acceleration in the modern age' (1992, 153). Although the consumption of alcohol had long been perceived as problematic, it became especially so during this period, particularly amongst women. This time it was not so much the overseas origin of the commodities that was the target of criticism, but the increased consumption of distilled spirits, particularly gin, amongst the poor, whose consumption habits were a more general focus of puritanical critiques about the waste of time and money. In mid-eighteenth century Britain, an increase in the supply of cheap gin – deliberately engineered by the government to resolve a grain surplus amongst distillers – made the spirit into an everyday beverage, encouraging a concomitant rise in drunkenness amongst the poor. Production in England rose from half a million gallons at the start of the century to eleven million by the middle. The 'Gin Craze' of the time was portrayed as an epidemic of working class life, causing widespread drunkenness and disorder, undermining the work ethic and causing mothers to neglect their children (Braudel 1979; Bancroft 2009). Such disorder is famously represented in Hogarth's sketch of 'Gin Lane' in which a drunken woman, oblivious, drops her baby. The destruction of family life, productivity and morality were associated with fears about reproduction, too. Henry Fielding worried about the effect on 'wretched infants' conceived 'in gin', linking birth defects with the health of future generations, and thus the strength of the nation, in a gendered discourse that anticipated concerns about foetal alcohol syndrome by some two hundred years, and that would re-appear around ideas about opium and alcohol in the nineteenth century, as we will see in the following chapters.

Gin, then, came to encapsulate more generalised fears of urban poverty and disorderly behaviour, as revealed through the 'excessive' consumption of the poor. Tobias Smollett summed up such concerns, writing that gin 'was sold so cheap that the lowest class of the people would afford to indulge themselves in one continued state of intoxication, to the destruction of all morals, industry and order' (in Courtwright 2001, 73). It was these concerns about productivity and morality that lay behind the introduction of heavy taxes and the prohibitionist Gin Act of 1736 (Braudel 1979; Bancroft 2009, 30): disciplinary attempts to govern the behaviour and morals of the poor.

Luxury, contagion and addiction

Running throughout these 'protean' criticisms of luxury are a number of common themes. In particular, we see a quasi-medical pathologising of imports that links the economic with the individual body in particular ways. Earlier, in *Leviathan*, Thomas Hobbes had warned that unrestrained 'forraign traffique' was 'noxious or at least unprofitable' to the body politic (in Harris 1998, 143). These 'noxious' invaders were even more acutely felt in the eighteenth century, however, when the term 'infection' was actually introduced to the vocabulary of international law to describe the cargo of any foreign ship, as the 'carriers' of symbolic disease' (Harris 1998, 143). Here, economic concerns over foreign trade are expressed in an exogenous explanation of illness, in terms of an invasion of foreign substances that attack and weaken the integrity of the body. A growing medicalisation of ideas about excess consumption was also apparent in the language of a number of writers and critics at the time: from the 'universal infection' and 'epidemical disease' of tea that Hanway wrote of, to what other eighteenth-century writers described as the 'contagion of luxury' that was being 'spread . . . amongst the lower ranks' (in McKendrick et al. 1982, 95). This would intensify in the nineteenth century, as we will see in the next chapter and, of course, it continues today, with both the emergence of medicalised ideas about addiction as a brain disease, and in the adoption of a quasi-medical terminology by some writers to describe, for example, the 'compulsive power' of fashion, or the 'irresistible drug' of novelty.

It was also around this time that a pathologised notion of consumption became a category of economic behaviour – a semantic development that was closely linked to the emergence of political economy as a distinct field of enquiry throughout the seventeenth century (Withington 2017). However, its pejorative connotations – derived from its earlier deployment as a medical word for 'wastage' and 'decay' – remained, and indeed, Withington argues, these 'pathological inferences' were 'a significant factor' in this initial, moralistic usage, which was specifically concerned with ways of regulating or taxing 'wasteful excess and luxury'(2017, 8). In this, it was particularly focused on alcohol, which laid waste to incomes, health and productivity, as well as intoxicating imports such as tobacco, coffee, wine and 'drugs', which represented both economic-national and physical-individual waste.

The physician George Cheyne articulated some of these connections between the economic and the physical realm in his examination of the relationship between affluence and health. In *The English Malady* (1733), he argued that the overindulgent lifestyles of the wealthy were the causes of a range of physical and nervous disorders, from obesity to melancholia. Far from creating well-being, consumerism was actually making people ill. Cheyne extended his analysis to the body of the nation, specifically linking ill health with capitalist expansion, writing, 'Since our Wealth has increas'd and our Navigation has been extended, we have ransack'd all the Parts of the Globe to bring together its whole Stock of Materials for *Riot, Luxury* and to provide *Excess*' (in Porter 1993b, 64). The cure for these enervating excesses? Significantly, Cheyne prescribed self-restraint and more frugal forms of consumption. He called the approach 'diatetick management' – the world's first diet – a very modern formula in which the obese body was to be returned to health through discipline and control: themes we will see again when we turn to look at food in Chapter 5. His admonition for dietary management was also animated by religious overtones, in which the defence of the soul against the temptations of the flesh was a Christian duty.[5] In Cheyne's articulation of the ailments of modern civilisation, we can see a convergence of the concerns of the body politic in the discourses of medicine, economics and morality. Luxury and excessive consumption were cast as forces that overwhelmed not only the individual's willpower, reason and self-control, but also their corporeal being, their very body. In this framework, self-control in the face of foreign luxuries was good not only for the economic health of the nation, but also for the physical health of the individual, as well as for their soul.

It is perhaps ironic to note that, at a time when capitalist expansion was built on the institutionalised slavery of the colonies, fears about the effects of the new commodities were focused on ideas about the enslavement of European consumers themselves, as we will see.

The semantic expression of criticisms of luxury has some convergence with what would later become expressions of ideas about addiction. To elaborate on this, we can note that the concern of both mercantilism and the critique of luxury was the avoidance of dependence and the preservation of autonomy, in both the economic, political sphere, and the individual and moral realm. In these discourses, luxury is presented as 'the Other'. As Sekora puts it, 'It provided its users with a powerful measure of self-worth, for it identified all they *were not*' (Sekora 1977, 50). This 'Other' is represented in negative imagery: in ideas and metaphors of enslavement, invasion, enervation, dependency and contagion that expressed fears of a nation being overtaken, an individual being overwhelmed. In this, it returns us to the original, negative meanings of consumption, or *consumere* – 'to make away with, to devour, waste, destroy' (OED 2003), as well as to the root of addiction, from *addictus*, where it designated a kind of enslavement – 'to devote, make over; to surrender, to enslave' (Oxford Latin Dictionary 2012).

Without wishing to overstate the case, I think it can be suggested that there is, nevertheless, some convergence here, in which 'protean' discourses of luxury anticipate some of the concerns that would later be expressed in discourses of addiction. The emphasis on the enervating nature of luxury and its potential to undermine self-discipline, reason and willpower and enslave the individual is suggestive of ideas around addiction. Similarly, the concern with its 'contagious' nature as something that could invade the individual and infect the social body, generating loss of productivity, idleness and crime, and eventually contributing to the decline of the nation, is resonant with claims that would much later be made for the problems caused by drugs such as heroin.

The suggestion here is not that the eighteenth-century critique of luxury can be 'mapped on' to later ideas about addiction, but rather the more limited point that each, in their own way, expressed concerns about consumption, control and desire in historically specific ways.

Stimulating commodities and the spirit of capitalism

Despite all these criticisms of their disorderly and damaging effects, the new colonial commodities were at the same time also subject to very different sets of meanings that associated them with the values of reason and productivity. In particular, as tea, coffee, sugar and tobacco gradually moved into the drawing rooms and coffee houses of the bourgeoisie, they became part of a symbolic economy of sobriety and respectability. Hot caffeinated drinks, loaded with sugar and accompanied by nicotine, can be regarded as a stimulating assemblage that encouraged wakefulness and concentration and fuelled the work ethic of a capitalising society. At a time when daily consumption of alcoholic beverages meant that large sections of the population were constantly slightly inebriated, this new orientation towards sobriety was notable and was integral to the creation of a bourgeois ideology of respectability and domesticity. Indeed, according to Nicholls (2006), the sobriety embodied in coffee actually became a 'political practice' that allowed a space for the public expression of reason. And so, at the same time that they were being denounced for their threat to moral and economic well-being, when consumed in different contexts, and by different actors, tea, coffee and tobacco were also being lauded for their virtuous properties.

Both tea and coffee were positioned largely through their opposition to the negative characteristics of alcohol, and the excesses of the aristocracy. The sipping of tea in domestic parlours and the taking of coffee was framed as a refined and moderate activity, in contrast to the conspicuous consumption of elites. As well as health benefits, the beverages were praised in religious and medical circles for their more spiritual attributes of increasing vigilance and piousness. Indeed, tea in particular found such favour amongst temperance groups concerned with the morals and behaviour of the poor that this 'Calvinist drink' came to be regarded as 'almost a divine alternative' to the evils of alcohol (Matthee 1995, 35).[6]

As well as being associated with tea and coffee themselves, the values of sobriety and respectability also came to be embedded in the public and private spaces in which they were consumed. As Matthee puts it, class and gender differences became 'inscribed in the nature of the stimulants and the places where they thrived' (1995, 46). The coffee houses that, as we saw earlier, were subject to gendered criticisms for encouraging the waste of time and money amongst men and for undermining their virility, were also key spaces for the redefinition of bourgeois masculinity, and indeed, for the development of the infrastructure of capitalism itself. Often located in stock exchanges and business districts, they played an important role in the development of new forms of business organisation as well as providing a forum for men to exchange ideas. In the course of these kinds of interactions, 'the coffee house became a significant part of the infrastructure of commercial capitalism and a real, observable element of what the classical economists described abstractly as "the market"' (Smith 2007, 152). The attributes of coffee itself promoted sharpened mental acuity and increased energy and wakefulness, so promoting business and the exchange of ideas, in opposition to alcohol, which dulled the wits and slowed the mind. Merchant capitalists and bankers indulged themselves with substances that suited their outlook, with the 'clear headed bourgeois intoxication' of the new stimulants of coffee, tea and tobacco (Hunt 1996, 90). In their promotion of the pursuit of business and discussion of serious subjects amongst sober and rational men, coffee houses – and coffee – became emblems of respectability, in contrast to the riotousness of alcohol taverns and, as Smith writes, 'a kind of living, present example of the ideal civil society' (2007, 155). As such, coffee could be said to embody the spirit of capitalism, a drink that substituted the natural rhythms of sleep and wakefulness with the more industrious time of the clock in a rush of caffeine. Indeed, for many writers, it was practically synonymous with modernity, reason and progress. Anthony Wild's *Black Gold*, for example, draws attention to the role of coffee houses as spaces of reason, writing that the Enlightenment was 'born and nurtured' in the coffee house (2005, 86), whereas Tom Standage describes coffee itself as the ideal drink for the Age of Reason (2007, 136).

If coffee was the beverage of masculine respectability, consumed in public and associated with the institutions of the market, tea was its feminine counterpart, consumed in the private space of the home and allied with the domestic institution of the family. Rather than a source of 'epidemical disease' when consumed by 'the very poorest Housewife', in the bourgeois parlour, tea became a mark of respectability and civilisation. Essentially a female ritual, the highly structured ceremony of 'taking' tea was conducted in parlours at set times, and overseen by the senior woman in the home, who organised the roles of servants, visitors and family members as well as supervising the making, pouring and distributing of the tea. In this role, women acted as 'civilisers', presenting an image of respectable femininity as well as acting out an ideal of relations between the sexes. They also acted as arbiters in the process through which the uses and meanings of tea were reappropriated and linked to issues of national identity. Such ceremonies as the pouring of hot water into delicate chinaware for afternoon guests encouraged new combinations of materials and practices that 'Europeanised' exotic items and attached distinctly British meanings to them (Mintz 1985).[7] The significance of tea extended beyond its role in the construction of family respectability to the establishment of the whole notion of private life, for tea did not merely symbolise family life, but also defined what it meant to *be* a family. If coffee was emblematic of 'the ideal civil society', tea was the epitome of domestic femininity, and the embodiment of the bourgeois family as the locus of virtue, stability and prosperity.

Tobacco, in the form of snuff, was an ideal accompaniment to the sweetened, caffeinated beverages, or 'complex of soft drugs' as Jordan Goodman (2007) puts it. In his history of the trajectory of tobacco, Goodman pays particular attention to the periods in which it was celebrated, in contrast to its position today, noting its attainment of respectability in the consumption rituals of the bourgeoisie in the eighteenth century. At this time, a fashion for snuff incorporated tobacco into the practices carried out in coffee houses and private homes, making it an acceptably respectable form of consumption, in contrast to 'cruder' practices such as smoking or chewing, which came to be associated with outdoor work, public houses and the consumption of alcohol amongst poorer social groups. This new-found status was thus generated by its association with middle class groups[8] and expressed through the material paraphernalia of snuffing, which became fashionable items in their own right. Snuff-box making, for example, became an art form, utilising a range of materials such as porcelain, ivory and shell in the creation of exquisite holders that were highly prized and prestigious items. And so, as part of a fashionable complex of stimulant beverages and consumption practices, tobacco became aligned with individuality, as it would for centuries to come. As Jordan Goodman put it, 'snuff proclaimed the individual' (1993, 82).

Productive consumption: sugar

Sugar was central to the ritualised consumption of the commodities discussed so far, acting as a sweetener for the bitter stimulants of coffee, tea and chocolate as well as an ingredient of many of the foods that accompanied them. Its importance extended beyond them, however, as a key commodity in the transformation of working class life. The popularity of sugar grew exponentially, and by the end of the eighteenth century, it was a staple of the nation's diet – particularly that of the poor, for whom it formed a far greater proportion of their diet than for the upper and middle classes. Sugar found its way into an increasing number of foodstuffs: breads and porridges, jams and spreads, and it was even incorporated as a 'sugar allowance' into servants' wages. By enlivening bland, cold or even stale foods, it provided a ready source of cheap calories for those whose diet was lacking in nutrition and, particularly given Britain's climate and the rigours of manual labour, it could also make a cold, frugal meal seem more satisfying. For Mintz, sugar is integral to the development of capitalism, and his neo-Marxist account portrays it almost as a drug – one of 'the people's opiates' – fuelling the workers of an industrialising nation. It was, he writes, the first consumable to express 'the capitalistic view of the relation between labour productivity and consumption' (1985, 148), in that it was a cheap, easily prepared foodstuff that gave workers energy, so increasing their productivity. Indeed, the consumption of sugar spread at the very point that the factory system was expanding, the movement from country to city was speeding up and time frames were compressing (Mintz 1985, 174). It adapted perfectly to the changing rhythms of an industrialising nation, helping to create fast, cheap meals for the labouring poor who had neither time nor money to spare and, combined with tea, provided an energy boost in the industrial breaks that divided the working day. Together with tea, it provided an appealing contrast to alcohol: an expedient alternative in a factory system that required a sober, orderly workforce.

If coffee could be said to stimulate the bourgeoisie for commerce, sugar fuelled the poor for work. Both were part of a wider symbolic economy of respectable and productive consumption in the development of capitalism. As Goodman put it, these commodities

> embodied moderation as opposed to excess, mildness, as opposed to harshness; sobriety and wakefulness, as opposed to drunkenness and wantonness. By ritualising the consumption of these substances within a domestic context . . . sobriety itself became a domestic strategy and quality.
>
> *(2007, 137)*

From the previous two sections, we can see the very different sets of meanings that were invested in the new commodities as they trickled down the social hierarchy. From being the rarefied luxuries of the elite, imbued with curative powers, they came to be the necessities of the mass of the population, and were variously regarded as pathological agents of disruption, or as aids to social and personal control. Their immensely malleable character meant that their meanings were continually adapted. Whereas alcohol assisted in the enslavement of indigenous peoples, sugar fuelled the workers of a capitalising economy and coffee stimulated the traders of a commercial age of reason. At the same time, they were all subject to range of critical discourses of luxury. They concealed these social relations within them 'like a hieroglyphic', their cultural biographies in constant flux as they weaved their way through the early modern capitalist period.

'Private vices, publick benefits': the transformation of luxury

During the course of the eighteenth century, ideas about luxury began to mutate. The shift was associated with the decline of mercantilism and the move towards more liberal, or laissez-faire, economics, which introduced the possibility that there might be benefits associated with the 'vice' of luxury. Writers such as David Hume, Bernard Mandeville, Daniel Defoe and Adam Smith proposed the radical notion that luxury could be a progressive social force, as Werner Sombart would later put it, that hedonism and extravagance were so fundamental to economic growth that capitalism was actually the 'illicit child of luxury' (1913, 27).

Mandeville's *Fable of the Bees*, published in1714, was one of the most controversial expressions of these ideas, and was one of the most widely discussed and reviled documents of its time. Although Mandeville was very much of his time, regarding luxury as a vice associated with fraud and vanity, he also pointed out a new dimension – that it also stimulated innovation and growth, fuelling national prosperity and ensuring the continued employment of the poor. He conceded that such consumption was a vice, but also that it had economic benefits – as he famously remarked, that 'Private Vices' were also 'Publick Benefits'. This notion of private vices and public benefits divorced the idea of virtue from self-denial – a marriage that had persisted for hundreds of years. The response to Mandeville's treatise was almost universally negative, and in parts of France, it was burned as a wicked, heretical document. It did, however, signify the emergence of a de-moralisation of luxury and a move towards a focus which concentrated on the benefits of the latter to trade. Throughout the century, more voices joined Mandeville, with David Hume and Adam Smith debating luxury almost exclusively in terms of commerce and (neutral) consumption. Indeed, Withington suggests that the very assimilation of the term 'consumption' into an emergent English political-economic discourse was linked to a recognition 'that ostensibly "vicious", wasteful, and harmful habits – like drunkenness – could nevertheless be economically beneficial' (2017, 3). In this context, we find economists such as Adam Smith arguing that desires and wants encouraged people to work harder, thereby stimulating trade, increasing prosperity and ultimately redistributing wealth. In *The Wealth of Nations* (1776), he stated that consumption was the sole purpose of production and was 'the sole end and purpose of all production', so legitimating the pursuit of profit and establishing consumption as the generator of economic growth (Berry 1994). This reinterpretation of luxury also recast images of the gendered market in a more positive light. Rather than capricious slaves to fashion whose quest for novelties damaged the social fabric, women's contribution to commerce through discerning consumption was being recognised and appreciated. Mandeville wrote admiringly that women were 'quicker of Invention and more ready at Repartee', an ability that reflected their role as arbiters of taste who were able to influence and stimulate consumption (in Berg and Eger 2003, 19). Away from the moralistic, pathologised use of the term 'consumption' that had emerged with the development of political economy itself, a more neutral usage was now emerging, in which specific commodities were no longer singled out as especially 'vicious', but rather, as Withington states, 'consumption [was] eventually describing the generic kind of economic behaviour intimated by Locke, with alcohol and imports two types of commodity among many' (2017, 8).

This shifting emphasis was encouraged by pragmatic concerns, of which tax is a prime example. Lacking the formal institutions to levy large-scale funds from the population, revenue-hungry states came to regard the new commodities flooding across their borders as a welcome opportunity to fund the development of their infrastructures and finance their militaries. Tobacco was subject to some of the heaviest taxation: in Britain, net duty rose to around two hundred per cent during the 1760s, whereas other European states extracted similarly large revenues, with, for example, France deriving seven per cent of its total revenues from tobacco taxation and Spain twenty-five per cent (Goodman 1993). With the growing popularity of coffee adversely affecting its revenues from beer, the English government made the decision to license coffee houses and tax the sale of coffee by the gallon, later replacing this with a straightforward customs duty of five shillings per pound sold (Matthee 1995, 37). The taxation of goods inevitably inflated their costs for consumers, often pricing them too high for many. In this, taxation was often regressive: disproportionally affecting the poor, who were also often the heaviest consumers of commodities such as sugar. However, the effects of taxation were mitigated by lively attempts to circumvent legal tariffs – that is, through smuggling. An illicit black market grew up around imports of the new commodities, professionally organised on a scale that frequently matched – if not surpassed – the legal one. In the late eighteenth century, duty was paid on more than five million pounds of tea, legally imported by the East India Company, although it was estimated that illegal imports amounted to the same amount again, ensuring that the British population got their favourite drink at an affordable price

(Hobhouse 2006, 140). Tea smuggling did not stop until 1784, when Willian Pitt repealed high government duties, and allowed enough imports to satisfy demand without raising prices (Matthee 1995, 43). The success of tea, and its eventual popularity over coffee and chocolate as hot drinks, was the result of political and economic factors rather than taste: the East India Company's monopoly over tea growing in India was backed by the state and provided one of the most lucrative sources of private and profit and state revenue in the Empire.[9]

A lengthy literature exists on the efforts to contravene state legislation on taxation and on the relations between smuggling, contraband and consumption, which is too voluminous to discuss at length here. But, in general, it underscores the trend in which consumption was increasingly seen less as a moral issue and more as a source of profit and, just as importantly, one which demanded the intervention of the economic, political and financial systems of the state. Such considerations accompanied the gradual dismantling of mercantile protections and the shift towards more laissez-faire, free market trading policies, in which consumer demand itself began to influence markets and generate wealth. In this new climate, the idea of excess was recast as surplus and vanity regarded as refinement and taste (Berg and Eger 2003, 9): a perspective that would gain increasing economic and political acceptance during the next two centuries.

End points

From the outset, the commodity culture that emerged in the eighteenth century was deeply ambivalent. The psychoactive goods that emerged from colonial commerce, in particular, had complex trajectories, where the distinctions between food, drug and medicine were unstable and fluid within shifting socio-economic and political relations of power. These relations were, in turn, bound up with the tensions of a modernising society, in particular, the influx of foreign trade and the break-up of traditional social formations. In such a climate, the new goods acted as players in a wider material and symbolic economy, where they served as repositories for ideas about control: of the self and the social body as well as the market.

Roy Porter has argued that at this time, the very notion of consumption gave rise to a paradox, expressed semantically and symbolically in both economics and medicine (1993a, 1993b). On the one hand, foreign commodities upset the mercantile balance of trade and threatened productivity in ways that were articulated around critical discourses of luxury. In these, the threat of consumption was articulated in exogenous terms of foreign commodities that came from beyond the borders of the state to undermine the autonomy of the individual and social body. Such an invasion created dependency that was regarded as particularly threatening for certain groups – namely the lower orders and women – who were indulging in the pleasures of commodity culture for the first time.

Such critical discourses of luxury and excess return us to the root of addiction as *addictus*, as form of enslavement or surrender. They also return us to the negative meaning of consumption, in the sense of *consumere*: to use up, to waste, destroy. As Porter puts it, 'What was expenditure but "spending", the dissipation of accumulated resources? Conspicuous consumption was conspicuous waste' (Porter 1993b, 7). Such meanings reflect the semantic roots of consumption, which was a term of medical pathology long before it became an economic descriptor in the seventeenth century. At the same time, however, another set of economic and political meanings complicated ideas about consumption, framing it as a source of economic wealth as well as an indicator of social status and respectability. It was this dialectic of wealth and waste, of respectability and excess, that made consumption what Porter called the 'sphinxian riddle' of early modern economics. The very word itself, he argued, was semantically ambiguous, 'suggesting both an enlargement through incorporation, and a withering away, both enrichment and impoverishment' (Porter 1993b, 7).

Part drug, part food, pathological agents of social disorder at the same time that they were indices of respectability, these commodities of early capitalism expressed wider tensions within a modernising society, and, in this, they can be read as 'social hieroglyphics', in Marx's sense of the term, 'surrounded by magic and necromancy' (Marx 1976, 76).

Over the next two hundred years, the associations of consumption with wealth would grow and come to dominate liberal and neoliberal thought. The critical reaction to consumption did not entirely end with the end of the luxury debates, however, and indeed, normative aspects persist, albeit in different forms, into the present day (Hunt 1996). Concerns around consumption continue to be expressed in a variety of ways, one of which, it is argued here, is through the development of a multifaceted notion of 'addiction', as we will see in the next chapter.

Notes

1 In this sense, arguing against a 'productivist bias' they make the claim that consumerism itself actually helped to drive the generation of the capitalist system, rather than simply being a by-product of it (McCracken 1988).
2 The massive influx of slaves generated by sugar production laid the infrastructure for the cultivation of coffee in the eighteenth century, which soon developed as a complementary commodity (Wild 2005, 123).
3 It stated: 'Whereas it is most apparent that the multitude of Coffee-houses of late years set up and kept within this Kingdom . . . and the great resort of Idle and disaffected persons to them, have produced very evil and dangerous effects: as well for that many Tradesmen and others, do therein misspend much of their time, which might and probably would otherwise be imployed in and about their Lawful Callings and Affairs; but also, for that in such Houses . . . divers False, Halitious and Scandalous Reports are devised and spread abroad, to the Defamation of His Majestie's Government, and to the disturbance of the Peace and Quiet of the Realm' (Charles 1675).
4 The city of Bern established a 'tobacco court' to try crimes associated with its consumption (Matthee 1995, 33), whereas Russian and Turkish smokers were beaten and tortured (Courtwright 2001, 16).
5 It was this discursive convergence that ensured the adoption of Cheyne's religious-moral regime by John Wesley, encouraging the spread of the values of self-control, asceticism and moderation from the pulpits to the middle classes (Turner 2008, 163).
6 The consumption of these beverages was viewed as an admirable regard for physical health, and also moral virtue, for those who were able to govern their bodies in this way were also deemed to be in control of their ethical faculties too (Smith 2007, 152).
7 The fashion for mixing milk and sugar with tea, for instance, anglicised the Chinese tradition of drinking it alone. Chinese porcelain was strong enough to withstand hot water and yet sufficiently delicate to be attractively decorated, so encouraging the further consumption of commodities such as us teapots, cups and saucers, which become integral to the symbolic as well as the utilitarian process of afternoon tea (Hobhouse 2006, 137–139).
8 Such as the clergy and doctors. In order to avoid the mess and inconvenience of smoking in churches, as well as the manipulation of cumbersome utensils, the clergy preferred to consume tobacco in the form of snuff. At the same time, some doctors were coming to advocate snuffing over smoking, not least through its encouragement of sneezing, a reaction that had been associated with various health, as well as spiritual, benefits, since Aristotle (Goodman 1993, 80).
9 In fact, British fiscal policy around tea culminated in the Boston Tea Party, in which the colonists rejected the British tax – and their tea – hurling chestfuls of it into the sea in a protest whose spectacle was as much symbolic as it was economic.

2
INDUSTRIAL MODERNITY
The birth of the addict

> Industrial prosperity unleashes 'an insatiable and bottomless abyss' of desire.
> — Emile Durkheim (1970 [1897])

Introduction

During the nineteenth century, shifting imperial and industrial relations lent renewed urgency to concerns about the disruptive effects of consumption, particularly as they interacted with the self-control and discipline of the individual. In an era in which these were increasingly important personal and well as political virtues, fears about consumption were expressed in terms of their being overwhelmed by the desire unleashed by increasing consumerism. Such fears were articulated by Durkheim (1970 [1897]) in terms of what he described as an 'insatiable and bottomless abyss' of desire which, he claimed, could lead to anomie and even suicide.

This socio-economic climate produced a shift in the location of problematic consumption. Whereas the tropes of luxury had expressed mercantilist fears over dangerous, usually foreign, commodities, the period of industrial capitalism saw the locus of the problem move deeper into the individual, and in particular, into their wills. The idea of addiction as a 'disease of the will' was conceived as a relation between powerful commodities and weak individuals who were too weak to resist the temptations of consumerism: a moral-medical hybrid that was part physical disease, part moral vice. Such ideas introduced new ways of conceiving the consumption of particular commodities and new ways of thinking about consumers themselves. In particular, it introduced the idea of the flawed consumer as a distinct type of person: 'an addict' who was, furthermore, a rightful object of governance.

It is these processes that are the subject of this chapter. It first looks at the spread of mass consumption as well as critical responses to it. It then moves on to explore the development of the idea of addiction as a disease of the will, which was argued to be a concept that linked ideas about vulnerable wills and physical pathology with the irresistible temptations of commodity culture. It goes on to argue that these ideas about addiction as a disease of the will were part of a 'great technology of power' that acted as a way of governing the consumption of the population, particularly the poor, immigrants and women. Using the example of opium, this section traces the ways that various organisations and groups drew on ideas about degeneracy and immorality to transform ideas about consumption in ways that reflected and reinforced social divisions, creating a 'stratification of the will' that reflected the stratification of industrial society itself. Such ideas produced a range of new identities, from degenerate working class alcoholics and 'hysterical' kleptomaniacs to oriental opium fiends, whose behaviour was subject to a stratified system of disciplinary governance. Finally, this chapter argues that, by expressing concerns about individuals' relations with commodity culture in terms that were both physiological and normative, the idea of addiction as a disease of the will created a broad epistemological framework within which all forms of problematic consumption could, potentially, be located.

The nineteenth century: 'addictive modernity'

In the nineteenth-century period of classical laissez-faire liberalism, industrialisation, urbanisation and immigration brought about new social relations based around social class, ethnicity and gender. In particular, the bourgeois emphasis on industrial productivity and labour discipline elevated the properties of self-regulation and control to personal as well as political virtues and also gave rise to an increasing intolerance of behaviour regarded as potentially disruptive.

In the midst of all this upheaval, and at the same time, seemingly symbolic of it, was a dramatic expansion of consumption itself throughout the population. Increased availability of inexpensive consumer goods, access to credit and rising material affluence brought about what Rosalind Williams (1982) described as a 'democratisation of luxury' that introduced the pleasures of consumption to wider sections of the population than ever before. Increasing numbers of consumers were expressing newly found desires and tastes in distinctive patterns of spending, while fashion and style animated the new consumer capitals of Paris and London. At the same time, technological and commercial innovations in transport, communications and advertising revolutionised the spatial, social and aesthetic organisation of consumption itself, a reorganisation that was embodied in the new department stores developing in urban centres. Such stores transcended the material basis of consumption, illuminating exotic merchandise with clever displays of lighting and mirrors, creating what Williams described as 'dream worlds' of fantasy and illusion with which to enchant their patrons. The spectacular nature of these environments contrasted with the utilitarian basis of traditional retailers, with their personal exchanges between customer and owner conducted on the basis of need. A whole new orientation lay behind the psychology of the new stores: purchase was no longer the sole end of the enterprise; rather, the goal was the more intangible – and more profitable – cultivation of desire. To this end, department stores encouraged a more drawn out process of browsing and window shopping, of stimulating imaginations and encouraging desires in potential customers, so generating a state of continual longing that, it was hoped, would lead to an ever-larger amount of actual purchases in the future. The socio-spatial organisation of the new department stores both reflected and encouraged the emergent, gendered division of space. Within them, middle class women found a space they could call their own – in Emile Zola's (2008 [1883]) novel, a 'ladies paradise' – where they were free to enter the public domain, unaccompanied by a male, to indulge in the temptations of commodity culture.

However, many social commentators watched these developments with dread and articulated their concerns in familiar eighteenth-century narratives about the enervating potential of consumption. In poetry, Wordsworth's sonnet 'The World Is Too Much With Us' (1807) lamented the destructive effects of materialism: 'Getting and spending, we lay waste our powers', while in medicine, the physician Thomas Trotter expressed similar sentiments, writing that the nation that had once ruled the waves 'had degenerated into a nation of slaves' (in Porter 1992, 186). Concerns about the negative effects of consumerism also ran as a leitmotif through the emerging discipline of social science, in the classic accounts of Karl Marx, Émile Durkheim and Thorstein Veblen. In *Economic and Philosophic Manuscripts*, for example, Marx described the structural tendency of capitalism to generate alienation in both the spheres of consumption and production as well as its drive to continually stimulate new forms of consumption in order to increase profits. In the more radical section on 'The Meaning of Human Requirements', he anticipated critiques of excessive consumption by over a century, arguing that capitalists had a vested interest in cultivating what he described as 'excess and intemperance' amongst the population. Profit depended on the constant stimulation of appetites and the introduction of novelties and fashions that were, however, discarded almost immediately as consumers were presented with a new array of temptations, and the cycle begun all over again. He accused producers of 'feeding imaginary appetites' to the point where real needs were replaced by 'fantasy, caprice and whim'. The end result, he stated, is that producers act as 'pimps' between consumers and their sense of need, generating 'morbid appetites, lying in wait for their weaknesses – all so that they can demand cash for this service of love' (Marx 1972 [1844], 148). The end result, for Marx, was the erasure of the line that separates desire from need and the generation of indulgence, hedonism and excessive consumption in the population.

It was also in this climate that Veblen observed the conspicuous consumption of the American bourgeoisie, publishing *The Theory of the Leisure Class* (1912 [1899]), as a sardonic indictment of what he regarded as the ostentation and greed that lay behind the new consumer behaviour. He argued that the leisure class used lavish displays of consumption in attempts to outdo their neighbours and demonstrate their standing in the social hierarchy. For Veblen, the joyless cycle of striving and envy was unending, and any satiation of the desire for wealth or goods was impossible, leading to a state of 'chronic dissatisfaction' (Veblen 1912 [1899], 20–21). Fundamental to the new consumer behaviour was waste: of time as well as goods, for it was primarily through its non-utilitarian nature that consumption acted as a marker of social status and prestige. As Veblen put it, 'In order to be reputable, it must be wasteful' (1912 [1899], 77). In Veblen's cynical appraisal of the 'invidious' basis of consumer ostentation, we can see a continuation of the critique of luxury: a tradition that was still widespread in the nineteenth century, although one that was being joined by critical commentaries that were formulating novel perspectives.

Émile Durkheim watched developments in France with dismay, and in both *The Division of Labour in Society* and *Suicide* equated excessive consumption with the regulatory breakdown of society itself. For him, society was regulated by a moral force which ensured that an individual's desires and the means of attaining them were balanced and finite; in other words, that 'an end and goal are set to the passions' (Durkheim 1984 [1893] 250). However, Durkheim feared that the increased affluence of the nineteenth century was destroying this regulatory force, unleashing insatiable appetites and bringing about a state of disequilibrium or 'anomie'. Industrialisation itself was regarded as a cause of this disruption, and described in terms of organic contagion: 'The contagious influence of large urban areas, [which] causes the needs of the workers to increase' (1984 [1893], 306). Without regulation, the constant search for fulfilment through the consumption of goods and experiences fell into 'an insatiable and bottomless abyss' (Durkheim 1970 [1897], 247), repeated over and over again in a form of behaviour that Durkheim described as pathological. This was 'the longing for infinity', of which he wrote, in *Suicide*:

> From top to bottom of the social ladder, greed is aroused without knowing where to find ultimate foothold. . . . A thirst arises for novelties, unfamiliar pleasures, nameless sensations, all of which lose their savour once known.
>
> (Durkheim 1970 [1897], 256)

This pathological state ultimately led to suicide, although according to Durkheim, not everyone was equally at risk. Unusually amongst social observers, he regarded the affluent, rather than the poor, as most vulnerable. The lower economic position and aspirations of the working class protected them from a more acute awareness of the infinite possibility extending above them. Durkheim declared:

> At least the horizon of the lower classes is limited by those above them, and for this same reason their desires are more modest. Those who have only empty space above them are almost inevitably lost in it, if no force restrains them.
>
> (1970 [1897], 257)

For Durkheim, then, unregulated consumption represented an almost literal gazing into the abyss.[1]

As with the response to the 'consumer revolution' in the eighteenth century, again we can see a fearful, critical reaction to increased consumption throughout the population. Running as a leitmotif throughout these classic texts is a portrayal of consumption and unchecked desire in terms of morbid appetites, false needs, alienation, anomie, waste and suicide. Durkheim's vision, in particular, is nothing less than the disintegration of civilisation. As Roy Porter has put it, during this period, modernity itself was coming to be regarded as pathological and portrayed as 'morbidly self destructive and self-enslaving: the acquisitive society was the addictive society' (Porter 1992, 180).

However, towards the end of the nineteenth century, a new paradigm was emerging which would articulate such sentiments in new ways, and which would become increasingly influential as an explanation for a wide range of human behaviour.

Addiction: disease of the will

Increasingly, fears over what was regarded as excessive consumption were being expressed in the language of medicine and pathology, where the concerns of both state and medicine coalesced around the moral–religious notion of the 'Will'. This would eventually produce the idea of addiction as a 'disease of the will', and it is to this development that we now turn.

Ever since the Reformation, the Will had been highly valued as the essential faculty that regulated all human behaviour, and that governed Desire (Smith 1992). In the nineteenth century, however, it became virtually hypostatised as a real agency that exercised a civilising force over the undisciplined animal instincts of the body (Valverde 1998). The increasing valorisation of the will was linked to the shifting socio-economic requirements and ethical formations of industrial society, which required high levels of self-discipline and an orderly, hard-working and sober labour force for the generation of profit and maintenance of social stability. In this climate, the idea of the will become a kind of moral code for the secular, rational individual – more specifically, the bourgeois male – within whom willpower intersected with notions of respectability, and 'character'. Here, masculine identity was conceived as a project of achieving control over not only one's external environment, but also one's self – overcoming temptations through discipline and continual self-monitoring in an exercise of what the nineteenth-century writer Hannah More called 'an habitual interior restraint' (1830, in Hunt 1996, 156).

It was at this time that new intellectual frameworks were being formed, which would radically alter conceptions of the will as well as its relation to desire, and which would lay the groundwork for the emergence of what came to be the notion of 'addiction' later in the century.[2] From the end of the eighteenth century, an assortment of physicians, moralists, reformers and religious leaders across Europe and in the United States had been taking an interest in the consumption of alcohol and opiates as the repositories of moral and physical pathology. The focus of many of these groups, and particularly the growing temperance movement in the United States, was initially alcohol, where consumption had increased dramatically. In 1820, per capita consumption was over seven gallons a year – a figure twice that consumed in the late twentieth century (Hickman 2007, 22). Heavy drinking was associated with violence and family breakdown and became a focus of temperance efforts to eliminate alcohol-related social disruption from society. Up until this point, drinking (and, indeed, all forms of consumption) had been regarded within the context of the Puritan doctrine of free will, which stipulated that individuals could always exercise choice in their actions (Levine 1978, 150). As such, drunkenness was regarded as the product of free choice and was described in terms of desire – however sinful. The drunkard loved to drink and found pleasure in the habit and, as such, was fully responsible for his or her actions, which were, therefore, evidence of sin.

Now, however, alcohol became the subject of new ideas about the will and of the power of particular commodities to overwhelm it. The American physician Benjamin Rush (1785) introduced the notion that the will could be damaged by disease, undermining its sovereignty over desire and leading to a state in which the individual was no longer free, but was rather *compelled* to behave in certain ways. The terminology shifted to accommodate the change: in place of love and pleasure, the emphasis was now on compulsion and irresistibility to describe the drunkard's desire for alcohol (Levine 1978, 148). Successive bouts of drinking weakened the will, leaving it unable to exercise any restraining influence over physical passions, a state of inebriety Rush described as a disease. Crucially, in this new framework, alcohol was now positioned as an inherently powerful substance that could undermine free will. Rush explained how 'the use of strong drink is at first the effect of free agency. From habit it takes places from necessity' (in Levine 1978, 152). He used the phrase 'disease of the will' to describe the enslavement of individuals by forces beyond their control, with the relation between the diseased individual and the substance they could not resist described by the notion of 'addiction'. The term had been used intermittently in this context before now. However, around the nineteenth century, its meanings changed, and it was increasingly associated with the negative effects of unwilled behaviour and used to describe a devotion or inclination to a habit or pursuit.

'Addiction' was not the only means of articulating ideas about compromised willpower, however, but was joined by a loose variety of medical-moral terms, including monomania, dipsomania, morphinism and inebriety. All of these could be described as belonging to the broad category of 'diseases of the will', which acted as a kind of shorthand for expressing a general loss of control. The physician Thomas Trotter, for instance, regarded uncontrolled drinking as more of a mental than physical ailment – 'a disease of the mind' – which, nevertheless, had physical aspects that rendered the afflicted individual incapable of either self-control or responsibility for their actions (Conrad and Schneider 1992, 78). Meanwhile the term *dipsomania* referred to a similar state of 'moral insanity', rooted in heredity, that was characterised by an uncontrolled craving for alcohol. The notion that the will could be 'paralysed' was expressed in the idea of 'inebriety' – a general concept that embraced excessive consumption of alcohol, opiates, tobacco and caffeine and various other substances. Its scientific authority was bolstered by key discoveries in chemistry that appeared to identify the 'addictive' component in various commodities, such as alkaloids in opiates, caffeine in coffee and nicotine in tobacco. Such techno-scientific advances were interpreted as evidence of the material basis of a variety of diseases of the will, now described as 'morphinism', 'caffeinism' and 'tobaccomania' (Goodman 1993, 115–117). Meanwhile, in France, the prominent alienist J.E.D. Esquirol located issues relating to the will within the notion of 'monomania', or partial insanity. Monomania of the will was characterised by overwhelming impulses and described a temporary lapse of reason that could be either physical or moral in origin. Emil Kraepelin drew on the idea of loss of impulse control to describe uncontrolled buying amongst women as *oniomania* (from the Greek *one*, for *shopping*, and *mania*, for *frenzy*) and compared it with men's impulsive gambling – *ludomania*, and Bleuler added *kleptomania* – compulsive stealing – to a growing list of disorders. All of these produced new medico-psychological ways of thinking about the excesses of consumption, and laid the groundwork for understandings of what would be reformulated as 'impulse control disorders' in the psychiatric literature of the twentieth century.

In his classic work on *The Diseases of the Will*, Theodule Ribot classified a range of these new pathologies in a way that linked the nineteenth century's materialistic epistemology of degeneration with its expanding consumerist landscape. He considered conditions such as kleptomania and dipsomania to be caused by an excess of impulse too strong for the will to control, writing that the patient 'feels that he is no more master of himself, that he is dominated by an interior force' (1896, 58). This undermining of the self formed part of Ribot's preoccupation with the problems of loss of control, freedom, action and choice that he saw as prevalent in nineteenth century society, and which he argued were reducible, ultimately, to physiological causes, that is, to degeneration.

In kleptomania, we can see an instance of gendered fears surrounding commodity culture, in which otherwise respectable, middle class women were being overwhelmed by the temptations of consumerism. Amongst this group, kleptomania was regarded as a mental disorder, linked to the biological vicissitudes of women's reproductive systems and their weak constitutions. Women who suffered from it were argued to be driven by irrational impulses and were painted as helpless victims of both their gender and their era. According to Elaine Abelson, it was a label 'that evoked understanding, if not genuine sympathy' (1989, 140). Amongst working class women and men, however, meanings were very different, and 'kleptomaniacs' were simply regarded as thieves and common criminals. The 'disease' of kleptomania undermined the probity of Victorian culture and hinted at a pathology that lurked behind the orderly façade of consumerism. It possessed connotations of sexuality and licentiousness in the image of women idly wandering through the new department stores, gazing upon and fondling luxurious displays of goods, then imagining and desiring what they had touched (Abelson 1989; Felski 1995). Discourses surrounding kleptomania articulated concerns about women's wider role in industrial society: their new-found visibility and freedom in public life and their increasing demands for suffrage. As Rita Felski (1995, 61) has pointed out, the period of modernity saw a general feminisation and denigration of consumption itself. Within this wider trend, the particular pathology of kleptomania can be seen as an articulation of the dangers of consumerism, the new ethos of gratification and the effects of mass produced luxury. These kinds of associations are not new, of course, and are part of a long running theme in which concerns around consumption are expressed in particular, gendered ways. The anxieties expressed by the disorder of kleptomania, for example, resonate with the sexualisation and gendering of eighteenth-century concerns about luxury that we saw in the previous chapter. Each critique, in its own way, articulates fears of the destructive, enervating effects of feminised consumption, contrasted with the order and stability of productive masculinity. Such associations shift over time, expressing cultural anxieties in particular ways, and we will return to them again throughout this book, in particular, when we turn to look at some of the issues around food in Chapter 5.

Returning to the main argument: the notion of the will that underlay the diverse formulations of kleptomania, monomania, inebriety, dipsomania and the like has been described as an 'ontologically hybrid entity' (Valverde 1998, 61). In her careful analysis of the period, *Diseases of the Will*, Mariana Valverde notes that it was both 'somatised' as a real entity, and yet it also had a moral presence. The 'disease' in question was regarded as physical in origin, with physiological states like craving and withdrawal taken as clear evidence of its physiological status. But at the same time, it was also defined in terms of behaviour that deviated from the norm – an essentially social assumption – while explanations of addiction itself were couched in moralistic terms, as a deficit of character or moral weakness: 'moral insanity' as it was known. And so, in this peculiar condition, the moral, the social and the physical converge in what one nineteenth-century physician described as a state of 'diseased cravings and paralysed control' (in Berridge and Edwards 1987, 155). Such a discursive formation, in which addiction is defined as a bona fide physiological state, and yet, nevertheless, explained in terms of social and normative assumptions, continues to shape ideas about addiction today, as we shall see over the following chapters.

Running through these ideas about 'diseases of the will', in all their variety, we can see the emergence of a new vocabulary of compulsion that represents new ways of thinking about consumption as well as new ways of thinking about consumers. It is a vocabulary that, I would suggest, reflects broader political-economic shifts. The essence of 'diseases' such as monomania, inebriety, dipsomania and the rest was loss of control or helplessness and involved the interaction between a physical substance that was inherently powerful and an individual will that was too weak to resist it. In this, it acted as a culturally expedient idea that linked ideas about vulnerable wills and physical pathology with the irresistible temptations of commodity culture (Weinberg 2005). Further, in such discourses, we can see a certain congruence between medical narratives and economic concerns. There is a shift from exogenous explanations that describe pathology in terms of an invasion of 'noxious' external agents, congruent with mercantile fears of foreign commodities, to endogenous explanations that focus on weaknesses and pathologies within the individual – whether located in their biology, morality or wills – at the same time that individual self-control becomes ever more important to industrial states. Whereas the tropes of luxury reflected colonial concerns over foreign commodities, ideas about 'the will' reflected an increasing emphasis on self-control in a period of economic liberalism.

The notion that wills could become 'diseased' through contact with powerful commodities such as alcohol was extremely timely and, according to Darin Weinberg (2005), articulated a 'growing existential anxiety' that attended the increasing urbanisation and industrialisation of modern society. Emergent quasi-medical ideas about addiction articulated concerns over loss of control and, initially at least, provided an exculpatory explanation for the excesses of middle class consumption. As Weinberg puts it, nineteenth-century concepts of addiction, as well as insanity, were first forged to 'preserve the integrity of otherwise respectable troublemakers, and serve as resources for their redemption' (2005, 6).

Although the problem of addiction would eventually come to be associated almost exclusively with those of lower socio-economic status, its initial recognition as an illness and, therefore, a matter worthy of investigation was related to its perceived incidence amongst the wealthy, where it was greeted with sympathetic concern and expensive medical treatment. As Mark Kohn dryly observes, 'Medicine did not explore the effects of industrial civilisation on those whose toil produced it with the same diligence that it brought to the infirmity of the bourgeoisie' (1987, 64). Disease theory was founded on a socially stratified materialism that regarded bourgeois brains as qualitatively different from proletarian ones. One Sir Ronald Armstrong-Jones, of Claybury Asylum, for example, articulated the distinction quite forcibly in his diagnosis of difference, writing that

> there is generally a physical difference between the brains of those in the private and rate-aided class . . . not only is the brain weight heavier, but there is also in the private class an added complexity of convolutional pattern . . . which mean a higher sensitiveness and greater vulnerability.
>
> *(in Berridge and Edwards 1987, 158)*

This so-called added complexity made their owners more susceptible to the strains of modem living and, in this, addiction, like neurasthenia (a culture-bound condition widespread amongst the Victorian middle classes), was regarded as an affliction partly induced by the rigours of civilisation (Porter 1993b). Like neurasthenics, addicts' delicate nervous systems were ill equipped to deal with the demands and excessive strains of modern life, making addiction particularly common amongst 'active brain workers' (in Conrad and Schneider 1992, 120). In this framework, middle class consumption of opium for recreational purposes – 'luxurious use' as it was known – was regarded as a respectable pastime, with addiction a regrettable lapse to be greeted with concerned sympathy and expensive medical treatment. Indeed, the consumption of Romantic writers like Samuel Coleridge and Thomas De Quincey was presented as an outlet for the artistic disposition, with narratives such as De Quincey's *Confessions of an English Opium-Eater* portrayed as a voyage of enlightenment and discovery, rather than one of addiction and decline.

Although ideas about addiction were initially worked out with the supposedly sensitive temperaments of the middle classes in mind, the concerns they embodied converged with wider fears over social disorder, so that the notion of addiction as a general loss of control came to be associated with specific social groups whose consumption was regarded as problematic. In particular, the willpower and self-control of the working classes, women and immigrants was regarded as especially weak: a 'stratification of the will' (Valverde 1998) that corresponded to the stratification of industrial society itself. A focus on these groups was tied up with bio-political attempts to govern the behaviour of the population, and it is to this that we now turn.

'The great technology of power'

The argument here that ideas about addiction as a disease of the will can be regarded as an aspect of what Foucault has described as the 'great technology of power' (1976, 140) or, in his later works, as the 'new physics of power' (1977) of the nineteenth century. Such a project, whose aim was the governance of the habits of the population, was intimately related to the development of capitalism and to widespread demographic change. The demands of economic productivity and military conflict required greater control over a growing population, whose movements were becoming ever more integral to the growth and stability of the modern state. The 'accumulation of men' had to be adjusted to meet the needs of the 'accumulation of capital', since the development of capitalism depended on the 'controlled insertion of bodies into the machinery of production' (Foucault 1976, 141). In other words, the practical requirements of economic productivity and efficient warfare demanded a healthy population: quite simply, the population had to be fit to work and to fight. And, in the nineteenth century, it was not up to standard. Illness and disease caused by poor diet, housing and sanitation were rife amongst the urban working class, a state which undermined the nation's productivity and security by debilitating the basis of both economic and military power (Turner 2008). At the same time, widespread infectious disease not only decimated the working class, but also threatened the health of the wider population – a particularly worrying state for the bourgeoisie, whose generalised fears of 'contagion' acted as both metaphor and focal point for widespread fears of disorder.

It was in this context that the life and health of the population, in all its various formations, became a matter of state interest and 'permanent, positive intervention' (Foucault 1976, 147). To assume responsibility for the care of its citizens, the state adjusted its gaze to focus on their every move: 'Their everyday behaviour, their identity, their activity, their apparently unimportant gestures' in order to better know – and so govern – them (Foucault 1977, 77).[3] Utilising the new statistical techniques of government, and drawing on medicalised forms of knowledge, a range of regulatory and coercive projects developed throughout the century, through which such biopolitical control was enacted. Some were religious, some secular, some associated with political reform, others with public health. All were concerned, in one way or another, with the reformation of the morals, health and lifestyles of the poor, and they attempted to instil middle class values of 'respectability' on the population: in other words, to promote the values of self-discipline and hard work for men, maternal domesticity and sexual purity for women.

It was these concerns, focused on particular disorderly groups, that brought ideas about addiction to life by, as Timothy Hickman puts it, 'personifying' addiction in recognisable stereotypes (2007). In particular, racialised and gendered 'others', as well as the urban proletariat, who were already regarded as lacking in the self-control demanded of modern society, became the tangible focus of fears about addiction. It is to these groups of 'others' that we now turn, focusing in particular on their consumption of opium and alcohol: two commodities whose trajectories were instrumental in the production of ideas about addiction. Ultimately, this shifting trajectory highlights the ways in which the development of ideas about addictive consumption acted as a form of biomedical governance, with a particular focus on the habits and bodies of the poor, and on women.

The habits of the population: opium and the addicted 'others'

The emergence of a working class, congregating in the quickly expanding, often chaotic, urban centres of the nation, was a source of ongoing concern for the bourgeoisie. The living conditions, values and habits of the poor were largely mysterious, albeit dimly perceived as threatening and disorderly to the middle classes, whose own orderly moral universe seemed a world apart. It was, as

Foucault put it, part of a '"great fear" of a people who were believed to be criminal and seditious as a whole' and who constituted 'a barbaric, immoral and outlaw class which . . . haunted the discourse of legislators, philanthropists and investigators into working class life' (Foucault 1977, 275). Temperance and public health concerns centred on the leisure and consumption practices of the poor, and especially their consumption of psychoactive substances for pleasure, or 'stimulant' use, as it was known. The image of unruly hordes of factory workers indulging in opium – or any other mind-altering substance, for that matter – undermined the requirement for a sober, manageable workforce, and was greeted with horror.

Opium had long been part of everyday life for the poor: freely available and widely consumed, it acted as both a palliative for a range of ailments and a pleasurable escape from the harshness and tedium of working life. In Berridge and Edwards's (1987) memorable phrase, it was truly an 'opium of the people'. However, in the nineteenth century, opium became a symbol of the growing political power of the working class and of the social disruption that was feared such power might lead to. Such fears were quite literally embedded in specific sociospatial contexts – namely, the densely populated urban centres that were expanding, unplanned and at breakneck speed, throughout the country. Kohn's depiction of the perception of menace is striking, and he writes in *Narcomania*:

> There they [the middle classes] were, extracting profit from the engines of the industrial revolution, building the cities which they themselves had to hack their way into, like jungles. They were corralling the poor masses, organising them into streets, mills and factories. Yet inside those alleys and workshops, a class was taking shape which its masters could not understand.
>
> *(Kohn 1987, 53)*

Overcrowded, insanitary slums were breeding grounds for infectious diseases such as cholera and typhus, which spread rapidly amongst their inhabitants. Medicalised ideas about contagion and 'miasma' went beyond physical diseases, however, to represent fears about the wider spread of immoral and disorderly behaviour, particularly those expressed through consumption. Such normative judgements provided the backdrop for statements like Durkheim's about 'the contagious influence of large urban areas' (1984 [1893], 289). Ideas about contagion were also caught up in the pseudoscience of degeneration that claimed the regression of the species through defective physiology and, because 'moral vices' were also regarded as both cause and effect of physical processes, certain types of 'defective' behaviour, including consumption habits, too. The fear, for respectable Victorian commentators, was that such degeneracy would spread beyond the slums to infect the wider public. In this, the contagious nature of degeneration was presented as a threat to the national stock that would undermine the gene pool and so the reproduction of the nation.

These fears were tied up with public health concerns over childrearing practices, and particularly directed towards working class women. As guardians of 'the future of the race', women's consumption, particularly of alcohol and opium, was subject to scrutiny as vices that squandered their time, money and attention away from their prime role of childcare. For degenerist writers such as Henry Maudsley, women who drank to 'excess' were regarded as not only lacking in willpower, but also mentally defective, and considered 'feeble-minded' or 'inebriate' – the possessors of mental defects that were hereditary and could be passed on to children. In the case of opium, childrearing fears centred specifically on the practice of 'infant doping', whereby mothers dosed their children with opium-based medicines that went by names such as *Mrs Winslow's Soothing Syrup* and *The Infant's Friend*, to ease colic and teething and to calm their babies while they went to work.[4] Outrage that women resorted to 'poisoning' their babies with gin while they enjoyed themselves in pubs also fuelled a debate that was driven in part by concerns over high child mortality figures as well as by disapproval over women's increased mobility in the labour market and public sphere (Valverde 1998, 54). Such 'infant doping' was the target of the public health movement, which agitated for restrictions on the sale of the preparations and campaigned to remould working class parenting into a 'respectable' form. Campaigners assumed that women's absence in the home was the root of the problem, although, as Berridge and Edwards point out, most infant deaths were actually caused by the poor sanitation, housing and diet endemic in working class life, and not by irresponsible mothers. In such a situation, opium actually had a positive role to play as a palliative for the ill health caused by poverty and an aid to women with little or no access to other forms of healthcare. Nor did the public health campaigns focus on the narcotising of middle class children – a practice which was at least as widespread as working class doping by nursemaids who regularly used opiates as a quietener on their charges (Berridge and Edwards 1987, 101).

All of these kinds of concerns about degeneracy, defective parenting and personal immorality, made visible through consumption, gave voice, albeit in disguised form, to wider fears about women's role in the nineteenth century. As with the anxieties around middle class female kleptomania, these ideas expressed unease around the changing social relations of an industrial society as well as concerns about Britain's ability to maintain its position of economic dominance on the global stage. In such a configuration, the whole area of female consumption became charged with issues of national and, in Britain's case at least, imperial concern.[5]

Opium was a key player in these issues. As a symbol of all that was disorderly or dangerous in working class consumption, it was increasingly the focus of public health concerns and, in this, the subject of biomedical control. Its trajectory was tied up with a convergence of interests between medicine and the state, which acted both to remove opium from everyday consumption and to increase dependence on more powerful commodities, such as morphine. In this context, tracing what Kopytoff (1986) would describe as the 'cultural biography' of opium is to study a substance that moved in and out of commodity status, shifting from an everyday form of consumption, to a restricted, medicalised substance, in ways that highlight the fluid boundaries between ideas about 'addiction' and those of 'consumption'. They also highlight the ways in which the development of ideas about addictive consumption act as a means of governance.

This shifting status, carefully outlined in Berridge and Edwards's classic study of *Opium and the People* (1987), to which this section of the chapter is indebted, was driven by legislative and scientific developments, in tandem with the ambitions of an embryonic medical profession. On the one hand, a series of Pharmacy Acts worked to restrict the sale of opium to medically qualified persons, whereas on the other hand, techno-chemical discoveries, such as the isolation of *morphium*, the active component of opium, and the development of the hypodermic syringe, acted to remove opiates from the hands of the people and place them exclusively in medically qualified ones. The synthesis of morphine and the shift from oral consumption to hypodermic injection established medical authority as a superior form of knowledge, separate from the mass of quacks and healers that made up the bulk of public understanding of medicine at that time. The exclusive dispensing of morphine by physicians changed the status of opiate consumers to patients or – depending on their social class – criminals. Techno-scientific developments also worked to create a faster acting, more powerful product, which provided a more intense consumption experience. Indeed, the cultural imagery of the hypodermic syringe itself has been depicted as a powerful symbol of the technological transformation of what Avital Ronell (1992) describes as 'narcotic modernity' and Timothy Hickman (2007) calls 'addictive modernity'.

This intensification would have implications for ideas about addiction, particularly amongst middle class women. Here, and in contrast to ideas about the 'degenerate' consumption of the poor, middle class female addiction was tied up with discourses of 'respectable femininity' and linked to women's complex reproductive functions, which were still a source for the diagnosis of many 'hysterical' complaints (Showalter 1985).[6] Their 'naturally' more sensitive constitutions were argued to make women vulnerable to the pressures of modernity: a weakness that was manifested, as we saw earlier, in the gendered pathology of kleptomania. It also made them vulnerable to *morphinism* – a new condition that was generated by the medical profession itself.

Whereas the consumption of opiates by women for their pleasurable physical effects was regarded as immoral, and was associated with prostitution, medicinal use was considered quite respectable, and was actually increasing, in the form of hypodermic consumption of morphine. The practice of hypodermic administration was jealously guarded as the prerogative of qualified professionals, who liberally deployed it in the battle against a range of ailments, from the pain of childbirth to sleeplessness and 'nerves', considered to be hysterical in origin, and from which women were considered to be particularly prone. The stupefying effects of opiates no doubt appeared as an effective treatment for the nervous excitability of hysterical women, in much the same way as Valium would be in the next century. Morphine was also regarded as a cure for alcoholism and opium addiction and, because injection was regarded as quite safe, many doctors weaned their patients off what were regarded as bad habits and into a lifelong relationship with morphine through liberal use of the needle (in Berridge and Edwards 1987, 141). However, over time, the problems relating to injection became impossible to ignore. Because doses were far more concentrated, the incidence of dependence increased, with the German physician E. Levinstein in 1877 coining the term 'morphinism' (later 'morphinomania') to describe the disease that was the 'morbid craving for morphine'. Most of the afflicted individuals were drawn from the upper and professional classes, and large numbers were female, for morphine was overwhelmingly a middle class drug, dispensed to those patients wealthy enough to pay for the services of a physician. Although the number of morphine addicts was not especially large, their status made them very visible to the professionals who had created them and who were responsible for treating them, so exaggerating the dimensions of the problem and highlighting the problems of addiction more generally (Berridge and Edwards 1987; Conrad and Schneider 1992). By the end of the century, then, it was clear that the medical profession had, to all intents and purposes, created, stimulated and then treated the problem of opiate dependence amongst certain section of the population.

Ethnicity: 'racialised others'

The consumption of opium was also caught up in a range of ethnic tensions, which centred on Chinese migration into the urban centres of Britain and the United States, and in Britain, opposition to the opium trade in the Far East (which as we saw in the previous chapter, resulted in the Opium Wars). This produced another variation of addiction in the racialised figure of the 'oriental opium fiend'.

A variety of anti-opium organisations, including the Society for the Suppression of the Opium Trade (SSOT) and the Anti-Opium Society, protested against what they saw as the immorality of trading in a dangerous, addicting commodity for profit. They found medical experts – many of whom had their own strategic interest in promoting perceptions of the dangers of opium – to rail against the harm caused by the drug, and to claim for it the power to create instant and lifelong addiction and to lead to vices such as crime and prostitution (Kohn 1987; Berridge and Edwards 1987). Together, these experts and organisations assembled an image of Chinese opium addicts as depraved and immoral, unable to control their appetites, and outwith 'respectable' society. Ethnic minority Chinese communities provided many Victorians with their first direct contact with a foreign culture, and although their numbers were generally quite small (at least in Britain), their impact was not. Into the urban labyrinths that formed the backdrop to bourgeois nightmares of social unrest came another element that appeared even more unsettling. The Chinese smoked, rather than ate, opium, a practice shrouded in mystery and whose very difference stimulated the creation of fearful stereotypes of 'smoking dens' as places of degeneracy, immorality and vice. Because it increasingly shunned this underworld, much of what 'respectable' Victorian society knew – or believed it knew – about it came from rumour, anecdote and the literary imagination. Writers such as Arthur Conan Doyle, Oscar Wilde and Charles Dickens painted vivid pictures of these mythical dens, where vicious 'drug fiends' lolled in drug-induced stupor. Although Wilde's hostile portrait in *The Picture of Dorian Gray* (1891) was a product of his imagination, it contributed to the popular image of Chinese subcultural life as though it were reality. His grotesque description of 'the twisted limbs, the gaping mouths, the staring lustreless eyes . . . . [of a] lascar dead drunk with opium' (in Berridge and Edwards 1987, 197) expressed growing popular hostility to opium, to Chinese culture, and to the perceived relations between them. Such fictional depictions also dehumanised the Chinese and contributed to the creation of a racial stereotype of Chinese opium smokers as possessors of 'depraved appetites', characterised by indolence, cruelty and laziness (Berridge and Edwards 1987, 198).[7]

The combination of Chinese immigrants, smoking dens and opium was fertile ground for ideas about contagion and degeneration, and out of them the image of Chinese addicts was turned into a vivid symbol for the dangerous foreign pollutants that could infect and undermine national stock. The possibility of contagion was particularly fearful because it suggested that the habits of these degenerate 'others' could spread to infect respectable, middle class society. In a striking, but typical, example of the conflation of moral-medical categories, couched in the language of Victorian imperialism, one Professor Goldwin Smith pointed to the influx of Chinese, bringing with them 'a hideous and very infectious vice' (in Berridge and Edwards 1987, 200).

Underlying fears of racial contagion were economic concerns: in particular, insecurity over declining productivity and anxiety over competition for jobs. The willingness of the Chinese to work for lower wages under poorer conditions was regarded as a threat to local labourers, particularly in America, where migrant workers were recruited and imported as cheap labour to work on large-scale projects such as railroads. Although economic tensions were not as acute in Britain, the figure of the Chinese 'opium fiend' invading, polluting and weakening the nation with foreign habits still served as a thinly veiled disguise for fears of unemployment and more general economic instability. The configuration of the racist 'other' was different in America and was focused on African Americans' consumption of cocaine. In particular, xenophobic ideas that cocaine made blacks violent towards whites, particularly women, who were at risk of rape by the 'cocaine-crazed Negro brain', originated in the Southern states (in Hickman 2007, 76). For Hickman, the power of this inscription of addiction lay in essentialist conceptions of racist identity. For many nineteenth-century commentators, African Americans were barely human and their actions governed by desire, passion and animal violence. In ideas about a 'brutal, bestial and predatory essence' (in Hickman 2007, 76) that was, supposedly, unleashed by the consumption of cocaine (and, indeed, any kind of intoxicants), we can see the racist application of tropes about the destructive effects of bodily Desire uncontrolled by the civilising force of the Will. As a result of these xenophobic stereotypes, by the end of the nineteenth century, the consumption of drugs by non-whites was regarded with widespread fear and met with coercive controls in a series of legislative restrictions on the non-medical use of cocaine and opiates in America (Weinberg 2005, 48).

Running through such racialised discourses was a dual focus: on the one hand, on weakness that was inherent in the individual themselves, and on the other, on the powerful commodity that overpowered them. Despite the degenerate power they were perceived to wield, Chinese addicts themselves were also regarded as victims of their vice, with one physician sympathising with those who were 'helpless slaves to this expensive indulgence' (in Berridge and Edwards 1987, 197). The SSOT condemned the 'weak and unmanly' character of the opium fiend, whereas others described the effects of the drug as rendering smokers 'dazed and helpless' as well as passive, 'anaemic and impotent' (Conrad and Schneider 1992, 118). In these kinds of ideas, we can hear echoes of mercantile concerns about the enervating and emasculating effects of powerful commodities, although now their power lies more in their conjunction with diseased wills and individual weakness rather than in their associations with foreign invasion.

The linking of specific practices of consumption with these medical-moral notions of degeneracy, miasma and contagion were expressions of Victorian morality: as Foucault put it, of the subordination of science to 'the imperatives of a morality whose divisions it reiterated under the guise of the medical norm' (Foucault 1976, 53). In some contexts, ideas about the 'contagious' aspects of consumption persist, particularly, for example, around current, largely working class, smoking, although today reconfigured in terms of disgust over the risks of second hand smoke, particularly when those who produce it tend to be non-white and poor, as we will see in Chapter 4.

To end this section, we can note that, in a broader sense, all of these diverse ideas about addiction as a disease of the will were tied up in a discursive framework that linked concerns about gendered reproduction and economic productivity with the consumption practices of specific groups. Such connections brought ideas about addiction to life, by personifying them, as we saw earlier, in recognisable stereotypes (Hickman 2007): the oriental opium fiend, the female inebriate, the morphine addict, the weak-willed kleptomaniac and the degenerate alcoholic. Together, these forged new ways of thinking about consumption, and new ways of thinking about consumers as 'addicts', as we will see in the final section of this chapter. They also established the idea that such individuals were the rightful object of governance, and it is to this that we now turn.

The disciplining of the will

Throughout the nineteenth century, a range of disciplinary practices was directed at those who were unable or unwilling to regulate their consumption. If individuals were unable to control themselves, then the techniques and institutions of medicine and the state would do it for them. Accordingly, a range of medical-juridical regimes aimed to install the values of self-control and reason by building up atrophied wills through discipline and hard work. This 'micro-physics of power' was made up of an uneven development of moral, legal and medical projects, realised through various acts and institutions, that were designed, in effect, to control the consuming population. Such a project was stratified along both class and gender lines. Generally speaking, the response to working class excess was realised through disciplinary efforts to regulate behaviour, from legislation and prisons to inebriate homes and asylums, whereas middle class problems were subject to the gentler approach of individualised treatment and pastoral care in private 'retreats'.

The Victorian era was littered with legislation that attempted to outlaw or regulate numerous forms of working class consumption. So, for example, the Inebriates Acts (1879 and 1898), the Pharmacy Act (1868), the Smoking Opium Exclusion Act (1908), the Gaming Act (1845) and the Street Betting Acts (1853, 1874 and 1906), amongst others, were disciplinary responses to fears of unruly 'others' that regulated the spaces and practices of working class consumption. Between them, they outlawed the sale of opium amongst the general population, as well as the practice of smoking it, and restricted the sale and consumption of alcohol, so corralling working class consumption into ever narrower, more regulated spaces, and in the process, turning large numbers of consumers into criminals. Working class gambling was subject to particular intervention. Its promise of unearned wealth undermined the basis of the Protestant work ethic and exemplified the disorder and loss of control that the bourgeoisie were trying to eliminate in both society and in the psyche of the poor (Reith 1999). Gamblers were targeted by specific reformist groups, such as the National Anti-Gambling League, and games of chance regulated through a succession of statutes and Acts, which forbade the playing of games of chance in public places (Reith 1999, 85–86). All of these disciplinary interventions in the lifestyles, morals and health of the working class was justified on philanthropic and public health grounds, with the Vice Society, for example, claiming that it aimed to 'extend the happiness and comforts of the poor by checking their destructive excesses' (1807, in Hunt 1996, 75).

In this legislative landscape, the Habitual Inebriates Acts of 1879 and 1898 stand out in their creation of a socially stratified division of disorderly consumers. Initially, alcoholics or addicts had been incorporated into the category of 'lunacy' and treated in insane asylums such as Bethlem. Now, however, the two Acts set out different pathways for treatment according to the class and gender of the consumer, designating some 'patients', the others, 'criminals'. Whereas the first Act focused on the establishment of private 'retreats' for the voluntary treatment of patients from the middle and upper classes, the second targeted both crime associated with drunkenness and groups accused of being 'habitual inebriates' (Berridge and Edwards 1987, 166). In effect, the second Act criminalised 'disorderly' men and particularly 'neglectful' mothers charged with child neglect, who made up the majority of those charged, and who were despatched to reformatories for discipline as well as treatment (Valverde 1998, 77). With their authoritarian regimes and coercive treatment, such reformatories were often indistinguishable from prisons. Their aim was nothing less than the reformation of weakened wills through discipline, abstinence and hard work in order to 'ensure the maintenance of productive relations' (Foucault 1977, 141).

Problems of middle class consumption, on the other hand, tended to be viewed with sympathy and indulgence and were treated through a range of therapeutic interventions, including pastoral care and private health retreats. Residence at these commercial retreats was voluntary and, because patients were also paying customers, there was little in the way of coercion or enforced discipline. In fact, many retreats were virtually health resorts, offering a range of sports and an invigorating mixture of fresh air, exercise and healthy food in regimes designed to instil good habits and develop character and moral fibre (Valverde 1998, 81). Such regimes worked together with the patient to return them to the status of free, self-actualising individuals, emphasising the aspects of courage and strength in their heroic battles against addiction. In this, and unlike the disciplinary policies of the reformatories, they 'worked through, rather than against, the patient's freedom' (Valverde 1998, 88). Because the affliction of addiction was regarded as moral as well as physical, treatment focused on reforming character and rebuilding atrophied self-control. It was a case of strengthening the will in order to free the patient from the bonds of servitude. As one physician put it, willpower 'buried under a heap of collapsed intentions, must be dug out' (in Berridge and Edwards 1987, 163).

Women's struggles with various forms of addictive consumption occupied quite a different discursive space in this landscape of treatment. Because their physiology and 'natural' irrationality supposedly rendered them helpless, women's willpower, 'character' and moral freedom was simply not part of the equation, far less the 'cure'. As such, female retreats were separate from male ones and tended to fall into the category of religious institutions, run by temperance movements, or medical homes for the treatment of various hysterical 'women's problems' through physical rest, spiritual guidance and medical treatment (Valverde 1998, 66, 78).

Cross-cutting this entire stratified system of treatment was an emphasis on the values of work and discipline, as well as moral guidance, as drivers that could repair diseased wills and so return their owners to a condition of self-control and productive freedom. The emphasis on morality as a causal factor in the undermining of the will was accompanied by a corresponding moral emphasis on cure: self-discipline, in every case, was key to recovery. So, in a somewhat contradictory position, although addiction was medicalised as a bona fide disease, the cure was the responsibility of the individual; failure to get well was a personal, not a medical, failure (Berridge and Edwards 1987, 156).

The birth of the addict

The medical-moral discourse on 'diseases of the will' introduced new ways of conceiving the consumption of particular commodities and new ways of regarding certain types of behaviour. Perhaps most importantly, it also laid the groundwork for the emergence of a new 'type' of consumer – an 'addict'. This process can be seen as an aspect of what Ian Hacking (1986) describes as 'making up people', from Foucault's (1976) notion of 'the constitution of subjects', where the observation and classification of specific features and types of behaviour provide the tools for new ways of thinking and talking about subjects. How things are said, who says them and what they say and do not say create an order of knowledge, a taxonomy, a discourse, and so make a particular subject visible. The ways that various groups – legislators, physicians, philanthropists, public health and the temperance movement – 'said things' about diseases of the will, what they said, who was included and who was left out of their conversations: all of this provided the tools for new ways of thinking and talking about addiction.

Foucault's genealogy of power has outlined the many categories that were 'made up' in this way during the modern period, including criminals, homosexuals and the insane, and the argument here is that 'the addict' represents one more figure in such a process. The similarities of the processes of construction have been noted elsewhere (Kohn 1987; Sedgewick 1993) but are worth returning to here, in the following passage from Foucault's *History of Sexuality*, in which 'addict' has replaced the original 'homosexual':

> The nineteenth century [addict] became a personage, a past, a case history, and a childhood, in addition to being a type of life, a life form, and a morphology, with an indiscreet anatomy and possibly a mysterious physiology . . . . [Addiction] was everywhere present in him . . . written immodestly on his face and body because it was a secret that always gave itself away. It was cosubstantial with him, less as a habitual sin than as a singular nature.
>
> *(Foucault 1976, 43)*

Although the Foucaultian image of 'the addict' outlined here is of a 'singular' figure, in practice, neither 'the addict' nor the idea of 'addiction' in general was a homogenous concept, but rather a fragmented set of practices and discourses. In reality, the concept of 'the addict' was made up of a combination of problematic groups: disorderly workers, troublesome immigrants, neglectful mothers and hysterical women, whose wills were, in one way or another, compromised and unable to provide the self-control necessary for the navigation of everyday life. As Valverde has pointed out, a coherent 'inebriate identity' was never created during this period, but was rather 'disaggregated' through the differential treatment of separate groups, and the more general inclusion of inebriety into already existing problems, whether nervous complaints such as neurasthenia amongst the middle classes, or 'feeble mindedness' and degeneracy amongst the poor (1998, 81, 87). Likewise with addiction, rather than a unified notion, we find instead a network of discourses on diseases of the will, pathological consumption and various kinds of mental illness and vice that reflect the various concerns and intellectual traditions of nineteenth-century psychology and medicine. And in practice, the specific problem of addiction was not initially dealt with as a separate entity but was rather incorporated into the general category of 'insanity' and/or criminality, so that, in treatment, addicts 'melted into the diffuse shadow zone between madness and reason' (Valverde 1998, 87).

However, although the 'expert' discourse of addiction never achieved complete epistemological hegemony in explanations or treatment of problematic consumption, its influence was vast. It might not have created a discrete type of 'addict', but it produced something arguably more important. It created an ideal of rational minds in controlled bodies; of consumers who were able to govern their desires in the face of the temptations of commodity culture. And in doing so, it also produced its opposite: the figure of the individual who was overwhelmed by them. In this, 'the addict' was conceived as a cultural figure who was lacking in willpower and whose consumption was characterised by loss of control. These individuals had failed to manage the new relations required by consumer modernity – rather than enriching them, consumption was overwhelming wills too weak to resist it. Addicts destablised the hierarchy of mind and body and transgressed the boundary that kept production and consumption in balance. In an era in which the continuous exercise of the will had become central to bourgeois ideals of respectability and was regarded as vital for the health of the individual as well as society, failure to exercise self-control was regarded with particular horror as a form of insanity in an industrial age of reason.

End points

The notion of addiction was not, then, the 'discovery' of some new disease but, rather, to return to Marx's phrase, the creation of a fetish. It was the emergence of a politically expedient discourse that articulated fin de siècle anxieties about social disorder in a way that connected the consumption practices of particular groups with wider social trends. By focusing on women, immigrants and the poor, nascent ideas about problematic consumption connected concerns over the individual body to those of the social body in very specific ways, linking economic, political and imperial relations with those of personal consumption.

The addict, then, was a 'made up' person, whose parents were a convergence of interests between the industrial nation state and various medical, moral and juridical groups and upon whose body a new moral–medical economy of consumption was inscribed. Although the concept of addiction articulated the rising tensions generated by the move to industrial modernity, addicts themselves personified widespread fears of disorder: a disparate group of 'others' who had a deviant identity stamped upon them, so that they could be just as forcibly 'cured'.

The legacy of the emergence of discourses of addiction is vast, in the creation of an idea through which *all* forms of uncontrolled consumption and dependency could potentially be understood. This is still with us today, perhaps even greater now, as the field of problematic consumption – designated by terms such as 'addictive', 'pathological', 'compulsive' and 'risky' – grows ever larger, seemingly in tandem with the exponential growth of consumption itself. It is to this growth that we turn in the next chapter.

Notes

1 As he put it, 'The man who has always pinned all his hopes on the future and lived with his eyes fixed upon it, has nothing . . . . ahead of him to fix his gaze upon' (Durkheim 1970 [1897], 256).
2 Although such a development was complex and uneven and produced a variety of definitions which were attached to different forms of consumption and types of behaviour.
3 Such a focus was made possible by new epistemo-juridical formations, that the administrative and bureaucratic apparatus of the state was based on, through which the population was transformed into an object of knowledge and governance (Hacking 1986).
4 A range of opium-based patent medicines were actively promoted by the growing drug industry as cure-alls, for a range of 'women's problems' as well as children's ailments, such as teething, sleeplessness or crying, as well as for general 'drug addiction', although many created dependency themselves.
5 The first female president of the British Society for the Study of Inebriety articulated this position when she urged study of the relation of alcohol consumption to degenerative conditions 'in view of the falling birth rate and of the imperative call from our colonies for a white population' (in Valverde 1998, 54).
6 As we saw in the previous chapter, middle class women had been elevated to guardians of morality and civilised values, embedded in the home – 'the citadel of bourgeois identity' (Hickman 2007, 81). Here they were arbiters of taste, fashioning the family's status through their consumption choices. Their power in this realm was also a source of weakness, however, because female addicts were unable to carry out their household duties and neglected their families' well-being, thus undermining the very heart of bourgeois domesticity.
7 Fears of inter-racial sexuality ran through these discourses, represented in the image of corrupt Chinese men luring young, white women into their dens, where they drugged and overpowered them and threw fears of degeneration into sharp relief (Kohn 1987, 13).

3
INTENSIFIED CONSUMPTION AND THE EXPANSION OF ADDICTION

> Every age develops its own peculiar forms of pathology, which express in exaggerated form, its underlying character structure.
> —*Christopher Lasch (1979, 41)*

Introduction

In the twenty-first century, the system of neoliberal consumer capitalism is a global phenomenon. Within it, innovations in technology and marketing, driven by cheap credit in deregulated markets, have worked to spread increasingly intensive forms of consumption further around the world, and deeper into the individual psyche, than ever before. At the same time, ideas about addiction have expanded to include an ever-wider range of commodities. Beyond substances like alcohol and opiates, today concerns about foods such as sugar and fats, as well as activities like gambling, shopping and smartphone use, are increasingly subject to medicalised discourses of pathology and excess.

Today, the enduring tensions within consumption are articulated in new ways. Whereas the concerns of the mercantile era were focused on the threat of new – particularly foreign – commodities, and the emphasis of the period of liberalism was on reforming damaged wills, in a neoliberal era of free markets and consumer choice, the project goes deeper into the individual. Ironically, at a time when commodity culture is proliferating both in terms of its global reach as well as in its intensity, explanations for the problems of consumption are becoming narrower. New forms of neuroscientific understanding have shifted the focus of addictive consumption to the brains, as well as the subjective states, of individual consumers. From a disease of the will, excessive consumption is increasingly coming to be understood as a disease of the brain as well as a disorder of the psyche.

This chapter aims to explore these issues, tracing changing ideas of addiction and their inter-relation with wider political-economic and social forces. First, it reviews the spread of increasingly pervasive forms of consumption that work to generate a climate of ongoing desire that acts as a motor of economic activity. It goes on to note that this climate of intensified consumption also produces the requirement for ever-more intensive forms of self-control.

As the state retreats from public life, such demands are realised in the ideology of 'responsible consumption' in which individuals are expected to navigate the freedoms and choices of the marketplace in order to demonstrate 'responsible' citizenship. In such a context, it is argued that the values of freedom and choice actually come to be sources of oppression and anxiety. The focus then turns to the expansion of ideas about addiction within the epistemological climate of neuroscience. The argument here is that as the ideology of consumerism and its attendant demands for self-control become more strident, understandings of excess become increasingly individualised and are articulated in medicalised discourses of pathology. Underlying them is a concept of problematic desire which is recast in terms of physiological craving and loss of control. Such an understanding works to expand the landscape of addiction and to encourage the spread of 'addict identities' throughout the population. The section moves on to examine the wider metaphorical aspects of discourses of addiction, arguing that they serve as a counterpoint to neoliberal ideals of 'responsible' consumption and the rational management of desire. In this, it is argued, they articulate long-standing concerns about the dangers of consumption in terms of neurological and psychological disorder.

The final section of this chapter briefly considers the notion of risk, which is interwoven throughout ideas of addiction, arguing that the former has not 'dissolved' the latter as is sometimes claimed, but rather intersects with it in complex ways.

The spread of consumerism: desire and excess

In the twenty-first century, the psychoactive commodities that we saw in the previous two chapters have become central to both the profits of Big Business and to critical discourses of public health. To get to this point, the social lives of these commodities have taken very different trajectories. Opium's biography ended in the general category of 'narcotics', defined in medical-juridical terms and subject to punitive prohibition as a key target of the War on Drugs. Alcohol, tobacco, tea, coffee and sugar, on the other hand, went on to world domination in commercial trajectories that produced multinational corporations, such as 'Big Alcohol', 'Big Tobacco' and 'Big Sugar'. The social lives of these commodities are complex, however. The changing status of tobacco in the Global North, for example, is bringing it closer to the category of illicit drugs, whereas sugar is increasingly coming under attack, and marijuana is increasingly normalised. Such shifts, which Virginia Berridge (2013) describes as 'repositioning', and Courtwright (2001) describes in terms of 'escalation' and 'de-escalation', will be the focus of the case studies later in the book.

The trajectories of these commodities, as well as the many others that make up our contemporary consumer landscape, are situated in the wider shift to a neoliberal era of consumer capitalism. It is an era that is characterised by sweeping socio-economic and political reorganisation. Since around the 1980s, Western governments have adopted political and fiscal policies that work to scale back state involvement in public life, encouraging deregulation, privatisation and the globalisation of capital at the same time that they promote the ideology of consumer sovereignty in free markets. This system continues to depend on an unequal geopolitical division of labour, however, whereby the production of commodities such as clothes and electronic goods has been increasingly outsourced to the countries of the Global South, where Western companies profit from cheap labour, low taxes and permissive regulatory structures. This has been described as a system of 'globally disarticulated production–consumption relationships' (Guthman 2011, 169), in which production is carried out by workers in sweatshop economies, who face poor working conditions and few or no rights. Meanwhile, consumption of the actual goods made in this system takes place in the Global North. Such geographically unequal relationships continue the dynamic between core–periphery states that we saw in Chapter 1 and underlie the foundation of plentiful, cheap consumption in the West. Shifts towards offshoring and downsizing have also had dramatic impacts on Western labour markets, which are characterised by the rise of a large, insecure, low-paid service sector, described as a new 'precariat class' (Standing 2011). This is a model of exploitative, low-cost retail, sometimes described as Walmart capitalism, and founded on a casualisation of labour exemplified by the kinds of employment that Douglas Coupland (1991) refers to as 'McJobs'.

Meanwhile, the economies of the Global North are increasingly based on consumption rather than the production of tangible goods: as Bauman (2007) puts it, the shift is from 'societies of producers' to 'societies of consumers'. With much of their production outsourced to developing countries, the business of many companies is less on producing goods than with marketing them. As Naomi Klein (1999) has argued in *No Logo*, during the 1980s, corporations began to view their physical assets – their warehouses, raw materials and labour forces – as costly and cumbersome, and began to focus instead on their most profitable assets – images of their brands. This is a move to downsizing and to dealing with ephemeral, lightweight images and ideas: towards, as she puts it, 'divestment of the world of things' (1999, 4). The result is a new kind of 'unproductive economy', in which materially unproductive services have become the largest, fastest growing sector of Western economies (Cerni 2007, 7). And so, the decline of industry, manufacturing and production is matched by the rise of services devoted to finance, technology, information and communication and characterised by an increased focus on marketing and branding. This is the post-industrial consumer economy that has been described variously as a system of financial capitalism or by Manuel Castells (1996) as the techno economic system of 'informational capitalism'.

Intensification, identity and desire

This political-economic system has been a key driver for the global expansion of ever-more intensive forms of consumption. In it, new technologies have revolutionised the ways that goods can be marketed and consumed, and the expansion of financial institutions has generated cheap credit, fuelling consumption in the present with debt in the future. These kinds of intersections of marketing with technology accelerate the pace of modernity (Virilio 1977) in a world that is 'informational, global and networked' (Castells 1996, 77), and they work to generate forms of consumption that are more intense and pervasive than ever before. They also act as a backdrop for the expansion of ideas about addiction, as we shall see in the next section. This is the landscape of one-click buying and instant downloads, of e-books and iTunes, where the marketing of multinational corporations embraces the globe as well as reaching into the smartphone in your hand.

In particular, the rise of mobile and social technologies signals a paradigm shift towards what has been described as 'networked publics' (boyd 2011) or 'mobile publics' (Goggin 2010), in which increasing numbers of consumers are shopping, banking and socialising via their smartphones and tablets, on their wearable technologies and on social networking sites. Mobile devices, and the technologies that drive them, have increased consumer connectivity and expanded its geographical reach, to paraphrase Jan van Dijk, 'to the most remote places and the deepest pores of the world' (2012, 57). They have also made it more personal: smartphones, for example, are far more than simply commodities. Torres and Goggin have described them as 'intimate, portable, flexible artefacts that are deeply and pervasively embedded in the social' (2014, 105). As receptacles of vast amounts of private information, from biometric data and bank details to text messages and family photos, they are intimately entwined with their owners. Some seventy-nine per cent of smartphone users check their device within fifteen minutes of waking in the morning; many sleep with them under their pillows and continue to check them up to a hundred and fifty times a day (Eyal 2014). Such relations with material goods recall Russell Belk's concept of the 'extended self' revised or, perhaps more accurately, upgraded for the digital age, in the notion of 'the extended iSelf' (Clayton et al. 2015). These kinds of technologies make consumption more immediate, more intensive and more ubiquitous, divorcing the act of purchase from the constraints of time and space and releasing it into the world opened up by cellular technologies. This is the enactment of what Giddens (1991) calls 'disembedding' – the overcoming of time and space and the removal of events from their local time frame.[1] To this, we could also add the removal of finances from the limits of one's budget, too, because an international system of cheap credit, as well as the rise of contactless payments and digital currencies, narrows the gap between wanting and having, making instant gratification a mere click away. Borrowing from Ritzer and Stillman's description of Las Vegas casino architecture, Torres and Goggin paint a picture of mobile devices as the future of consumption, arguing that they stand to become miniaturised 'cathedrals of consumption' (2014, 103).

These technologies act as conduits for new forms of marketing as well as mediums of surveillance, and in this, they represent what Bauman described as both the seductions and the repressions of the marketplace. Geolocational and tracking technologies, social media activity and financial and smartphone transactions record where, when and how often consumption goes on, converting behaviour and desires into quantified units of Big Data that are fed into algorithms to produce new forms of what Cheney-Lippold (2011) calls 'algorithmic identity'. Such shifting categories of code allow marketers to better understand – and so better target – their audiences. And so, personalised marketing targets online shoppers with a continually updated feed of products that are uniquely determined by their past browsing habits and purchase history, presenting them with a stream of possibilities that matches the shifting contours of consumer desire itself. Such exquisitely targeted marketing works through guidance, persuasion, suggestion – what Deleuze (1992) calls 'continuous control' – in ways that gently direct individuals towards ever-greater engagement with consumption. As Amazon's personalised marketing tells its customers, based on past orders, 'if you liked that, you'll love this!'

Although the system of advertising has long worked to associate goods with idealised selves that can be realised through commodity purchase, new technologies take marketing to new heights – or, perhaps more accurately, into cyberspace. Increasingly, corporations are moving to develop a social media 'presence' in ways that allow them to generate, as well as guide, conversations about their brands, 'seeding' content into conversations that are then disseminated by networks of consumers themselves. Such 'social influence marketing' allows them to embed branded imagery in the interactions of millions of people, through Twitter and Facebook, highlighting brand-related events and services that are 'liked', 'tweeted' and shared by others, so disseminating more pervasive forms of desire-generation throughout wide networks of consumers. Such strategies are far more sophisticated than the 'engineering of consent', as Edward Bernays (1947) famously described the art of manipulation through advertising. Through social media, it may come to seem that consent isn't so much 'engineered' as co-produced by consumers themselves, who engage as active participants in the generation of content. By embedding branded goods and experiences in the social networks and everyday lives of millions, companies intensify the power of their marketing and '[create] intimate relationships and a sense of kinship between users and brands' (Jernigan and O'Hara 2004, in Nicholls 2012, 490).

New technologies have also been harnessed by companies in conscious efforts to engineer what are described as habit-forming products, with consultants employed to advise on how to design the most compelling mobile devices, the most addictive games, the most indispensable services. As the subtitle of Nir Eyal's recent book, *Hooked: How to Build Habit-Forming Products* (2014) suggests, such a quest now appears as a legitimate business aim. Eyal uses his book as a manual for the creation of 'hooks': manufactured experiences that result in habits, and so increased consumption. As he puts it, the increased connectivity and the ability to collect and mine larger amounts of customer data at faster speeds means 'we are faced with a future where everything becomes potentially more habit-forming'. Or, as a Silicon Valley investor puts it, merging the aims of capital with the language of addiction: 'The world will get more addictive in the next forty years than it did in the last forty' (in Eyal 2014, 18).

In this expanding consumer landscape, built-in obsolescence, product upgrades and personalised marketing present us with newer, faster, slimmer products, while promotions and special offers super-size choice, giving us ever-cheaper drinks and ever-bigger burgers. There is an increase in the sheer range of products and experiences on offer and an expanding choice of outlets – from mega malls and vintage boutiques to eBay and Amazon – from which to purchase them. All of this is part of what Antonio Hardt and Michael Negri (2000) have described as a shift, within late capitalism, towards the intensification of existing resources rather than the production of new ones, in which consumption is speeded up to generate immediate gratification and ongoing desire. Theorists have coined different terms to write about this trend, with Juliet Schor (2008) using the phrase 'turbo' consumption to describe the squeezing of consumption into shorter, more intense time frames, and George Ritzer (1999) describing new forms of consumerism that manipulate time and space in order to encourage the continual and ever-increasing consumption of commodities in what he terms 'hyper consumption'.

These formations are also productive of specific kinds of subjectivities in which desire is central. Bryan Turner (2008) has argued that modern individuals are 'desiring subjects' – a state of being that is not only integral to the project of the self, but also crucial to the reproduction of consumer capitalism itself. As Bauman has noted, the very basis of consumerism is not the gratification of needs, but the 'ever-rising volume and intensity of desires' (2007, 18). It is here that the seductions of consumerism lie: in the constant generation of fleeting desires and novelties and in an exponential speed of change. Indeed, for Bauman, the promise of satisfaction is seductive only insofar as desire itself remains unsatisfied. As he puts it, 'It is the *non*-satisfaction of desires, and a firm and perpetual belief that each act to satisfy them leaves much to be desired and can be bettered that are the fly-wheels of the consumer targeted economy' (2005, 80). Predating Bauman's observations, Colin Campbell described the most distinctive feature of modern consumption as its insatiability, writing in *The Romantic Ethic and the Spirit of Modern Consumerism* that capitalism is characterised by not only the consumption of goods, but also an unlimited hunger for an apparently endless list of desires. He writes that 'the modern consumer is characterised by an insatiability which arises out of a basic inexhaustibility of wants themselves, which forever arise, phoenix like, from the ashes of their predecessors' (1987, 37). This conception of desire is unique to contemporary consumer culture, having had, as we saw in Chapter 1, very different meanings as something that was limited and finite, for much of its history. New formations of consumption in the eighteenth century, however, began to invert such teleological understandings of desire, and today, the maintenance and – perhaps most importantly – the governance of an almost perpetual state of unrealisable desire is regarded as crucial for the fulfilment of the modern self and for the continued reproduction of consumer culture itself. Modern desire, which Campbell calls 'autonomous imaginative hedonism', is founded on novelty and the anticipation of as-yet unknown pleasures in the future, because it is on to these that fantasies and ideals are projected. In Grant McCracken's (1988) terminology, consumer goods act as 'bridges' to 'displaced meaning', insofar as they are invested of a range of cultural meanings and personal aspirations involving an idealised version of the self. However, they can act as 'bridges' in this way only when they are coveted, but not actually owned because, in Campbell's account, reality is seldom able to live up to expectations, and so the actual object is almost guaranteed to disappoint and so is discarded. At this point, the process of chasing, longing for and discarding some obscure object of desire begins again, in a continual cycle of obsolescence. This is the process that is captured in Barbara Kruger's image: '*You want it, You buy it, You forget it*', suspended over the heads of oblivious shoppers in the Selfridges sale (see Image 3.1).

The corollary of this dynamic is waste. As Bauman puts it, consumerism is 'an economics of waste and excess' (2007, 48), meaning that just as quickly as novelties fill the shelves, the discarded goods that have failed to meet expectations fill the garbage bins. Further, for Bauman, inequality is inscribed within this system, because those who engage with it successfully – 'the seduced' – need only act out their demand for ever-new goods and experiences, whereas those who are seduced but unable to act – 'the repressed' – are the 'collateral casualties' of consumerism, forced to witness the spectacle of lavish consumption but unable to join in (2007, 124).

In such accounts of consumerism, the modern self is fuelled, in equal measure, by both endless longing as well as continual dissatisfaction. This state drives consumer capitalism, for which permanent satisfaction is equated with economic stagnation – despite the commercial rhetoric to the contrary. And so, as McCracken points out, 'It is absolutely essential for us never to receive what it is we want' (1988, 116). This, in turn, means that the supply of goods themselves must be inexhaustible. It is this aspect that generates the constant expansion of wants and 'helps to enlarge our appetites so that we can never reach a "sufficiency" of goods and declare, "I have enough"' (1988, 104).

And so, the production of habit-forming products, guided by the persuasions of personalised marketing and facilitated by systems of instant finance, works to stimulate desire and encourage repeated consumption. Indeed, the dynamic of consumerism raises instant gratification and self-fulfillment to personal virtues, because – as the L'Oreal advert tells us – 'you're worth it'. And impulsivity certainly appears to be 'worth it' in economic terms: it is estimated that some $4 billion in annual sales is generated from impulse buying in the United States (Kacen and Lee 2002).

This valorisation of desire and self-indulgence has some convergence with popular tropes of addiction, with images and metaphors of excess woven into advertising itself: albeit in ironic and knowing ways. For example, Christian Dior's best-selling lipstick – 'Dior Addict' – plays on the longing that products might generate, folding the idea of addiction into the cultural imaginary of consumer capitalism itself.

Throughout all of this, we can see that the idea of desire is central to consumer capitalism, as both a driver of economic activity and a personal, subjective state. It is also key to current,

IMAGE 3.1 *Barbara Kruger, 'You want it, You buy it, You forget it' (2006).*
Source: Photo by the author.

medicalised notions of addiction, which are underlined by a concept of problematic desire, as we will see later in this chapter. First, however, we turn to look at the ways that consumption is governed in neoliberal societies.

Freedom and governance

These features of neoliberal consumer capitalism that generate excess and desire on an increasingly intensive scale also generate the requirement for correspondingly intensive forms of governance.

Since the 1980s, the retreat of the neoliberal state from the regulation of public life has been matched by a heightened emphasis on individual self-control. As the state reduces its presence in the regulation of commerce and the provision of services, so individuals are expected more and more to take responsibility for their own well-being and to govern themselves, through the medium of the market. The seductions of the market are to be countered by self-governing individuals, who manage desire and restrain excess in culturally appropriate ways. And so, at the very point that the state rolls back its regulation of markets and consumerism proliferates on a global scale, responsibility for its control becomes increasingly individualised.

The ideology of 'freedom' is central to this demand, both in terms of the increasing deregulation of markets and in the sense of the unrestricted choices of consumers within them. In this formulation, economic growth is regarded as best served by competition in free markets, in which consumption is driven by the actions of enterprising, autonomous agents. These sovereign consumers are, in Milton Friedman's (1980) famous shibboleth, 'free to choose': fashioning a self-narrative through the purchase and manipulation of commodities on the market. And so, in the process of self-formation, Giddens says, the modern individual engages in a series of questions: 'What to do? How to act? Who to be?' (1991, 70). The answers to these questions are to be found mainly in acts of consumption, because it is by exercising consumer choice that the project of the self is formed into a coherent 'narrative' of identity that makes sense of the past, shapes the present and motivates future behaviour, so generating a sense of ontological security in an otherwise uncertain world. It is through consumption, then, that the modern self is fully realised and expressed, and in this sense, as Bauman puts it, today, simply 'being' is not enough, rather, '*making* oneself, not just *becoming* is the challenge' (2007, 57). In this perspective, with supposedly limitless freedom to indulge in the temptations of consumer capitalism, the formation of identity comes to be presented almost as a matter of personal choice. As Ewen and Ewen (1982, 249) put it: 'There are no rules only choices . . . Everyone can be anyone'.

All this freedom of choice comes with a number of caveats, however. The first is that it is not really free: as Bauman put it, 'granted in theory but unattainable in practice' (2007, 141). The second is it acts as a form of control, as we will see. Ultimately, however, the rhetoric of freedom along with its corollary – responsibility – helps to legitimise the workings of neoliberalism by diverting attention towards the individual and away from wider structural features. The ideology of responsibility is thus the cornerstone of neoliberal systems of governance. It rests on the key normative values of autonomy and rationality and is an aspect of what Pat O'Malley (1996) describes as a 'new prudentialism' in which responsible consumption is evidence of the 'right' way to live, the 'right' way to be. Indeed, it becomes the duty of the sovereign consumer to furnish themselves with relevant knowledge and information and take appropriate steps to safeguard their health and well-being by avoiding risks and consuming 'correctly' as they map out a trajectory of the self into the future. As a corollary of this individualising and normative project, the individual is also the site of blame when things go wrong. So, as we shall see in later chapters, problems of excessive consumption – overeating and obesity, binge drinking and alcoholism, smoking and gambling – tend to be framed in terms of poor choices and failures of individual consumption, rather than as structural features of the system of consumer capitalism itself.[2]

We can see from this that the central value of neoliberalism – freedom – is actually highly ambivalent. It acts as both a form of liberty and a kind of governance. As Rose puts it, individuals are 'obliged to be free' (1999) because it is through the exercise of their freedom that they not only realise themselves, but also control themselves in visible and culturally appropriate ways. This contradictory aspect of freedom is lived out in consumption. Crucially, then, it is not 'consumption' *per se*, but specifically 'responsible' consumption that lies at the heart of the neoliberal ideal. As such, it is properly managed consumption that is cast as a means of self-realisation and authenticity, carried out by individuals who are able to both successfully respond to the seductions of the marketplace and exercise 'responsible' self-control, by at the same time limiting their freedoms.

This formulation means that the state is able to govern 'at a distance', without actually governing society itself, but rather through shaping the subjectivities of autonomous individuals who, conveniently, undertake the task of self-control themselves. Such an orientation is an aspect of what Foucault describes as 'governmentality', in which the modern subject 'assumes responsibility for the constraints of power . . . he [sic] becomes the principle of his own subjection [sic]' (1977, 202). Mariana Valverde (1997) describes this as the move from 'act' to 'identity'-based governance, where individuals are governed not so much through what they do, but rather through who they *are* – through the shaping of particular kinds of subjectivity. Rather than the enforcement of discipline, which is experienced as external to the self, self-control is effective precisely because it bridges the divide between self and other: between authority that appears as alien to the self and desires which are perceived as being part of it. Failure to exercise such self-control, however, activates what Valverde (1997) calls the 'hidden despotism' of liberal society, whereby various forms of penal, medical and therapeutic interventions are invoked to control those whose consumption is regarded as excessive. These range from, for example, imprisonment for the consumption of illicit drugs, fines for the inappropriate consumption of alcohol or compulsory forms of therapy for those who are deemed to gamble too much or who eat too little. In this sense, Foucault argues for the existence of a 'triangle' of control: 'We need to see things not in terms of the replacement of a society of sovereignty by a disciplinary society by a society of government; in reality one has a triangle, sovereignty-discipline-government' (1991, 102). It is such a 'triangle' that Denise, whose excessive shopping we saw in the Introduction, was subject to, in a series of punishments that made her atone for her excessive consumption with its opposite – unpaid work – with compulsory therapy intended to reform her inner self. Despite the ever-present threat of this kind of 'hidden despotism', in general, governmental approaches act as gentler, as well as more pervasive, forms of control than those meted out to the nineteenth-century underclass, whereby the values of autonomy, freedom and choice are internalised as subjective states; as part of one's very identity. And so, individuals embark on a continual process of self-surveillance and introspection: monitoring their interior states, scrutinising their consumption habits, forever on the lookout for signs of unchecked desire or deficient self-control. Integral to this project of self-governance are the forms of knowledge and authority generated by what Nikolas Rose (1999) terms the 'psy sciences' – the disciplines of psychology and psychiatry, which produce notions of normality and abnormality and so continually 'make up' new types of people; new types of consumer identity. Like all forms of knowledge, their epistemological assumptions, as well as their therapeutic aims, are embedded in particular socio-economic climates and shaped by their values. In a climate of neoliberalism in which freedom is valorised as key to individual well-being, this means that, ultimately, the psy sciences, 'fabricate subjects capable of bearing the burdens of liberty' (Rose 1999, viii).[3]

And it is quite a burden. Although individuals may be 'free to choose', in fact, as Giddens has pointed out, they have 'no choice but to choose' (1991, 81). They are forced to choose from amongst a range of constantly changing and ever-increasing alternatives. Virtually every aspect of life in the Global North comes with a range of options: Between the mid-1970s and late 2000s, for example, the number of products on offer in the average supermarket increased from around 9,000 to 50,000 (Food Marketing Institute 2014). But one of the great paradoxes of all this variety is that genuine choice is not, ultimately, increased. Because many apparently distinct commodities are supplied by the same multinational producers and because stylistic changes seldom affect the basic design of many fashionable items, differences between products often remain superficial. They provide the illusion of choosing amongst alternatives but do not enable customers to make meaningful decisions. It is this overabundance and seemingly limitless freedom that, for many writers, generate the negative psychological impacts of consumerism, a point that has been repeated in a number of polemics with titles such as *Affluenza: The All-Consuming Epidemic* (2001) and its variant, *Affluenza: When Too Much is Never Enough* (2005) and, most recently, *Stuffocation* (2014), whose title conveys the sense of overwhelming materiality that is, in one way or another, a focus of them all.[4] It is in this vein that Barry Schwartz has argued in the *Paradox of Choice* (2009) that when it is too vast, the need to make ongoing decisions in the light of constant change comes to be seen as a burden rather than a freedom; the response to which is more often confusion and anxiety rather than satisfaction. Similarly, Bauman (1988a) has argued that because individuals are obliged to create their own identities through the selection of such a wide range of goods, the possibility of making the 'wrong' choice, and so suffering anxiety, embarrassment and feelings of inadequacy, is ever present.[5] He links this with the horror of responsibility – the flip side of freedom. Giddens also recognised the potential for consumption to generate feelings of being overwhelmed and oppressed and linked these specifically with ontological insecurity, writing that 'addiction comes into play when choice, which should be driven by autonomy, is subverted by anxiety' (2000, 64).

At the end of this section, then, we are left with a dualistic notion of consumption as both a means of freedom as well as constraint. Consumers are presented with a paradox: on the one hand, they are, indeed, 'free to choose': to carve out a lifestyle and identity from the marketed options available. But on the other, they are also obliged to subjugate aspects of themselves, to mould their subjective states and inner desires in accordance with cultural norms and social institutions. They must balance the temptations of consumer culture with the appropriate levels of self-control and restraint. Desire – although limitless – must also be managed 'responsibly'. And so begins an ongoing process of governance in which individuals must be constantly vigilant: monitoring their consumption habits as visible makers of self-control and responsible freedom – as well as signs of their loss. The task of modern consumers is a delicate one, and they have to maintain a careful balance: succumbing to desire – but only in culturally appropriate ways. As Eve Sedgewick memorably put it, they must negotiate the 'twin hurricanes' of 'Just Do It' and 'Just Say No' (1993, 140).

The argument here is that this tension is played out in the expansion of ideas about 'addictive consumption'. The next section turns to look at the understandings about excess that are produced in this kind of environment. It focuses on developments in ideas about addiction, which we left in the nineteenth century, as they are reformulated within the epistemological climate of the twentieth and twenty-first.

The expanding landscape of addiction

It was in this political economic climate of consumer proliferation, ambiguous freedom and oppressive responsibility that the notion of addiction re-appeared with renewed vigour, expanding its reach into ever more areas of social life and embracing larger sectors of the population to become the disease of commodity culture *par excellence*.

We saw in Chapters 1 and 2 how ideas about addictive or problematic consumption were historically associated with changing concerns about the disorderly effects of new, especially luxurious, commodities in the eighteenth century, and with the 'diseased' or compromised wills of particular types of individual in the nineteenth. In the twenty-first century, formations have changed again as new understandings of addiction locate the problem increasingly deeply within the individual. Today, ideas about addiction are produced through two distinct but complementary forms of knowledge: neuroscientific understandings of the brain as well as psychological understandings of mental health. In these, a problematised version of the desire that, as we have just seen, is central to consumer capitalism, is recast in terms of physiological craving and loss of control. Such understandings locate the 'causes' of problematic consumption in the body of the sufferer, peering into the pathways of neurological activity and even examining the subject's past in the genetic codes of their DNA. Although most accounts also recognise that these processes interact with the environment in complex ways, they nevertheless produce an understanding of addiction as an essentially biological condition and addicts as physiologically distinct 'types' of person.

These types of knowledge typify the recent march of neuroscientific explanations across increasingly diverse fields of human behaviour, from ethics and law to social life and culture (e.g. Tallis 2011). This is part of what Nikolas Rose describes as a profound transformation in understandings of personhood, as the twentieth-century sense of ourselves as 'psychological' individuals gives way to what he terms 'somatic individuality', or 'neurochemical selfhood', in which the mind and the self are understood primarily in terms of our brains and bodies (2004, 2). In his essay 'Becoming Neurochemical Selves', Rose details how desires, personality, subjectivity – in fact, personhood itself – is increasingly understood at the molecular level, as the outcome of biochemical and neurological processes, particularly those that go on in the brain. Further, this embodied self is something to be acted on, whether through the exterior modifications of diet and exercise or by reshaping the interior 'organic' space of subjectivity through pharmacological interventions (2004, 18). To this end, drugs such as naltrexone aim to erase the craving associated with particular kinds of opiates, whereas lithium and SSRIs aim to balance moods, so levelling out the neural pathways of desire.

The understanding of the self as formed through biochemical processes is increasingly influential in policy and practice circles, where it has been argued that it at least partially ameliorates the moralism associated with addiction by shifting the source of the problem from the wills or personality of the individual to the material workings of their bodies. This shift also has pragmatic implications: rather than blameworthy, weak-willed and possibly criminal, such individuals can be reconceived as suffering from physiological dysfunctions – a morally neutral problem, for which medicine holds out pharmacological solutions.

This ascendance of neuroscientific forms of knowledge is embedded in economic and political relations and has, I would argue, an elective affinity with the ideology of neoliberalism as well as the aims of capital. In its privileging of the brain as the source of human subjectivity, it also returns us to eighteenth-century and nineteenth-century debates about free will, selfhood and morality, although here reconceived as the result of organic processes. We shall look at these wider implications later in this chapter but first turn to look in more detail at the application of neuroscience to the field of addiction.

From diseased wills to diseased brains: the rise of addiction neuroscience

Towards the end of the twentieth century, neuroscience came to attain scientific and cultural hegemony in understandings of addiction, initially with respect to narcotic drugs, but later gradually expanding to encompass a wide range of commodities and experiences. This perspective was spearheaded by the influential U.S.-based National Institute on Drug Abuse (NIDA), who defined addiction as a 'chronic relapsing brain disease'. As its director, Alan Leshner (1997) put it: 'Addiction is a brain disease, and it matters'.

From the outset, this epistemological shift had political origins: in this case, those of the 'War on Drugs' in the United States. As Scott Vrecko (2010) has pointed out in his account of 'addiction neuropolitics', NIDA was founded, in part, by the Nixon administration in the 1970s, in response to concerns about drug use and social disorder, which it regarded as interlinked. Hence, funding was directed towards scientific research that suited the disciplinary goals of the War on Drugs,[6] in a political convergence that Suzanne Fraser calls the field of neuroscience's 'collaboration with drug war politics' (Fraser 2015, 18). The very specific views of addiction that emerged were thus driven by particular political agendas and supported by large-scale government funding, which had the effect of turning a marginal field into a 'state sponsored speciality' (Vrecko 2010, 54). Today, the epistemic climate of neuroscience has expanded far wider but continues to be embraced by particular political rationalities. The former Republican President George H.W. Bush's declaration of the 1990s as 'the decade of the brain', for example, can be seen as part of a politically partisan project to enhance public understanding of neurological research.

As well as specific political perspectives, the development of this paradigm depended on expensive and specialised technologies, most notably fMRI (functional Magnetic Resonance Imaging) and PET (Positron Emission Tomography). These produce very particular 'ways of seeing' their subject, which are represented by digitised visualisations of brain functioning. They are often used to produce striking images of human brain activity, particularly in terms of blood flow and glucose metabolism, that can be frequently used to contrast 'healthy' with 'addicted' tissue. Operating within these technologies, interpretations of brain scans themselves produce a particular way of understanding neurological functioning. They posit a common biological substrate – a 'common pathway' – in the brain's pleasure centre that is ultimately responsible for the generation of addiction. Powerful substances or pleasurable sensations stimulate the neuronal circuits in the pleasure centre, 'lighting them up', and sending signals that demand their repetition. In fact, these neurobiological signals are so powerful that the metaphor of 'hijacking' has been vividly deployed to describe the effect of drugs taking over the brain and, by extension, the agency of their owners. In such a takeover, the brain's synapses and circuits are permanently remodelled by desire and come to require greater amounts of consumption for the same levels of activation in a cycle driven by neurochemical pleasure and reward. Furthermore, according to the former NIDA director Adam Leshner, such processes show that prolonged consumption of drugs causes long-standing changes in brain function in the areas responsible for judgement, decision-making, memory and self-control. Such a physical rewiring means that, as he puts it, 'the addicted brain is distinctly different from the non-addicted brain' (Leshner 1997, in Hickman 2014, 219).[7] The epistemological basis of neuroscience has also boosted research into the quest for understanding what Agrawal et al. (2012) call the 'genetic architecture of addictions', so tracing a hereditary tendency for excess even further into the past, as well as projecting it into the future, of the individual.[8]

These powerful neuroimaging technologies produce equally powerful representations of the workings of the mind: it is a portrait of desire in the brain, the ghost in the machine. Less sophisticated deployments of the images also proliferate, however: most notably, the Partnership for a Drug-Free America's infamous slogan 'This is your brain on drugs', which was accompanied by the image of an egg being fried in a pan: a rather blunt visualisation of the effect of narcotics on the brain.

The implications of these techno-scientific kinds of knowledge are considerable. They produce an understanding of 'the addict' as a qualitatively different type of subject, so paving the way for the notion of an 'addict identity' as a distinctive type of person. Not only are brains different, but also their owners are, too. As Leshner put it, the addict exists in a 'different state of being' (1997, in Fraser et al. 2014, 53). It is worth pointing out here that, ironically, although much of the neuroscientific focus on features such as plasticity and epigenetics suggests the social and adaptable nature of the brain, addiction neuroscience presents a different interpretation. Although the addicted brain may be plastic enough to be changed by addiction, once 'hijacked' it is not sufficiently adaptable to change back again. The disease is a chronic one; the state of addiction is a permanent (see, e.g. Fraser et al. 2014).

However, despite the conviction of the statements produced by NIDA and other neuroscientific authorities, the assumptions upon which this form of knowledge is based are actually highly contested. The production of brain scans is a profoundly social and subjective act, and the interpretation of the information they generate remains controversial, with disagreement over associations of causality and correlation. In *Picturing Personhood* (2004), the anthropologist Joseph Dumit eloquently shows how social assumptions, expectations and biases are built into the entire process of scanning, from setting up experimental protocols to interpreting results. He argues persuasively that the images produced by scanning technology make effective use of visual patterns and colour but do not, in fact, show us the direct workings of the brain. Rather than a snapshot of scientifically occurring 'fact', they actually produce a representation based on a process of selection and omission as researchers decide how to group the quantitative data produced by the scan, which aspects are significant and how they should be presented. Dumit notes that coloured and 'lit up' patches in images of brains create the illusion that brains are far more differentiated than they are, and that the areas of activity are of significance independent of researchers' selection of them. Meanwhile, adding colour to the pictures invests them with particular sets of cultural meanings that, again, are selected by researchers themselves. The complexities involved in producing and interpreting scans have led to criticisms of researchers' overstating the correlations between brain activity as 'revealed' in scans and actual human behaviour, with Ed Vul talking of 'voodoo correlations' and Stanton Peele deriding the entire exercise as one of 'high tech phrenology' (in Hickman 2014, 211). As these critics, and other social scientists have pointed out, neuroimaging technology does not simply provide a 'window' into the brain, because brains are located in human bodies, which, in turn, are situated in culture and influenced by a range of social, historical and political factors, all of which underline the point that human behaviour rests on reasons, not simply neurochemical causes.

However, what is more certain is that this shift to a focus on the materiality of the brain not only generates new ways of thinking about agency and causality, but also creates the potential for 'addiction' to expand into ever more areas of behaviour. In particular, the 'common pathways model' allows that changes in brain function can occur in response to any number of pleasurable stimuli, resulting in what Granfield and Reinarman describe as 'an embarrassment of riches' (2014, 6) – the incorporation of an ever-greater number of substances, activities and experiences into the field of addiction. In short, the brain's pleasure centre does not differentiate between the kinds of substances or activities that can generate desire and does not recognise normative or legal categories: heroin, Coca-Cola, fast food, shopping, gambling and sex – all have been found to 'light up' the zone. Dopamine neurons are sensitive to a wide array of activities, and in this paradigm, almost anything that the individual finds enjoyable can illuminate the brain. In a single sweep, this new form of knowledge dramatically expands the landscape of 'addiction'. As Fraser et al. put it, the existence of a common neural dysfunction as the root of addiction 'unites non-substance and substance addictions and in some sense renders the specific object of addiction irrelevant' (2014, 46), so paving the way for an almost potentially infinite expansion of the field of addiction itself, from gambling and sugar to smartphones and Facebook.

These forms of scientific and technical knowledge are also being increasingly used to explain 'normal' consumer behaviour in an effort to create more effective advertising. In the fusion of neuroscience and marketing, the emergent discipline of 'neuromarketing' utilises fMRI scans in an effort to uncover the neurological processes behind consumption, revealing consumers' hidden motivations and desires by literally examining their brains. One such experiment involved scans of subjects' brains as they were exposed to Pepsi and Coca-Cola cues, in order to establish which parts of the brain are responsible for recognition, desire and preference. It found that most people preferred Pepsi, with fMRI scanning revealing the drink lit up a region called the ventral putamen, one of the brain's 'reward centres', far more brightly than did Coke. However, when the names of the products were revealed, most participants said they preferred Coke (McClure et al. 2004). Such an underwhelming result stands in contrast to the dazzling technology that produced it and suggests that less glamorous factors such as branding and social expectations are more powerful factors in shaping consumer desire. As Naomi Klein has noted, 'Corporations may manufacture products, but what consumers buy are brands' (1999, 7).

At this point, we can note what could perhaps be described as an elective affinity between the kinds of knowledge produced by neuroscience and the aims of capital. In different ways, both the tracking of consumer behaviour through algorithms in the commercial world and the scanning of brains in medical labs work to make visible and quantify intangible properties such as desire, pleasure and longing. The 'algorithmic selves' of the marketplace are matched by the 'neurochemical selves' of the lab: both attempting to uncover the material substrate of desire, the source of profit. As new forms of technology and marketing drive intensified forms of consumption deeper into the psyche of the individual consumer, so explanations for excess also move inwards, probing their neuronal circuits for evidence of 'hijacking' and, as we shall see in the section that follows, examining their interior states for proof of uncontrolled desire.

Diagnosing desire

The forms of knowledge produced by neuroscience work in tandem with the clinical authority of the 'psy sciences', where addiction is conceived in terms of mental disorder. In particular, the official compendium of the American Psychiatric Association, the *Diagnostic and Statistical Manual of Mental Disorders* (*DSM-5*) provides the standard definition of addiction in medicine, psychology and epidemiology and acts as a diagnostic screening tool used by clinicians to classify behaviour. If neuroimaging is sometimes interpreted as a kind of 'window' through which to observe the workings of desire in the brain, the psychiatric screens provide a quantifiable list of symptoms with which to diagnose it in the psyche. In doing so, they translate ideas about 'excessive' consumption into distinct types of psychiatric conditions.

The latest edition of *DSM-5* was revised in 2013 in order to incorporate the new types of knowledge being produced by neuroscience and genetics. In it, the label of 'addiction' was dropped in favour of the category of 'substance use disorder' (SUD), and the criteria widened to include a much wider range of substances and behaviours that people can form pathological relationships with. The new category of SUD now involves a cluster of substances, including tobacco, cannabis and opiates, that are seen to possess a common 'addictive' quality, whereas gambling has been newly classified as a behavioural addiction, 'binge eating disorder' added and Internet gaming and 'caffeine use disorder' marked out as 'conditions of interest' requiring further research. Furthermore, the criteria that need to be satisfied for diagnosis are loosened, so that the symptoms of what counts as addiction become more diverse, and its manifestations proliferate. The expanded criteria have the potential to reach wider sectors of the population: male and female and young and old as well as a broader range of ethnic and class backgrounds (Fraser et al. 2014, 36). The changing terminology is significant for, despite the somewhat confusing downplaying of the term, it marks what Fraser et al. describe as a 'major change in the constitution of addiction as a medical entity' by opening it up to non-substance or behavioural addictions (2014, 46). Like the 'expansionary mode' of neuroscientific research, the revisions to the *DSM* have produced what the researchers describe as 'diagnostic . . . creep' (2014, 36).

Making up addictions

At this point, it is useful to step back to consider in more detail the wider epistemological basis of neuroscientific and psychological understandings of addiction. As a number of scholars have pointed out, what is perhaps most immediately striking about both types of knowledge is that, despite being ostensibly based on 'objective' scientific evidence, their accounts of addiction are actually founded on a range of social and normative assumptions and diagnosed in terms of impairments in social functioning and/or subjective feelings of loss of control (Keane 2002; Fraser et al. 2014; Vrecko 2010). As Fraser et al. put it, medical models are 'hybrid medical-ethical assemblages, built on culturally specific ideals such as self-control and autonomy and inevitably involving normative judgements about how to live and how to prioritise pleasures' (2014, 28). Even accounts that evoke the authority of neuroscience are full of normative and social assumptions, as the following extract from the American Society of Addiction Medicine (ASAM) demonstrates. It starts with highly specialised medical terminology, declaring that 'addiction affects neurotransmission and interactions within reward structures of the brain, including the nucleus accumbens, anterior cingulate cortex, basal forebrain and amygdala'- before sliding into judgements about the effects of such processes-, 'such that motivational hierarchies are altered and addictive behaviours . . . supplant *healthy, self-care related* behaviours' (ASAM 2016, italics added). Ultimately, the ASAM expresses what it regards as defining features of addiction in non-medical terms, stating, 'once the brain has been changed by addiction . . . choice or willpower becomes impaired. Perhaps the most defining symptom of addiction is a loss of control over substance use'.

Likewise, the knowledge produced by the disciplines of psychiatry and psychology rests on a range of social assumptions about 'normal' behaviour based on ideals of autonomy and self-control, properly managed time and money and appropriate desire as well as particular kinds of social and personal relations (see, e.g. Keane 2002; Fraser et al. 2014). When we look at them more closely, we can see that the criteria of the clinical screens actually embody these assumptions, reflecting back a mirror image of the neoliberal ideal. The diagnostic checklist for Opioid Use Disorder, which acts as the template for all other disorders in the SUD category, is presented below, with social, subjective and normative criteria italicised. It can be seen at a glance that most of the list is annotated in this way.

DSM-5 *opioid use disorder*

A: A problematic pattern of opioid use leading to clinically significant impairment or distress, as manifested by at least two of the following, occurring within a 12-month period:

1. Opioids are often taken in larger amounts or over a longer period than was *intended*.
2. There is a *persistent desire* or unsuccessful efforts to cut down or control opioid use.
3. A great deal of *time* is spent in activities necessary to obtain the opioid, use the opioid or recover from its effects.
4. *Craving*, or a *strong desire* or *urge* to use opioids.
5. Recurrent opioid use resulting in a failure to fulfil *major role obligations* at work, school or home.
6. Continued opioid use despite having persistent or recurrent *social* or *interpersonal problems* caused or exacerbated by the effects of opioids.
7. Important *social, occupational* or *recreational activities* are given up or reduced because of opioid use.
8. Recurrent opioid use in situations in which it is physically hazardous.
9. Continued opioid use despite knowledge of having a persistent or recurrent physical or *psychological problem* that is likely to have been caused or exacerbated by the substance.
10. Tolerance, as defined by either of the following:

    a   A need for markedly increased amounts of opioids to achieve intoxication or *desired effect*.
    b   A markedly diminished effect with continued use of the same amount of an opioid.

Note: This criterion is not considered to be met for those taking opioids solely under *appropriate medical supervision*.

11. Withdrawal, as manifested by either of the following:

    a   The characteristic opioid withdrawal syndrome (refer to Criteria A and B of the criteria set for opioid withdrawal).
    b   Opioids (or a closely related substance) are taken to relieve or avoid withdrawal symptoms.

(APA 2013)

Here, diagnosis of addiction is produced through criteria that are social, subjective and culturally specific, and framed in terms of excessive desire, loss of control and damaged relationships.[9] Even 'tolerance' – an ostensibly biological criterion – is discounted if it is produced under 'appropriate' conditions; that is, within the authority of medicine. For instance, the criteria that refer to 'social impairment' and failure to fulfil 'major role obligations at work, school or home' essentially relate to the impacts of spending what is judged to be too much time or money on particular forms of consumption and from spoiled relationships, unsatisfactory jobs and general existential ennui (Keane 2002, 40). Even Adam Leshner's definition of addiction ultimately rests on the idea of consumption that gets in the way of social relationships; that is 'uncontrollable', as he puts it, 'even in the face of negative social consequences' (Leshner 1997, 191). These are all judgements about what productive citizenship should look like and how 'conventional' – typically middle class – relationships ought to be organised, which, in turn, are embedded in particular formations of gender, class and ethnicity. They are an example of what Mike Savage (2003) has elsewhere described as the 'particular-universal', whereby values and practices that are specific to the middle class are regarded as universal. Ideas about addictive consumption can be seen as a similar kind of projection of particular normative ideals as universal values. Rather than being universal values, notions of appropriate relationships, particular kinds of employment and acceptable ways of spending time and money are specific to Western Protestant ideals in which time is treated like a commodity, to be used, saved and spent in productive ways, rather than 'wasted' or simply 'experienced' in consumption for its own sake (Granfield and Reinarman 2014, 4).

Furthermore, rather than material criteria, the 'gaze' of the clinical screens is on affective internal states like intentions and emotions. In this, they are fairly typical of the neoliberal emphasis on subjectivity more generally. As Helen Keane (2002) has pointed out, fundamentally, the concern is with how people *feel* about their behaviour, and more specifically, how they feel about their ability to *control* it. This focus tells us much about the subjective experience of addiction, which in this framing is constituted as uncontrollable desire, but almost nothing about the putative material processes involved. This focus on subjective feelings of loss of control as criteria of addiction is significant, for ultimately it means that the concept of addiction itself can become potentially infinite, expanding to embrace ever-increasing commodities and behaviours, across wide swathes of the population. Furthermore, as Valverde (1998, 27) has pointed out, such an emphasis leads to the peculiar position whereby those who are committed to conventional social roles, structured around stable routines, and who worry over what may be relatively minor aspects of their behaviour are more likely to be pathologised than those who are less concerned about their actions. As such, definitions of addiction are increasingly coming to include the middle classes into the newly 'addicted' population.

Perhaps most strikingly for this study of consumption and excess, a concept of problematic desire is a central diagnostic criteria of pathology in the clinical screens, with the *DSM* basing its definition of addiction on 'a persistent desire' to consume a substance and 'a need for increasing amounts of the drug to achieve the desired effect' (APA 2013). As we have seen, such pathologised desire is also key to the conceptualisation of addiction in neuroscience. Earlier in this chapter, we saw the centrality of desire to the logic of consumer capitalism – a system that writers such as Colin Campbell and Grant McCracken argued was driven by the generation of insatiability and excess. Today, the globalisation of financial and technological systems, the production of habit-forming technologies and the expansion of cheap credit produce intensified forms of consumption that generate an almost perpetual state of longing. These are the drivers of what Marx described as 'excess and intemperance' and the 'insatiable and bottomless abyss' of desire that Durkheim feared uncontrolled consumption could unleash. It is a narrative of desire as an uncontrollable force with the potential to enslave the individual to 'base' instincts, reconfigured today in terms of neurological and psychological disorder.

Addiction as metaphor

So we are faced with a peculiar notion of addiction. On the one hand, the forms of knowledge and authority associated with neuroscience produce it as something 'real', visible and physiological. On the other, the perspective of the psy sciences renders it an experience that is rooted in subjective states. Interestingly, both forms of knowledge work to expand ideas about addiction: at the molecular level of the pleasure centre in the former, and at the level of individual subjectivity in the latter. Both types of understanding also conceal socio-economic issues at the same time that they reflect normative values. This peculiar epistemological status has led some to describe the notion of addiction as one that 'derives more from magic than from science' (Peele 1985, 1).

However, the argument here is that its significance lies more in its symbolic power than its scientific veracity. This is true of understandings of a number of ailments, as Susan Sontag has made clear in her *Illness as Metaphor*. In it, she writes that the language used to discuss certain diseases can also reveal much about the wider fears and aspirations of their societies:

> Any important disease whose causality is murky, and for which treatment is ineffectual, tends to be awash in significance. First, the subjects of deepest dread (corruption, decay, pollution, anomie, weakness) are identified with the disease. The disease itself becomes a metaphor. Then in the name of the disease . . . that horror is imposed on other things. The disease becomes adjectival.
>
> *(1978, 58)*

This is what has happened with addiction, which has 'become adjectival' to articulate fears about pathological relationships with consumption. In neoliberal consumer cultures, understandings of the 'disease' of addiction are expressions of long-running concerns about loss of control: a condition that hovers around the boundaries of Cartesian dualism, part physical disease, part mental disorder, and located somewhere in the hybrid zone between the body and the mind. Although ostensibly more sophisticated, contemporary accounts share many similarities with their nineteenth-century predecessors: namely, the appeal to physical processes as 'causes' of behaviour and the tendency to fall back on internal states as ultimate explanatory factors – in the nineteenth century, the will, today, subjective emphasis on feelings and emotions. Peele's criticism of MRI scans as little more than 'high tech phrenology' is a prescient reminder of this lineage.

By making subjective assessments of loss of control and excessive desire themselves diagnostic criteria, the notion of addiction comes to act as a kind of shorthand for a wider cultural malaise, expressing a range of relationships with which individuals feel unable to cope. Just as nineteenth-century ideas about diseases of the will expressed a range of *fin de siècle* anxieties, current formulations of addiction embody some of the specific tensions within neoliberal consumer capitalism. More specifically, ideas about addiction articulate growing anxieties in a culture of consumer proliferation and oppressive choice. As we saw earlier, individuals may be free to choose but, they have 'no choice but to choose' (Giddens 1991, 81), a situation that generates anxiety and confusion rather than satisfaction, and in which the 'horror' of responsibility is the converse of freedom. Such ideas of anxiety and insecurity are implied in the very term 'pathological' itself, which was described by Georges Canguilhem as that which 'implies pathos, the direct and concrete feeling of suffering and impotence, the feeling of life gone wrong' (1978, 137). Today, the concept of addiction can be read as a kind of shorthand for 'life gone wrong' in consumer societies.

Disordered identities and the proliferation of addictions

And so, from its roots in psychoactive substances such as alcohol and opiates, today notions of addiction have spread out to encompass a wide range of commodities and activities now considered 'pathological' in various ways. Eve Sedgewick (1993) has described these as 'epidemics of the will' – paralyses of the freedom that is so highly valued in consumer society. Epidemics of the will undermine free choice and are possible only in a society where the freedom of the will is so highly valued and, correspondingly, where its loss is so feared.[10] And, indeed, wherever it is applied, we see consumer pathologies expand to embrace individuals who feel they are unable to control their consumption in a variety of areas, from shopping and gambling to eating McDonald's and surfing the Internet. Even the smartphone – that ubiquitous item of commodity culture – has been described by researchers as a potentially 'addictive technology' (Lee et al. 2014) and the disorder of *nomophobia* (an amalgam of 'no mobile phone' and 'phobia') named as a pathological fear or anxiety associated with being out of touch with technology (King et al. 2013). Although not an 'official' disorder (yet), Norwegian researchers have recently incorporated the diagnostic criteria of the *DSM* to produce a 'Bergen shopping addiction tool' to quantify – and, hence, make 'real' – the 'pathology' of excessive shopping (Andreassen et al. 2015). In it, 'compulsive' buying is regarded as evidence of impulsivity and contrasted with reasoned or utilitarian considerations (e.g. Kellett and Bolton 2009), translating Kraepelin's nineteenth-century notion of *oniomania* as a disorder of the will into the language of twenty-first century pathology as it does so.

These medicalised understandings of disordered consumption are not limited to formal, medical paradigms, but have been incorporated into a range of legal-juridical discourses as well as cultural, ethical and policy debates. Perhaps most interestingly, they are also sometimes actively adopted by consumers themselves, with individuals drawing on the tropes of addiction to lend authority and legitimacy to their condition. In such cases, 'addict identities' are not forced upon unwilling subjects but exist in a dynamic sense in which they are actively selected and interpreted by individuals themselves. Co-production of the language of addiction can be seen in the growth of the myriad self-help groups that have recently developed around forms of problematic consumption, especially the twelve-step Alcoholics Anonymous (AA) model, which has expanded to include groups for narcotics, gambling, cocaine, pills, nicotine and food, amongst others. Indeed, the tone of the foreword to the 2001 *AA Handbook* is almost celebratory as it describes the increased membership and diversity of the organisation across the world and the translation of the handbook into seventy languages. In the proud statement that 'in country after country where the AA seed was planted, it has taken root, slowly at first, then growing by leaps and bounds' while the membership, in terms of 'age, gender, race and culture has widened and deepened' (Alcoholics Anonymous 2001, xxiii), we can see the globalisation of consumer capitalism matched by the global march of addictions.

Although they may not indicate the presence of new diseases, more interestingly, such groups act as testimony to individuals' subjective identification with behaviour they feel is out of control – with 'life gone wrong'. The ideology of these twelve-step groups articulates a very specific concept of identity: one that runs counter to the neoliberal ideal of rational autonomous selfhood, and that in many ways mirrors the neuroscientific understanding of addicts as distinctly different 'types of being'. It is based on an image of addiction as a physical disease and the addict as a distinct, unchangeable type of person. It rests on members' identification with an essential 'addict identity' whose very nature it is to consume to excess.[11] The primary role of AA, for example, is to help members accept their distinction from non-drinkers: 'The delusion that we are like other people, or presently may be, has to be smashed. We . . . have lost the ability to control our drinking. We know that no real alcoholic *ever* recovers control' (2001, 30). And so, an essential identity, defined by a complete and irreversible loss of control, is established. Like other addictions, alcohol addiction is a moral-medical hybrid, and in this, AA also advocates its disease status: 'alcoholics of our type are in the grip of a progressive illness. Over any considerable period, we get worse, never better' (2001, 35). This view of addiction converges with the claim of neuroscience that, as Alan Leshner put it earlier in the chapter, the addicted brain is 'distinctively different from the non-addicted brain', and that 'the addict exists in a different state of being'. In this dovetailing of neuroscientific with AA-style ideas of addiction, we can see an expression of what Rose would describe as 'neurochemical selfhood', whereby a disordered brain is at the root of a disordered identity.

Unlike the nineteenth-century addict, the fault here is framed in terms of the nature of the individual's very being, rather than in a defective will, which could, nevertheless, be strengthened. AA warns, 'Will power and self knowledge will not help these mental blank spots' (2001, 33). Central to the philosophy of AA is this notion of an essential identity, and it is because of this that it aims to affect only behaviour change, because it admits that identity itself cannot change.

This view of addiction acts as a counterpoint against which dominant cultural values can be asserted. It is anathema to the neoliberal ideal of autonomous agents making up a biography of the self through the discerning manipulation of commodities and the responsible management of desire. By failing to manage their freedom, addicts have given up the crucial attributes of autonomy and choice and replaced the dynamic, sovereign self that is constructed through consumption with an essentialist state of being that is destroyed by it. This is a view of identity as a static, ontological state of being, rather than an enterprising process of movement towards the future. It is a distinction that is illuminated in the contrast between Bauman's vision of the enterprising self – of whom he wrote, simply 'being' is not enough, rather, '*making* oneself, not just *becoming* is the challenge' (2007, 57) – and Alexander Trocchi's statement that in addiction, 'one is no longer grotesquely involved in the becoming. One simply is' (1960, 11).

This framing of addiction turns the sovereign consumer on its head, transforming freedom into slavery and desire into need. Addiction is uncontrolled, pathological desire, and it replaces consumption carried out to fulfil wants with consumption that is carried out to fulfil needs, exchanging the pleasurable tension of longing for the agony of craving. Such a state undermines the freedoms of consumer culture, returning us to the realm of necessity: whereas the consumer *chooses* to act, addicts are *forced* to do so – here, there are no choices, only rules. Here, we return to the etymological root of 'consumption' – from the Latin *consumere*, 'to devour, waste, destroy' (OED 2001). This is the 'insatiable and bottomless abyss' of desire that Durkheim warned of. In this formulation, addiction becomes shorthand for those who fail to exercise responsible autonomous subjectivity: who fail to consume the right things, in the right quantities, and who do not – or who cannot – utilise consumption to create a socially sanctioned identity. In this, we can see the construction of a figure that embodies the contradictions of consumption at the same time that it is expelled by them.

To go back to Christopher Lasch's observation that 'every age develops its own peculiar forms of pathology', we can suggest that addiction is the 'peculiar pathology' of the era of neoliberal capitalism, where it acts as a metaphor for wider contradictions within that system. At a time when the admonition to choose from a barrage of commodities and experiences is at its most insistent, the active adoption of the 'addict identity' may even be interpreted as the embrace of a state that rejects the need for choice at all: a refusal of choice that has become overwhelming, a denial of freedom that is illusory. In a climate in which individuals are urged to be active participants in their own self-project, discourses of addiction provide an alternative 'narrative' of identity: one that absolves them of the responsibility of freedom and choice entirely. One final choice ends the tyranny of all the little choices. The addict – at least in the formulations of the self-help groups – is finished with all that.

The addict-protagonist Renton in Irvine Welsh's (1993, vii) novel about heroin addiction, *Trainspotting*, sums it up, explaining his decision to remove himself from consumer capitalism altogether:

> Choose us. Choose life. Choose mortgage payments; choose washing machines; choose cars; compact disc players and electrical tin openers; choose sitting on a couch watching mind-numbing and spirit-crushing game shows, stuffin' fuckin' junk food intae yir mooth . . . Well, I choose no' tae choose life.

Risky subjects

Before leaving this discussion of the contemporary consumption landscape, I will briefly reprise the notion of risk that has been woven throughout ideas about addiction, control and identity in this chapter. In particular, I want to address the suggestion that a shift towards ideas about risk has overtaken discourses of addiction (May 2001; Dean 1999), replacing them with a combination of factors and relationships, expressed in terms of a continuum of behaviour and degrees of harm, rather than the 'absolutist' binaries of addict/non-addict. As Robert Castel put it, the argument is that ideas about risk 'dissolve the notion of a subject or concrete individual, and put in its place a combination of factors, the factors of risk' (Castel 1991, 281).

Although some of this is persuasive, the argument here is that discourses about 'the problems' of consumption, broadly interpreted, are more complicated than this. The ways in which addictive consumption is understood and governed does not necessarily entail either a dissolution of the subject, or a wholesale transition from one set of discourses to another. It is rather a more 'messy' overlapping of dialogues and the forms of governance associated with them. It is not the case that the subject is 'dissolved', because, as we have seen, a distinct (if multifaceted) 'addict identity' persists in a number of dialogues and narratives, from sections of the medical profession to self-help groups and popular discourses. It exists both as an identity that is embraced by self-defined addicts themselves as well as an identity to be avoided by prudent risk negotiators. Ideas about addiction are also frequently deployed by industry, whose focus on a 'pathological minority', counterposed to a 'responsible majority', serves to detract attention from the role of structural factors in the generation of problems relating to excessive consumption. Here, the problem is framed as lying not with the production or marketing of particularly tempting kinds of products, but rather with the supposedly defective individuals who are unable to resist them. This perspective has expedience for the operation of capital in neoliberal markets, where the focus on individual pathology downplays the role of both big business and the state in generating the environments that such commodities are made available in.

Ideas about addiction and risk are entwined in other ways too. Particular 'risky' types of consumption, such as smoking or drug taking, are often presented as something that can lead to a state of addiction in themselves. In this, it could be said that the language of risk actually reinforces the notion of 'addiction' as a state that the individual is actually at risk *from*. On the other hand, in some narratives, addiction itself is presented as something that can encourage risky consumption. For example, the American Society of Addiction Medicine's definition of addiction is of something that causes 'deficits in executive functioning', which, in turn, 'predisposes youngsters to engage in "high risk" behaviors, including engaging in alcohol or other drug use' (ASAM 2016). A NIDA blog entitled 'Peering Into the Teen Brain' presents images of 'lit up' sections of brains to ask, 'What does risky behaviour look like?' (NIDA Blog Team 2016). The short answer is that it looks very like addictive behaviour. Through the medium of brain scanning technology and the normative assumptions that power it, risky behaviour is conflated with substance use disorders and both contrasted with 'cautious' behaviour to produce two very different physical 'types' of brain, and by extension, two different types of identity.

It is not, then, a case of transition or dissolution, but rather a more complex intersection of discourses and the forms of governance associated with them. And, in fact, notions of addiction and risk happen to intersect in a very particular way. Both articulate a general sense of insecurity, conceived in the former as a subjective sense of loss of control, and in the latter as vulnerability to potential danger. The location of risks in a miasma of inter-relations expands the potential for danger across a range of factors and spreads vulnerability throughout the entire population – anyone can be 'at risk' from a huge variety of – often invisible – elements. Similarly, the identification of addiction with a subjective sense of loss of control creates a climate in which 'addiction' is felt to lurk everywhere; there are a potentially infinite number of situations and products that can catch the consumer unawares and undermine agency. It could be said that addiction becomes a potential danger, a risk, in itself. The intense focus on the analysis and monitoring of their own subjective states makes individuals hypersensitive, ever alert to signs of loss of control. And, because innermost thoughts and emotions are the medium through which freedom is controlled, as well as the measure of its loss, there seems to be no limit to the situations and substances that can erode it and undermine agency. Such a focus makes the burdens of liberty even greater, so that it becomes imperative to be vigilant, to regulate behaviour, to guard against risk and keep watch on subjective states – to continually monitor one's freedom.

End points

Since its creation in the nineteenth century, the 'addict' has grown up and spawned many more 'types' of disordered consumer identities that, like the proliferation of consumption itself, are increasingly widely dispersed throughout the population. But whereas the nineteenth-century addict had a deviant identity stamped upon them, today's consumer pathologies are increasingly characterised by individuals' identification with subjective states, backed up by the authority of neuroscience.

In the twenty-first century, an increasingly global system of consumer capitalism has driven intensified forms of consumption deeper into the psyche of the individual consumer. At the same time, explanations for excess have also moved inwards, peering into their neuronal circuits for evidence of 'hijacking' and examining their interior states for proof of deficient reasoning, in a move that expands the potential for pathology to increase throughout the population, along with the exponential growth of consumerism itself.

The social processes behind the production of these forms of knowledge, like those of their predecessors, obscure relations of power and authority as well as normative judgements about productive citizenship and properly managed desire. So whereas the mercantile era focused on the threat posed by foreign commodities, and the period of liberal capitalism was concerned with weak wills, today's era of deregulatory capitalism locates the source of problematic consumption at the level of individual biology.

Such a framing has expedience for capital. The focus on the (flawed) individual consumer downplays the role of big business in producing excess, and the role of governments and regulators in creating the political conditions for them to do so. And so, the production of increasingly intensified forms of consumption, relayed through habit-forming technologies and persuasive forms of marketing, are elided in a generalised focus towards the deficiencies of the individual. The result is a gaze that largely absolves the producers, legislators and regulators of commodities from responsibility for the effects of consumption. This tendency also possesses a normative aspect. The ideology of responsibility rests on judgements about autonomy and rationality, and in it, responsible consumption is evidence of the 'right' way to live, the 'right' way to be. Indeed, it becomes the duty of sovereign consumers to furnish themselves with relevant knowledge and information and take appropriate steps to safeguard their health and well-being by consuming 'correctly'. As a corollary of this individualising and normative project, the individual is also the site of blame when things go wrong.

So, as we shall see in later chapters, problems of excessive consumption – overeating and obesity, binge drinking and alcoholism, smoking and gambling – come to be defined as failures of individual consumption, suffered by the minority who are unable to control their behaviour, so diverting attention from the wider political-economic environment that consumption goes on in. These are some of the issues that we now turn to in the Case Studies in Part Two.

Notes

1 Castells has pointed out that technology drives the expansion of capitalism, as he puts it – 'always trying to overcome the limits of time and space' (1996, 101).
2 It has been noted that the discipline of public health itself is part of a normalising project with Lupton (1995), for example, drawing attention to the ways it tends to stigmatise and reinforce social divisions based on class, gender and ethnicity.
3 Although this governance of the self is the individual's responsibility, there are plenty of experts within the psy sciences, such as counsellors and therapists – whom Rose (1999, 3) calls 'engineers of the human soul' – to provide guidance on the management of behaviour, so that, as Cruikshank puts it, 'the police, the guards and the doctors do not have to do so' (1996, 234).
4 Although many of these veer into moralistic critiques of what is regarded as mass consumerism, what is perhaps most interesting about these essays is their continuation of a long line of arguments against the negative effects of the spread of mass consumption: the adverse effects on health and well-being,

the threat to the integrity of the individual, the community and the nation state through the enervating effects of materialism.
5 Although, according to Bauman, salvation comes in the form of guides to 'correct' behaviour, which are generated by the market itself. Advertising, celebrity endorsements, scientific validation all work to reassure anxious consumers that their choices are 'right and rational' and that their behaviour is culturally acceptable (Bauman 1988a, 65).
6 Described by Vrecko as being focused on 'monitoring, optimising and organising drug using individuals and populations' (2010, 62).
7 NIDA scientists Volkow and Li describe addiction as 'the neurobiology of behaviour gone awry' and liken it to heart disease, so establishing the physical – and visible – 'reality' of the condition. They write that drug addiction 'is a disease of the brain, and the associated abnormal behaviour is the result of dysfunction of brain tissue, just as cardiac insufficiency is a disease of the heart' (2004, 963; in Fraser 54).
8 Although it accepts the influence of environmental and social factors on behaviour, this kind of research postulates the 'substantial heritability' of substance-specific addictions (Agrawal et al. 2012). Researchers have also calculated and quantified the heritability of a number of forms of consumption – or addictive disorders – ranging from hallucinogens, stimulants, cannabis, sedatives, opiates and cocaine to alcohol, smoking, caffeine and gambling (Bevilacqua and Goldman 2009).
9 The criteria for SUD in *DSM-5* are classified into four main groupings: impaired control, social impairment, risky use and pharmacological criteria (i.e. tolerance and withdrawal).
10 Sedgewick writes that, in modern society, not only is free will is hypostatised and ethically charged, but also a corresponding 'compulsion' is equally hypostatised to oppose it. Such a notion has to be 'available as a counterstructure always internal to [freedom], always requiring to be ejected from it' (Sedgewick 1993, 134).
11 Ironically, to find any kind of respite or absolution, this most out of control consumer must abnegate control altogether and admit powerlessness over their consumption in order to accept for themselves the statement that 'I am an addict'.

Part II
Addictive consumptions
Drugs, food, gambling

In Part II, we turn to look in more detail at how some of these issues are realised through three specific case studies. At this point in the book, we change focus again. Away from the wide historical sweep of the first two chapters and the analysis of the contemporary landscape of consumption that we have just seen, we now turn to zoom in on three specific areas. Closer examination of the consumption of drugs, food and gambling are designed to illustrate central themes of the previous chapters while also highlighting unique aspects of consumption.

The exploration of the different dynamics within and across these case studies is intended as a counter to the kind of essentialising logic that locates the 'source' of addiction in the individual consumer. Instead, here we look further: towards the political, economic and cultural environment that produces the epistemological basis for such understandings in the first place. Exploration of the differences in the three case studies also aims to highlight variation within the idea of addictive consumption itself, and to show that it is not some kind of uniform practice, but rather a relationship whose meanings are socially situated and context specific. In a culture of super-sized foods, mobile gambling and legal highs, ideas about addiction come to have very particular meanings.

So, for example, issues around the excess consumption of food can be said to quite literally embody the contradictions of consumption and bring us back to nineteenth-century ideas of willpower where issues around control are played out at the level of the body. In contrast, gambling appears almost as its opposite: as a dematerialised form of consumption whose pathologies are articulated in narratives of irrationality and 'waste', in ways that have resonance with the wider economy of finance capitalism. Meanwhile, the intoxications involved in the consumption of drugs highlights both Western ideals of sobriety as well as, ironically, the ambivalence involved in ideas about addiction, as some substances move along trajectories of increasing normalisation. Furthermore, when applied to drugs, food and gambling, the drivers of intensified consumption that we have just seen in Chapter 3, along with particular formations of geography and class, work to produce whole environments in which consumption is increasingly pervasive, which are described here as variously 'intoxicating', 'obesogenic' and 'aleatory'.

The subjects of the case studies highlight the shifting trajectories of a number of commodities as they move in and out of commodity status, towards or away from social acceptability, their course shaped by cultural, normative and scientific drivers, that are situated within socio-economic relations of power. We find that, ironically, many of the 'drug foods' and 'private vices', such as alcohol, tobacco and sugar, that were subject to the critique of luxury in the eighteenth century and the disciplinary gaze in the nineteenth, have become the focus of the 'risky' gaze in the twenty-first, their threat to the social order relocated, along a social gradient, to the health, bodies and brains of mainly poor and excluded groups.

As well as distinctive aspects of each type of consumption, taken together, the case studies also highlight key themes of the book: in particular, around issues of control and excess, freedom and responsibility, identity and desire, the role of the state and the freedoms of the market. Together, they begin to show how ideas about 'addictive consumption' act as a form of biopolitical governance in neoliberal societies, at the same time that they highlight ongoing tensions within them.

4

DRUGS

Intoxicating consumption

> Drugs make us question what it means to consume anything, anything at all.
> — *Avital Ronell (1992, 63)*

Introduction

In *Plato's Pharmacy*, Derrida (1981b) noted that the concept of 'drug' derived from the Greek *pharmakon* and had a dual meaning as something which could act as both a medicine and a poison, providing relief at the same that time it caused harm. This ambivalence complicates ideas about consumption, as expressed in Avital Ronell's observation that 'drugs make us question what it means to consume anything, anything at all'.

And today, the consumption of drugs is a practice still shot through with ambiguity. On the one hand, as intoxicating commodities, they promise pleasure and self-fulfilment; on the other, they threaten addiction and self-destruction. And, although consumers' desire for illegal substances creates a global trade worth billions, policymakers' determination to rid the world of them creates an anti-drugs industry that costs a roughly similar amount.

The psychoactive commodities of the eighteenth and nineteenth centuries – alcohol, tobacco, opiates and cannabis – have been supplemented by a cornucopia of new ones today: empathogens, hallucinogens, smart drugs and designer drugs; some of which are legal, some not. In this increasingly intoxicating landscape, the consumption of drugs is characterised by a blurring of boundaries. As some substances, such as cannabis and Ecstasy, become increasingly normalised and incorporated into commodity culture, others move in the opposite direction, becoming repositioned as dangerous substances, like tobacco, or risky ones, like alcohol. Meanwhile, others have appeared – new commodities such as 'legal highs' and e-cigarettes – that have yet to find a stable set of meanings. In the twenty-first century, the boundaries between licit and illicit, risky and respectable, drug and commodity are fluid and are tied up with shifting configurations of power, morality and technology.

This chapter explores these issues. Following the dualism of the *pharmakon* itself, its focus is two-fold. On the one hand, it is concerned with a trend towards the increasing normalisation and commodification of psychoactive commodities in the spread of what are argued to be 'intoxicating environments'. On the other, it is concerned with the governance of intoxication or, more specifically, with the governance of particular groups of individuals through their consumption of drugs.

So the first section considers the issue of intoxication itself, which, although central, has long been regarded as problematic for the order of societies, especially when associated with particular social groups of 'outsiders'. It moves on to argue that the consumption of intoxicating commodities has thus historically been subject to moral panics and attempts at governance: an approach that has been exemplified by the 'War on Drugs', whose disciplining of marginalised groups constitutes an attempt to impose the values of sobriety and productivity on unruly populations of consumers. The next section moves on to consider a key contradiction of drugs: the fact that, although problematic, they are also pleasurable, as well as highly profitable, commodities in consumer capitalism. Here, the argument is that the current psychoactive landscape has been shaped by the wider deregulatory climate of neoliberalism and the structural drivers of intensified consumption within it, that we saw in Chapter 3. These have produced an expansion of both the spaces and the opportunities to consume drugs, in the spread of intoxicating environments. To explore this in more detail, the section briefly reviews the shifting trajectories of Ecstasy, cannabis, legal highs and alcohol. The third section moves on to explore the more complex forms of governance that are elicited by such processes. Away from the disciplinary approach of the war on drugs, it argues that the policing of sobriety is now being incorporated into neoliberal ideals of individual responsibility and risk management as well as being backed up by more disciplinary measures. It describes how these processes have been operationalised largely through a focus on smoking and the excessive consumption of alcohol in ways that continue to focus on the problematic pleasures of marginalised social groups. Finally, it argues that these processes highlight the fluidity of ideas about both drugs and concepts of addiction and, as they do so, exemplify wider tensions within ideals of sobriety and productivity.

Intoxication and governance

Throughout much of the twentieth century, the policies of Western governments[1] were underlined by a pathologising rationality which constituted drugs – especially 'hard' drugs like heroin and cocaine – as uniquely dangerous commodities. When people talk of addiction, it is still drugs in general, and these drugs in particular, that are their implicit or explicit subject. These are the bearers of harm: of ill health, social disruption, crime, misery and death. Despite the proliferation of various types of addictions seen in the previous chapter, the object of addiction par excellence is still (illegal) drugs: a specific group of psychoactive commodities that are defined through a range of penal and medical discourses as uniquely harmful to both societies and individuals. Indeed, there is a semantic elision between the term 'drug' and the concept of addiction, with the former generally believed to 'cause' the latter in some way.

The threat of these uniquely powerful commodities is tied up with their promise of intoxication: a state which has long threatened the ideals of reason and productivity of orderly societies. Indeed, the historian Phil Withington has privileged the more encompassing term 'intoxication' over the more ideologically loaded 'addiction' or 'drugs' to refer to a wide range of consumption practices that posed a challenge to social order. From what he describes as 'the mild stimulation of afternoon tea to the inebriation of rounds in the pub' (2014, 12), such practices demanded self-control, which was integral to the pursuit of intoxication itself as well as a means of demonstrating status. Controlled consumption was thus historically important, and Withington argues that the way societies recognise and deal with the threat of latency is one that has long been integral to culture (2014, 15).

Deliberate intoxication through the consumption of drugs stands as a counter to the hegemony of sobriety as well as the ideal of rational, autonomous subjectivity. As Stuart Walton (2003) noted in *Out of It*, put another way, intoxicated subjects are unproductive subjects, whose capacity to work, plan, or even consume in a rational manner is compromised. Intoxication undermines liberal and neoliberal ideals of productivity, inviting instead unruly pleasure, excess and idleness. The contemporary vernacular of intoxication – 'wasted', 'annihilated', 'obliterated', 'out of it' – reflects the insult to the values of reason and purposive action and the overwhelming of the 'civilised' body by irrational disorder. Such a non-rational, non-productive state is the precursor to the destructive state of addiction.

Contrary perspectives exist, however. George Bataille, for example, positions intoxication, along with waste, luxury and excessive consumption, as aspects of the 'principle of excess' within his general critique of classical political economy. In *Visions of Excess* (1985), he argues that intoxication through intense forms of consumption acts as a means of transcending the 'bourgeois' values of restrained expenditure and reason. Elsewhere, he writes of 'these moments of intoxication, when we defy everything. . . . those moments when consumption accelerates' (1991, 20). Here, then, intoxicating consumption is a hedonistic escape from 'straight' society and a deliberate rejection of the values of sober, autonomous subjectivity. Its value as a form of self-expression has also run as a leitmotif throughout history, especially in bohemian and literary circles. In the nineteenth century, for example, William James described the power of drugs to stimulate those capacities 'usually crushed . . . by the cold facts and dry criticisms of the sober hour. Sobriety diminishes, discriminates, says no. Drunkeness expands, unites and says yes' (James 1902, 387). And, as we saw in Chapter 2, in certain circles of Victorian society, consumption of opium was regarded as an outlet for the artistic temperament, expressed in literary offerings such as Coleridge's *Kubla Khan* and De Quincey's *Confessions of an English Opium-Eater*.

Today, this Romantic association of drugs with self-actualisation continues to be, for many, one of the most meaningful aspects of drug use, where it stands in opposition to the demands of autonomous rational subjectivity which, as Walton (2003) has pointed out, is above all, a sober subjectivity. For many, 'the zone' of drug consumption is an area which offers escape from the routines of everyday life in 'straight' society. Indeed, Walton argues, intoxication makes us question the very values of sobriety and rationality and is the one area, he says, that 'allows us radically to question the point of moderation as a desirable goal in itself' (2003, 205).

This kind of 'radical questioning' tends to be perceived as more threatening when it is carried out by 'problematic' social groups, whose embodied and disorderly pleasures have long been associated with the more material aspects of Cartesian dualism. The association of drugs and intoxication with such 'outsiders' (Becker 1973) have been persistently portrayed as a threat to the moral order of society. Such fears are expressed in what Reinarman and Levine (1989) call 'drug scares' that link social disorder and moral decline with social divisions based on ethnicity, gender, sexuality and class and that regularly erupt as a precursor to prohibition and attempts at social control. Scares about marijuana, the 'killer weed' of Mexicans, and of 'cocaine-crazed Negroes' in the early part of the twentieth century, and of hippies dropping acid and beatniks smoking cannabis in the later part, echoed similar fears to those we saw earlier of nineteenth-century Chinese opium 'fiends' and working class 'degeneracy' in an ongoing narrative about preternaturally powerful commodities that were able to enslave their consumers and undermine the social fabric.

Discipline and punish

In this framework, the very definition of certain commodities as 'illicit drugs' can be seen as a means of policing those who consume them as well as defending dominant social values of sobriety, productivity and order. In this vein, a number of writers have argued that ideas about addiction in general, and about 'the problem of drugs' in particular, act as a means of governing consumption, particularly amongst marginalised groups (Bourgois 2000). Indeed, Julie Netherland has argued that today, such discourses have become 'one of our most expansive and influential systems of social control' (Netherland 2012, xvi).

In 1971, this disciplinary approach culminated in a declaration of war, with the enemy identified, generically, as 'drugs'. The War on Drugs originated in the Nixon-era administration, as part of the political-economic response to social disorder which, as we saw in Chapter 3, also encouraged the development of neuroscientific understandings of addiction. It was thus a political concern with population control that drove both the funding of brain science and the drug war's linkage of drugs with crime and disorderly groups.

The War on Drugs – which still rages today – has been a vastly expensive, ultimately futile campaign whose real target has been not so much illegal drugs but, as Noam Chomsky (1991) has noted, the narco terrorists in the countries that produce them as well as the 'superfluous' underclass population who consume them at home. In the 1980s in particular, the threat of crack cocaine in urban ghettos in the United States and heroin in inner city council estates in Britain was portrayed as an epidemic, reducing productivity, decimating youth and linked to crime, prostitution and, especially in Britain, HIV, AIDS and death. As Craig Reinarman and Harry Levine have convincingly shown, this approach to drugs acted to deflect attention from wider economic and political conditions, acting as what they call 'an ideological fig leaf to place over unsightly urban ills' (Reinarman and Levine 1989, 562).[2] It operated in a climate in which neoliberal policies had overseen the scaling back of public spending and the undermining of the power of organised labour in order to boost corporate profits; all of which worked to increase unemployment and generate poverty and insecurity for millions. As we saw in the last chapter, the globalisation of the consumer economy was supported by, on the one hand, the exploitation of labour in the Global South, and on the other, the creation of 'McJobs' as well as increased poverty and the expansion of drug addiction throughout deprived urban neighbourhoods in the Global North. However, in a political inversion of the problems that were created or exacerbated by neoliberal policies, the illicit consumption of heroin and crack cocaine by the poor on either side of the Atlantic was regarded as the cause, rather than the consequence, of wider social problems. In what Reinarman and Levine (1989) call a 'vocabulary of attribution', drug use was presented as an individual problem – of weak wills, compromised reason, lack of self-control – that elicited an equally individualised response, expressed in the rhetorical language of consumer choice: 'Just Say No'.

The approach of the War on Drugs has been operationalised through a range of penal, medical and moral practices that seek to produce docile and, importantly, sober bodies. On the one hand, punitive racial and class-based policies have filled prisons with mainly poor and ethnic minority consumers. On the other, those members of the underclass not incarcerated have been increasingly monitored through the police, courts and parole systems; their homes, public spaces and even their bodies becoming sites of state surveillance as police powers extend to increasingly invasive practices of interrogation, tagging and 'stop and search'. Meanwhile, for the rest of the population, mandatory drug testing is widespread for employees of many U.S. companies and is also being considered for applicants for welfare, food stamps, unemployment or housing assistance. As of 2016, fifteen U.S. states have enacted legislation requiring the poorest and most needy in society to submit to drug testing before essential benefits are paid (NCSL 2016), with similar proposals to cut the benefits to those taking drugs who refuse treatment being considered in the United Kingdom (*BBC News* 14 February 2015).

The system of methadone maintenance can be viewed as a concrete as well as a symbolic example of the exercise of this kind of disciplinary authority or, more accurately, of biopower: the disciplining of bodies through various forms of social control. It is, as Philippe Bourgois notes, a state-endorsed attempt to 'inculcate moral discipline into the hearts, minds and bodies of deviants who reject sobriety and moral discipline' (2000, 173). Intended as a replacement drug for heroin, methadone is designed to chemically negate pleasure, to eliminate intoxication. As an opiate agonist, it blocks the reception of heroin in the synapses of the brain, eliminating sensations of euphoria and desire as well as craving, in what Bourgois sardonically describes as a 'technocratic magic bullet that can resolve social economic and human existential quandaries by intervening almost surgically at the level of the brain's synapses' (2000, 176). Its symbolic qualities are no less impressive, for it represents the resistance of the pleasurable and unruly effects of intoxication and the promotion of the state of stable and productive sobriety. The fact that methadone does not, in practice, work in this way, being itself resisted and subverted by those who consume it, does not detract from its power as a marker of biomedical control.

From prisons to methadone clinics, these approaches to Chomsky's 'superfluous' populations act as a means of disciplinary and biopolitical control over problematic groups, working on their bodies and brains through their consumption habits. In them, we can see some convergence with the nineteenth-century disciplining of the urban underclass: a population whose non-productive and potentially disruptive nature marked it out for particular forms of penal-moral regulation and surveillance. However, in today's system of twenty-first century consumer capitalism, current models of control are becoming more complex. The policing of sobriety is increasingly being incorporated into neoliberal ideals of self-governance and responsibility, backed up by the regulation of public space and a 'mobilisation of morality', as we will see later in this chapter. This is, in turn, related to wider processes of normalisation, commodification and to the spread of what can be described as 'intoxicating environments'. It is to these developments that we now turn, through a consideration of the shifting trends in the consumption of Ecstasy, cannabis, 'legal highs' and alcohol.

Commodification, normalisation and the spread of intoxicating environments

> Junk is the ideal product. The ultimate merchandise. No sales talk necessary. The client will crawl through a sewer and beg to buy.
>
> *(William Burroughs 1977, vii)*

As we noted at the beginning of the chapter, the *pharmakon* has a dual aspect as a source of both pleasure and pain. Drugs are characterised by similar ambivalence: as well as acting as conduits for discipline and governance, they also serve as seductive commodities of the self. Indeed, as

Burroughs's quote suggests, drugs can be regarded as exemplary products of consumer capitalism. They can provide excitement, pleasure and instant gratification as well as offering release from stress and escape from boredom. Their effects are transient; their pleasures fleeing, and sometimes habit-forming. All require repeat purchase, as Burroughs was aware. This latter point means their lucrative potential is particularly salient in a system of consumer capitalism, a feature that Robin Room has drawn attention to, writing that alcohol, as 'a quintessential habit-forming commodity. . . . along with other psychoactive substances, is [ ] ideal for building and sustaining markets' (2011, 141).

As we saw in the previous chapter, a Romantic ethic that valorises desire, novelty and pleasure as means of self-expression is a driving force of capitalism. The generation of new and exciting commodities and experiences is central to this quest. Drugs fit the bill well. They embody the values of a culture committed to the pursuit of instant gratification, hedonism and individual self-fulfilment and that repeatedly urges its citizens to indulge its desires – because, as the L'Oreal advertisement reminds us, 'you're worth it'. The quest for illicit drugs is, for O'Malley, evidence of continued Romanticism in modern life and an expression of the increasing freedoms and 'exciting transgressions' (1999, 173) of the post-war period. It can also be seen as part of the neoliberal 'project of the self', in which autonomous consumers choose the commodity best suited to their particular desires from amongst a variety of (black) marketed options (Blackman 2004).

In this context, the political-economic drivers of intensified consumption that we saw in Chapter 3 have also worked to reshape the landscape of psychoactive consumption. Throughout the 1990s, a range of commercial, political and licensing interests converged, in different ways, to produce an expansion of the spaces and opportunities to consume drugs, in the spread of 'intoxicating environments'. During this period, a range of 'soft' drugs were joined by new types, such as 'legal highs' and designer drugs, and both merged with the consumption of licit substances such as alcohol and tobacco. This psychoactive cornucopia increasingly came to feature in the leisure patterns of young people and was described as a shift towards 'normalisation' whereby the recreational consumption of drugs moved from the margins to the centre of youth culture (Parker et al. 1998; Aldridge et al. 2011).[3] In particular, consumption of Ecstasy, cannabis, 'legal highs' and, in some contexts, alcohol have worked to normalise intoxication, reflecting the expansion of the environments in which it can be carried out. The shifting trajectories of these commodities and the new meanings they bring to ideas about the consumption of 'drugs' are the subject of the rest of this section.

Commodifying Ecstasy

The appearance of Ecstasy did much to draw increasingly commodified images of drug use into mainstream culture. Unlike 'outsiders', many of the young people who were its most enthusiastic consumers were affluent, middle class and suburban: a demographic that undermined long-standing associations of drugs with urban deprivation and social dislocation. Throughout the 1980s, as its popularity increased, the drug itself became the focal point of a new subculture, accompanied by distinctive styles of music and fashion. By the end of the millennium, rave culture had developed into a mainstream leisure industry with commercial ventures such as Ministry of Sound organising clubs and recordings of the music played in them, a range of specialised magazines such as *i-D* and *The Face* showcasing new fashions and the rise of the DJ as a celebrity in their (although usually his) own right. Indeed, after four years,

Ministry of Sound had launched itself as a brand, developing its own radio show and lifestyle magazine as well as links to other brands such as Pepsi and Sony in corporate sponsorship deals that amassed an annual turnover of some £10 million. As Matthew Collin put it, Ecstasy was the first mainstream illegal drug that came packaged 'as the ultimate entertainment concept, with its own music, clubs, dress codes' (1996, 285).

Ecstasy pills themselves were key actors in this commodified assemblage: fashionable items in their own right, featuring designs that often aped the logos of corporate capitalism (at the same time that they subverted them), such as Nike, Versace and McDonalds, with each brand associated with particular qualities and effects and used to establish credibility and the identity of particular products (see Image 4.1).

Such designs encouraged the creation of a truly global drug culture, uniting chemical generations around the world with instantly recognisable symbols of consumption and shared meaning. Meanwhile, the imagery of Ecstasy, as well as of other illicit drugs, was also being increasingly adopted by mainstream industries to advertise their own legal products. So, for example, fashion houses play with the iconography and language of both drugs and addiction, with Christian Dior presenting its *Addict* lipstick like a cigarette (see Image 4.2) and advertising for Yves Saint Laurent's *Opium* perfume suggesting the sexualised abandon of an opium den.[4]

In making knowing, ironic references to commodities that are illicit or risky, mainstream manufacturers aim to transfer some of the countercultural status of the forbidden to their own commodity: a 'trickle up' of street credibility and cool into the sober mainstream in which the products, as well as the imagery, of intoxication become central, and highly lucrative, features of

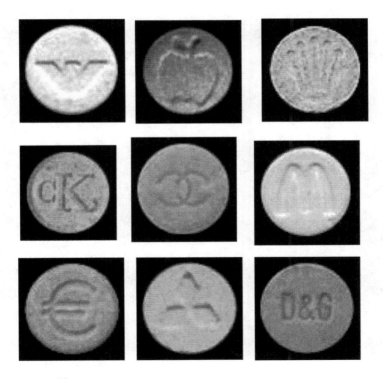

IMAGE 4.1   Ecstasy tablets

IMAGE 4.2 Jennifer Lawrence for Dior Addict lipstick.

consumer capitalism. Within this commercial environment, Ecstasy itself was part of a process of the repositioning of drugs that was taking place on a broader social scale. Its shifting status was exemplified in the now (in)famous statement by Professor David Nutt, then Chair of the U.K. government's Advisory Council on the Misuse of Drugs, that Ecstasy was less risky than horse-riding (2009). Many consumers agreed, regarding it as less harmful than alcohol or tobacco and as a fashionable pill, free from much of the paraphernalia associated with drug use, rather than a heinous agent of destruction.

Cannabis: from the counterculture to the mainstream

A similar process of normalisation has also characterised the trajectory of cannabis, where controls over consumption are being increasingly relaxed throughout North and South America as well as Europe. The shift is part of widespread calls for a more pragmatic approach to drug regulation, but it has also been helped by the shifting status of the groups who use drugs like cannabis and who advocate for them in drug debates (in the Global North, at least). As Joseph Gusfield pointed out in 1963, definitions of acceptable or unacceptable behaviour are partly formed by the power and status of those social groups doing the defining. Such 'status politics' are also at work in the case of cannabis. Away from the dropouts and hippies of the counterculture, many of the people who openly admit to taking the drug now, or who argue for its benefits, are increasingly the 'respectable' middle class: medical professionals, academics, law enforcement agencies. Alongside this association with more powerful, mainstream groups is the linking of cannabis with medicinal benefits. Its role in alleviating pain and sickness has conferred legitimacy, as has advocacy from groups associated with illnesses such as multiple sclerosis, with users reconceptualised as 'deserving' patients, and the drug itself repositioned as a 'treatment'. Legislative realignment has followed, with a number of U.S. states approving the medicinal use of cannabis (Duvall 2015). Colorado became the first U.S. state to approve recreational consumption in 2012; Uruguay became the first country to legalise it altogether in 2014, while Canada announced the legalisation of recreational consumption in 2018.

As its trajectory shifts towards legality, cannabis has become commodified in ways that work to erode associations with the problematic pleasures or addictions of the underclass and realign it more closely with the respectable mainstream. The recreational consumption of marijuana has now produced an entire industry, estimated to be worth approximately $7.1 billion in America (Arcview 2016). It is organised along the lines of regular, mainstream business, with regulations around product quality and packaging, the appearance of specialist stores and the development of luxury products to expand the customer base. A new Silicon Valley start-up company called Eaze – a mobile app that arranges cannabis deliveries – exemplifies the entrepreneurial spirit driving the growth of the cannabis industry. Described as 'Uber for pot', Eaze utilises big data, digital marketing and technology to organise the supply and delivery of medicinal marijuana throughout the state of California. Customers can browse through high-resolution images, detailed descriptions and lab results of various products before placing their order, which is then delivered to them by a courier, with text updates allowing them to track its progress. As one business commentator puts it, 'From vape pens to edibles to raw flowers, patients can select what they would like to smoke, vaporise or ingest and have it delivered in less time than it takes to get a pizza' (Carmody 2016).

In its upwardly mobile trajectory, we can see the shift of cannabis from the counterculture to the mainstream – a move that has made legal marijuana the fastest growing industry in

America (Arcview 2016), and a respectable option in an expanding, commercial psychoactive culture. In the example of ventures such as Eaze, we can also see the embodiment of some of the features that drive neoliberal consumer culture more generally: in particular, the effects of deregulatory licensing policies that allow the marketing and branding of cannabis as just another consumer product, the neoliberal emphasis on freedom and choice and the intersections of marketing with technology, as the company utilise Big Data and mobile technologies in order to personalise and expand consumption for newly discerning customers.

Drugs 2.0: legal highs

Along with these trends of normalisation and commodification, the emergence of new types of intoxicating commodities (as well as the consumption of established ones in new ways) trouble the distinction between licit and illicit consumption and occupy a kind of liminal psychoactive status.

'Legal highs' are substances whose molecular structure is deliberately redesigned to create new versions of traditional substances in ways that circumvent legislation. Often the chemical composition of a new – legal – drug is only one or two chemical tweaks from an existing – illegal – one, a nicety that shows up the porosity of the concept of legitimacy and, indeed, of 'drug' itself. The Internet is the primary medium of this type of psychoactive trade: a place where commodities and, just as important, information about how to consume them is traded in a mirror image of neoliberal commerce. The intersections of digital technologies and social media that, as we saw earlier, work to intensify licit forms of consumption also accelerate and expand illicit forms, too. Similar to its mainstream counterpart, the so-called dark net acts as a virtual marketplace for the trading of illicit substances, but one where identities remain hidden and where buyers and sellers can trade in digital currencies such as Bitcoin. This underground system frustrates penal attempts to regulate or even define consumption, with one dark net site, the 'Silk Road', having approximately $1.2 billion worth of revenue from two to five years of operations (World Drug Report 2014). As Mike Power puts it, 'Welcome to Drugs 2.0 – an anarchic free market world in which drug legislation is being outpaced by chemistry, technology and ingenuity' (2013, xii). The drug mephedrone – closely allied to Ecstasy – was what Power describes as the first 'mass market downloadable drug' (2013, xii). Initially available only online, its popularity spread as users recommended it to friends via social networks in a form of narcotic viral marketing. Many British manufacturers outsourced production of mephedrone to China for similar reasons cited by manufacturers of licit goods: cheap labour and relaxed export regulations. The resulting products were sold openly on public websites, whose sophisticated designs, one-click ordering systems, customer databases, user review sections and overnight delivery options mirrored the most successful legal sites. With a click of the mouse, British consumers could obtain their cheap, legal mephedrone in the Royal Mail in a move that turned postmen into what Power describes, slightly tongue-in-cheek, as 'unwitting drugs couriers' (2013, 139). As it often does in the case of licit commodities, the Internet accelerated and intensified trends in drug consumption, with mephedrone achieving a popularity in weeks that Ecstasy had taken years to reach.

Alongside legal highs, off-label consumption of pharmaceuticals whereby 'medicinal' drugs spill out of controlled, regulated contexts into informal and illicit economies constitute a case of what Lovell (2007) describes as pharmaceutical 'leakage'. In doing so, they transgress the boundary from 'good' to 'bad' drug, cure to poison and regulated to unregulated consumption.

The history of pharmaceuticals is replete with examples of such spillage, from the emergence of 'uppers' in the 1930s, 'downers' in the 1960s, amphetamines and barbiturates in the 1970s, and painkillers such as Vicodin and OxyContin – described as an addictive form of 'hillbilly heroin' – into the twenty-first century (Inciardi and Cicero 2009). Most recently, off-label consumption of cognitive enhancers or 'smart drugs' (*nootropics*, from the Greek *noos*, for *mind*) are the latest example of pharmaceutical leakage. Originally intended for use in sleep disorders, these drugs of the new millennium are timely additions to the pharmacological landscape. However, rather than hedonistic abandon and pleasure, these embody a kind of 'pharmacological work ethic', acting as productivity enhancers by sharpening focus, concentration and memory. In this, they appear closer to an ethic of self-improvement and sobriety than one of intoxication and excess. Writing in the *New Yorker*, journalist Mary Talbot (2009) considered the aspirations opened up by these very twenty-first century commodities dispiriting, writing: 'Every era, it seems, has its own defining drug. Neuroenhancers are perfectly suited for the anxiety of white-collar competition in a floundering economy'. These drugs were not about realising the self or expanding consciousness, rather, Talbot continued, 'they facilitate a pinched, unromantic, grindingly efficient form of productivity'. In this, smart drugs are to the twenty-first century what caffeine was to the eighteenth. Whereas the latter stimulated the commercial activities of the merchant bourgeoisie, nootropics promote endurance amongst the high-achieving professionals of the competitive neoliberal era. Both are located within discourses of productivity and efficiency: stimulating forms of 'clear headed bourgeois intoxication', as we saw in Chapter 1, that work to fuel the spirit of capitalism, rather than to transcend or challenge it.

Alcohol and the night-time economy

These trends of normalisation and commodification are embedded in wider intoxicating environments, in which the shifting political economy of alcohol plays a central role. Since the 1970s, a period of post-industrial decline oversaw the erosion of the traditional customer base of many British pubs; a trend that was exacerbated in the 1990s, when large numbers of young people turned away from pubs and alcohol in favour of raves and Ecstasy. In response, the alcohol industry attempted to reinvent itself by creating new markets and transforming not only its products but also the spaces they were consumed in. Backed up by the power of the state and the interests of local authorities and urban planners, this venture produced a new landscape in which alcohol became cheaper, stronger and more ubiquitous than ever before.

Brain describes this as a 're-commodification' of alcohol within a 'post-modern alcohol market' of hedonistic excess (2000, 2). The shift was propelled by the liberalising agenda of New Labour, who used the 2003 Licensing Act to promote the role of alcohol in the regeneration of urban centres. The Act made it easier to obtain alcohol licenses, extended opening hours and allowed cheap drink promotions and happy hours. Meanwhile, supermarket discounting practices resulted in a situation in which alcohol was sometimes cheaper than water. Such policies were intended to appeal to the youthful electorate, a strategy witnessed in the text message sent out by the Labour Party to young voters on the eve of the general election in 2001, 'cldnt give a XXXX 4 lst orders? Vote Labour on thsday 4 xtra time'. The policies were also embraced by local authorities, optimistic about the role of alcohol in creating modern, twenty-four-hour night-time economies and keen to attract business and visitors to generate revenue. And, indeed, the economic effects of liberalising the alcohol landscape were significant, creating jobs and generating wealth so that by 2012–2013, revenues from alcohol taxation was around £10 billion, with around three quarters of a million people employed in licensed premises and a further million employed in the wider economy (Institute of Alcohol Studies 2013).

These commercial-legislative shifts produced a whole new landscape of alcohol-related products and drinking practices designed to promote what Measham and Brain (2005) describe as 'determined drunkenness': quite simply, the act of drinking to get drunk. Alcohol tricked into the spaces of everyday urban life, from shopping centres to sports clubs, and into a range of demographically targeted spaces, from chains of corporate 'megapubs' to upmarket wine bars, from pre-club 'feeder' bars to post-club 'chill out' bars. Inside these spaces, drinks became stronger and cheaper, and sessional consumption, promoted with special offers and happy hours, increased. Although the strength of traditional beers and wines increased by up to fifty per cent, newer, designer drinks were blended with caffeine, sugar and strong spirits, with Alcopops such as *Raver* and *Rocket Fuel* promising what appeared to be closer to a hallucinogenic 'drug' experience than an alcoholic one.

The expansion of a culture of intoxication has not only been restricted to the high street but has also permeated digital space via social media. We saw in Chapter 3 how corporate marketing has harnessed the power of new technologies, such as smartphones and geolocational software, as well as social networks, to generate more intensive and personalised forms of marketing. Nowhere is this more apparent than in the case of alcohol, where companies like Diago and Bacardi have all but abandoned brand websites in favour of partnerships with social media sites such as Facebook, generating what Griffiths and Casswell (2011) describe as the creation of 'intoxigenic digital spaces'. Marketing on social media allows alcohol companies to create a constant presence in the intimate social spaces of consumers lives, stimulating or 'seeding' discussions on Facebook, weaving images and ideas about their brand into Twitter feeds and so embedding the very idea of intoxication into online social interactions in ways that increasingly normalise it. The somewhat blunt language of marketers themselves illustrates what the alcohol industry regard as the powerful commercial utility of this approach. For example, in an online blog, Andy Vale, of the social marketing platform *Audiense*, emphasises the importance of user-generated content for reaching and engaging a large audience and, significantly, for indirectly promoting alcohol consumption in legal ways. He writes,

> Tieing [sic] the message of the brand in with something that their own target audience created can massively help in driving the brand's. . . . conversation in their market . . . [and] . . . helps alcohol brands to spread awareness of their brand while not directly promoting their product in a way that could fall foul of the regulations of their industry.
> *(Vale 2015)*[5]

Heineken, for example, recently launched its '@wherenext' campaign, which it describes as 'an innovative digital compass' that uses geolocation technology to provide followers with information on events that are happening around them (The Heineken Company 2014). The mobile app uses an algorithm to scan tweets, check-ins and photos across Twitter, Instagram and Foursquare, analysing popularity and customer review data to make recommendations about which restaurants, bars and social events users should head to next. The company tells us that 'The real-time recommendations engine' will help consumers answer that eternal night-out question, 'Where next?' – presumably, hoping that the answer will involve somewhere selling Heineken. The platform was described by one online marketing consultancy as 'a brilliant example of a brand using data to create an experience altogether more engaging by being so relevant to people's lives' (Contagious Marketing 2014). Such a personalised, user-centred campaign also allows alcohol companies to establish relationships with their followers, to learn their likes and preferences, their movements, their favourite places and, ultimately, to align these with their drinking habits. In Vale's words again, brands like Heineken can 'be given a nuanced personality via micro-conversations with their fans . . . [which] . . . could be all-important when those people arrive at the bar'. (2015). And, of course, the larger aim of all this social media activity is the generation of what Deleuze described as 'continuous control': the persuasion and suggestion that gently guide individuals towards greater engagement with their product. In the case of @wherenext, the guidance is almost literal: all the conversations and recommendations and tweeting and 'liking' aim to direct individuals throughout the corporate night-time economy, gently guiding them towards the ultimate destination – the bar.

The effect of the alcohol industry's move into social media is the creation of what the BMA (2009, 21) describe as 'excessively pro-alcohol real and virtual environments', in which the idea, as well as the reality, of alcohol is ubiquitous: as James Nicholls (2012) puts it, it is 'everyday, everywhere'. And so, alcohol joins Ecstasy, cannabis and legal highs in an environment in which intoxication becomes ever more ubiquitous throughout the spaces of consumer capitalism. These trends start to undermine the distinctions between licit and illicit forms of consumption. With the imagery of drugs like Ecstasy adopted by the mainstream, with cannabis increasingly reconfigured as respectable, with legal highs available online and with the increasing variety and availability of strong, cheap alcohol, the boundaries between legal and illegal, between drug and commodity and between forbidden and licit pleasures are becoming increasingly blurred. Many drugs have come to be seen as much as branded fashion accessories as objects of addiction, in a situation in which, as Parker et al. put it, 'illegal drugs have become products which are grown, manufactured, packaged and marketed through an enterprise culture whereby the legitimate and illicit markets have merged' (Parker et al. 1995, 25).

As we have already noted, the boundaries of this new, intoxicating landscape are porous. Whereas certain illegal drugs have been subject to claims of normalisation, the trajectories of other, legal ones are moving in the opposite direction and are becoming repositioned as dangerous or risky substances. Shifting assemblages of power, knowledge, technology and morality are increasingly moving perceptions of tobacco and 'excessive' alcohol consumption towards the margins of social acceptability. This repositioning undermines traditional dualisms that aligned 'legal' drugs with (relatively) safe and socially acceptable practices and illegal ones with risky and unhealthy ones. All of this is a more complicated and 'messy' landscape, and its navigation requires new forms of governance. These are the subject of the next section, which explores the shifting trajectories of alcohol and tobacco as they are increasingly subject to more stringent types of control.

Denormalisation and new forms of governance

Today we are witnessing a gradual shift away from the universalising prohibition typified by war(s) on drugs towards more complex 'capillary' systems of governance that demand ever greater levels of control from individuals themselves. These are typical of the neoliberal forms of governance that we saw in the previous chapter and are operationalised through an increasing emphasis on self-control and ideals of responsibility. Applied to the consumption of drugs, this kind of governance is based less around binary distinctions between legal/illegal and more around ideals of controlled/uncontrolled consumption. Ultimately, it works to produce what Angus Bancroft (2009) describes as a 'carefully managed hedonism' as a counterpoint to the expansion of psychoactive consumer culture. Particularly in Britain, Europe, Australia and Canada, recognition of the widespread public consumption of drugs has encouraged the adoption of pragmatic approaches, described as harm reduction and risk minimisation, rather than on more draconian attempts to prohibit consumption altogether. Such approaches embody neoliberal ideals of the sovereign consumer, whereby the provision of information about risk enables individuals to make informed – and, therefore, it is assumed, rational – choices. So, to this end, tips for 'safe clubbing' provide information about the dangers of mixing drugs and the importance of hydration, and needle exchanges aim to reduce the risks of contaminated equipment. Such a shift in perspective undermines the absolutism of the category of 'addiction', replacing it with a continuum in which consumption is described in terms such as 'harmful', 'excessive' or 'inappropriate' and contrasted with 'controlled', 'informed' or 'responsible'. The embrace of drugs by neoliberal ideals of responsibility and self-control reformulates the idea of the 'drug user' as a choosing consumer: a position articulated by Alexander Shulgin, the inventor of Ecstasy, in his classic statement: 'Be informed, then choose' (1991, xv). This shifts the locus of control from external to internal mechanisms of self-governance, so that, as O'Malley puts it, 'as rational, calculating risk-takers, [consumers] enter the sphere of responsible drug use' (1999, 205). This kind of governance is both more liberal and yet also more pervasive than what went before. It is no longer simply a small, discrete group of 'addicts' who are disciplined, treated and punished but the majority of people who consume psychoactive substances, who are now 'constantly responsible for monitoring their behaviour, governing themselves without pause' (1999, 206).[6]

Such a rationalist approach to drug use has been described by researchers in various ways. Margaretha Jarvinen (2012), for example, writes of drug users as 'rational risk managers', Kevin Brain (2000) talks about 'bounded hedonistic consumption', and Fiona Measham (2004) describes the 'controlled loss of control' which occurs within carefully demarcated limits of time and space. These ideas are part of a wider tradition that Elias and Dunning (1986) described as a 'quest for excitement', in which the cathartic release of tension through risky activities resulted in what they called a 'controlled de-controlling of the emotions', and that writers such as Steve Lyng (1990) developed in the idea of 'edgework': the managed experience of risky states.[7] Such concepts exemplify long-running themes that we have returned to many times throughout this book – around the tension between order and disorder and control and excess – and they are highlighted particularly well in these kinds of ideas about the possibility of responsible self-management in the consumption of drugs. For example, the Ecstasy users interviewed in a study by David Shewan et al. (2000) epitomised this kind of rationalistic approach, talking about consumption that was characterised by strategic planning and meticulous preparation. From the purchase of the drug from trustworthy dealers to the choice of a reliable venue in which to take it, nothing was left to chance – with some careful hedonists even going so far as to match dosages of drugs with body weight in order to predict the optimal experience. True, they did allow themselves to get 'out of it', but only within carefully constructed parameters that would not interfere too much with the rational demands of the everyday world that they knew they would return to. As one individual put it: 'When I'm using drugs, I plan it in advance, just to fit in with my lifestyle. If you're going to work on Tuesday, then at the weekend, you know you can't . . . not have recovered fully by the time you're back [at work]' (in Shewan et al. 2000, 445). His comments sum up the tropes of 'work hard, play hard' and articulate a managed kind of hedonism that stands in stark contrast to the excessive, unruly intoxication described by Bataille. There are no one-way trips here: this is responsible intoxication, neoliberal style.

As Shane Blackman puts it, this rationalist approach to drug consumption is not so much about facilitating as about shaping choice – and, therefore, behaviour – in particular ways. This technique of 'ruling at a distance' – government through shaping the free choices of others – is based on the assumption that the provision of information and the facilitation of choice will, in demonstrating the realities of drug use, allow the responsible individual to come to a rational decision: the 'rational' option being limited and controlled consumption. In aligning reason with particular sets of decisions, such approaches are, in many ways, just as prescriptive as more direct forms of prohibition (Seddon 2009). This is 'just say no' wrapped in the rhetoric of responsibility and choice and, like many of the choices available in consumer capitalism, actually involves very little choice at all.[8]

The governance of space and the mobilisation of morality

It is at this point that we witness the appearance of what Mariana Valverde (1997) calls the 'hidden despotism' of liberalism: a form of authority that serves to back up the individualised self-monitoring of these new forms of governance. This disciplinary approach introduces a variety of medical–penal interventions, as well as a moralising agenda, to persuade, cajole and ultimately steer consumers into 'responsible' patterns of behaviour. It is argued here that it has been enacted largely through the regulation of public space as well as through what Alan Hunt would call a 'mobilisation of morality': the increasing denormalisation and stigmatisation of behaviours once deemed acceptable, such as smoking or being drunk in public. Both of these processes work to reinforce unequal power relations by focusing particularly on the problematic pleasures of women and poorer social groups.

The recent widespread 'denormalisation' of both tobacco and the excessive consumption of alcohol can be seen as instances of these trends. Although legal, both commodities have been repositioned as risky forms of consumption: a shift that has been actioned largely through a focus on the governance of public space, both symbolic and material. Although the drugs in question have not been outlawed, their consumption in particular spaces, such as public areas and workplaces, has been banned, and their consumers excluded. O'Malley describes these as 'zones of prohibition': places in which the consumption of particular substances is restricted. Legislation that produces 'alcohol-free zones' in urban areas and bans on smoking in public places reposition both tobacco and alcohol as forbidden substances as well as stigmatising the individuals who consume them.

The 'blacke stinking fumes' of smoking (and vaping)

The cultural biography of tobacco is a case study of denormalisation: the fall from grace of what Brandt (2009) described as an 'icon' of twentieth-century consumerism. Despite the mass popularity of smoking (in the early 1980s, for example, one third of all American adults smoked) and the commercial and political power of the industry, Big Tobacco is under attack. Since the 1990s, medical and scientific knowledge, public health and anti-smoking lobbies, consumer litigation and advocacy groups combined to create a powerful alliance that contested the commercial and political influence of the tobacco companies, forcing legislative and cultural change that has dramatically reduced smoking amongst the populations in the Global North. From a socially acceptable practice that could signify a range of desirable personal characteristics, cigarette consumption has been repositioned both medically, as a cause of death and disease, as well as morally, as an irresponsible and selfish act. The World Health Organization has declared tobacco 'one of the biggest public health threats the world has ever faced' (WHO 2014), and cigarettes themselves have been defined as objects of addiction. In a process similar to the ways in which biochemical understandings of the active components in morphine encouraged new views of addiction in the nineteenth century, today new understandings of the properties of nicotine have encouraged the incorporation of cigarettes into biomedical discourses of addiction. Indeed, Nicotine Anonymous states that nicotine is 'as addictive as heroin' (Nicotine Anonymous 2015). Its clear risks to health and the vested interests of the industry that promote it are not in question here. Rather, what is of interst in this discussion is the trajectory of tobacco as a case study of the shifting status of a type of addictive consumption.

The radical denormalisation of a once-popular product has involved the re-directing of a range of medical, penal and normative discourses against a legal commodity: the war on drugs has shifted to the war on tobacco. Or perhaps it would be more accurate to say, not so much tobacco itself, given that its production has never been outlawed, but rather the *consumers* of tobacco, and the spaces they consume it in. This is significant, because the repositioning of tobacco in the Global North has been largely operationalised through the governance of public space. A number of state governments have introduced measures against the practices and spaces of smoking, including mandatory heath warnings, price increases and taxation as well as the erasure of cigarettes from the public realm through the removal of cigarettes, smoking and smokers from public spaces and the banning of advertising, promotion and sponsorship. Uruguay's strict tobacco legislation severely restricts the consumption and marketing of cigarettes (in contrast to its liberal marijuana laws) and made the country the target of a lawsuit by Philip Morris. In Britain, smoking was banned from all indoor public spaces in 2005. Elsewhere, discussions about outdoor bans are gaining traction. At the time of writing, New York, Hong Kong and Toronto have outlawed smoking in key public places, and Bristol became the first British city to pilot smoke-free zones in 2015. In 2012, the open display of cigarettes in British shops was outlawed, requiring retailers to conceal packets behind counters. Penalties and fines demarcate the new smoke-free landscape as well as disciplining those who transgress by, for example, smoking where they shouldn't or displaying tobacco when it should be hidden. These measures have more than material impact and are full of symbolic significance. In reducing its visibility, tobacco has been detached from mainstream culture and recast as a forbidden substance. This shifts it closer to illegal drugs like cannabis, which, moving in the opposite direction, is coming to be seen as less harmful in terms of its pharmacological properties (Berridge 2013, 237).[9]

This governance of public space works along with what Hunt (1996) describes as the 'mobilisation of morality' in ways that increasingly stigmatise once-acceptable behaviours as well as individuals who practice them (Yeomans and Critcher 2013, 311). Furthermore, they do so in ways that inscribe the deep class and gender divisions around cigarette consumption. The mass reduction of smoking in the Global North has a steep social gradient, with the majority of those who do still smoke now belonging to lower socio-economic groups (Barbeau et al. 2004). As the tobacco industry increasingly pursue a 'spatial fix' (Harvey 2006) by shifting their focus to target the enormous, largely impoverished populations of the Global South, the disparities become striking: eighty per cent of the world's smokers now live in poor and middle-income countries (WHO 2014). As Marsh and McKay argued in *Poor Smokers* (1994), with around one third of smokers belonging to the bottom ten per cent of income distribution in Britain, smoking has become 'the defiant badge of the underclass', with poor smokers not only 'the last refuge of normative smoking', but also actively *expected* to smoke (Marsh, in Berridge 2013, 183). Indeed, its very popularity amongst the poor has contributed to its downward trajectory. In another example of the kind of status politics we saw at work with cannabis, changing attitudes to cigarettes have been influenced by the social position of smokers themselves. Extending Gusfield's arguments to smoking, Tuggle and Holmes (1997) make the argument that, although undeniably the cause of major health harms, there also exists a normative aspect to the denormalisation of tobacco that goes beyond medical evidence, and that is bound up with the influence and social capital of particular social groups and the relative lack of power of others. As smoking moved down the social hierarchy, the pace of criticism quickened, with the lower status of consumers making it easier to criticise the industry that supported the habit. As Berridge points out, it followed a classic public health trajectory, in that 'it was only when the problem was confined to the working class, and working class women especially, that the rest of society began to fear it' (2013, 184). Along with the other 'problematic pleasures' of the underclass such as drinking, criticisms of smoking are highly gendered, and women in particular subject to practices of normative and biomedical governance. Concerns about smoking have been persistently couched in discourses about damage to foetal and reproductive health – concerns that, as we will recall from Chapter 2, are redolent of nineteenth-century fears about the 'future of the race' – and pregnant women screened for their habit. Public health campaigns about the impact of passive smoking on babies and children focus largely on women, utilising images of infants 'forced' to breathe their mother's smoke, and, beyond pregnancy and motherhood, smoking has been reconfigured more generally as 'disgusting', unfeminine, and indicative of low social status.

In their drive to eliminate the habit, the global health campaigns that have denormalised smoking have actually endorsed stigma as a 'legitimate public health tool' (Bell 2011, 7) – a tactic that is made easier by the social class of smokers, and that is rendered visible and 'real' through the bans that enact a normative division of space into smoking/non-smoking, or healthy/unhealthy areas. Such symbolic qualities also adhere to smokers, too. The ejection of smokers from bars, restaurants, workplaces, hospitals and so on renders them highly visible, and it also separates them from the rhythms of 'normal' work and leisure.[10] The separation is material and temporal as well as symbolic and reinforces the image of the 'dirty habit' of the other: the poisonous fumes that must be kept away from the clean, responsible majority. Much of the rationale for restricting smoking hinges on medicalised understandings about the physical harms of second hand smoke; a position that Kirsten Bell has critically appraised in her deconstruction of its 'offensive' qualities. She describes smoke as a liminal substance that dissolves the boundaries between bodies and invades the space of the non-smoker. Thus, second hand smoke offends Westernised, middle class ideas about personal space and undermines the separation of self/other – particularly problematic when 'the other' happens to be poor or non-white: a social consideration that casts smoke as disgusting, corporeal and 'unclean' (2011, 9). This kind of symbolism has historical antecedents, which we saw in the first two chapters of the book. Current normative-medical discourses around smoke recall fears of the so-called contagious miasma of the nineteenth-century underclass, in which working class urban dwellers were regarded as bearers of disease and infection that could be passed on through the very air that they breathed. Although expressed in discourses of medicine and health, such fears were driven by social and normative considerations, as Durkheim's comment about 'the contagious influence of large urban areas' (1984 [1893], 306) suggested. And in some ways, the invective against smoke itself has hardly changed since King James I's *Counterblaste to Tobacco* (1604), in which he railed against the 'blacke stinking fumes' of a 'filthie noveltie' which was 'loathsome to the eye, hateful to the Nose, harmefull to the braine, dangerous to the Lungs'.

It will be interesting to see whether the vapour generated by emerging products such as e-cigarettes will elicit similar responses as tobacco smoke. The practice of vaping divorces the materiality of smoking – the raising of the cylinder to the lips, the inhalation and exhalation of plumes of air – from the harmful substances at its core, so providing a simulacrum of smoking itself. As a commodified response to the health issues of cigarettes, the production of Electronic Nicotine Delivery Systems (ENDS) have been embraced by Big Tobacco, with many tobacco companies developing their own e-cig brands and marketing them as glamorous lifestyle products in ways that they once did with traditional cigarettes. The television commercial for *Blu* e-cigs (owned by a subsidiary of Imperial Tobacco), for example, updates Marlboro Man for the new millennium: a sophisticated female replaces the rugged cowboy, her helicopter is a more efficient cow-herder than his horse. But both still gaze into the distance, holding the iconic cylinder to their lips; the strap line, 'take back your freedom' invoking familiar neoliberal ideals of personal autonomy and choice. A whole vaping culture has quickly grown up around e-cigarettes, with specialist shops and boutiques selling hand-crafted pipes and different flavoured juices: an entrepreneurial market, similar in many ways to the one developing around legal cannabis. However, e-cigarettes have also been criticised for renormalising cigarettes and acting as a 'gateway' form of consumption that will draw young people into smoking itself (de Andrade et al. 2013). In 2013, the EU regulated e-cigarettes as medicines, although some countries have banned their advertising. Such juridical moves, and the medical-normative discourses around them, are producing a blurring of the boundaries between e-cigarettes and 'real' cigarettes, between vaping and smoking and between health and illness, in which the products and practices of vaping are emerging as a new battleground in debates over the science and morality of consumption.

Issues of tobacco consumption go beyond medicine and health to construct what Tuggle and Holmes (1997) call a 'polarised symbolic-moral universe' in which smokers are constituted as dirty, weak-willed and selfish, whereas non-smokers are cast as the bearers of bodily purity and abstinence. In the context of current understandings of health, smoking appears as a supremely irrational form of consumption, one that threatens individual self-destruction as well as imposing a burden of disease and financial costs on wider society. Given widespread knowledge of the risks involved, why would anyone smoke? The focus on irrationality and addiction tends to elide consideration of broader possible meanings, whereas the issue of pleasure – neglected in much of the research on drug consumption (O'Malley and Valverde 2004) – is even more notable by its absence from debates around smoking.[11] Whereas some have studied the complex ways that smoking acts as a means of youthful identity creation (Nichter 2015), others have drawn out the symbolic properties of smoking as a source of relaxation and 'time out', that delivers autonomy, release and, hence, some degree of control over the rhythms of everyday life, with a long-standing place in the cultural practices of poor and excluded groups. As Courtwright has noted, cigarettes segue into the rhythms of working life: designed to burn for the optimal length of time, smoking breaks demarcate the working day just as easily as they signify leisure and relaxation in recreational spaces. Their fluid meanings have made them vehicles for the construction of individual and social identity, able to signify a range of desirable characteristics, ranging from sophistication and masculinity to femininity and independence, depending on context (Courtwright 1992). Most provocatively, Richard Klein has argued that 'cigarettes are sublime', in a polemic that pays homage to the cigarette as cultural icon and signifier of individual personhood, at the same time drawing out the sensual and aesthetic dimension of the act of smoking itself. In Klein's account, smoking is a 'negative pleasure' that threatens death at the same time as it fulfils desire (1994, 2). Indeed, it is in precisely this danger, and in the repression and stigmatisation of smoking, that much of the pleasure of the activity lies. As he puts it, 'If cigarettes were good for you, they would not be sublime' (1994, 1–2). In all of this, smoking emerges as a uniquely contradictory form of consumption, embodying the dualism of the *pharmakon* as a practice that provides pleasure at the very moment that it delivers harm.

Despite the very real issues of industry manipulation and the immense harms generated by tobacco, the issues of class, gender, place and pleasure that are wrapped up in the denormalisation of smoking seen here complicate medical-normative ideas about addiction and harm. Similar themes are at work in the case of alcohol, which we turn to next.

The binge drinkers of Gin Lane

The economic and political processes that saturated British culture with more bars, stronger drinks and longer opening hours also produced a contradictory trend, in which 'excessive' drinking came to be defined as a counterpoint to neoliberal ideals of responsible consumption Although some suggested that young people had been both 'seduced' into a culture of heavy drinking and 'pathologised' as disorderly and unruly consumers (Measham and Brain 2005), media images of drunken people rampaging through the city at night, fighting and vomiting in the streets, served as a violent counter to the gentrified portrait of alcohol as a player in a vibrant night-time economy. In particular, the figure of the 'binge drinker' staggered out of the new political economy of alcohol. She was created through, on the one hand, the increasing dissemination of cheap, easily available alcohol, and on the other, through the political-medical production of information about 'risky' versus 'responsible' levels of alcohol consumption. With 'safe' levels of consumption defined as twenty-one units per week for men and fourteen for women (unless pregnant, when no level is judged to be safe), the focus on 'bingeing' shifted attention away from absolute amounts to the manner of consumption, creating what Nicholls describes as a 'hopelessly ill-defined concept' (2006, 145) that a number of medical and political forms of authority continue to disagree over. So, for example, whereas the British Medical Association defines bingeing as consuming five or more drinks in one session, the Office for National Statistics suggests eight or more units in any one day. Meanwhile, the Government's own Alcohol Harm Reduction Strategy defines binge drinkers as those who drink to get drunk, whereas the Institute of Alcohol Studies defines bingeing as drinking that results in the drinker 'feeling at least partially drunk' (IAS 2005). Given that most people drink to get 'at least partially drunk' – a tendency that is understood by alcohol manufacturers and consumers alike – the distinction between 'responsible' consumption and bingeing seems tenuous, at best. Such tangled definitions undermine the optimistic neoliberal association of information provision with rational consumption, and they also work to conflate medical claims with normative values.

The idea of bingeing also produces the value-laden ideal of responsibility as a kind of sober self-management. Binge drinking is heavy drinking, but it is also 'excessive' and 'irresponsible': a mobilisation of morality that has been eagerly deployed by government and industry in the tagline 'drink responsibly'. And so, even as they extend licensing and availability and reduce the real price of alcohol, the shibboleths of 'responsible drinking' work to individualise the consumption of alcohol products. Within this environment, the issue of binge drinking has been produced as a moral panic: a familiar historical narrative of individual destruction and national decline, woven around fears of lost productivity and social disorder. It is a narrative that was articulated in British Prime Minister David Cameron's announcement that binge drinking 'drains resources in our hospitals, generates mayhem on our streets and spreads fear in our communities' and his consequent warning that 'we have to tackle the scourge of violence caused by binge drinking', and promise to 'attack it from every angle' (Cameron, in *The Government's Alcohol Strategy* 2012).

All this excess is also extremely lucrative, however. Binge drinking accounts for a majority of the profits of the alcohol industry, with researchers from Southampton University estimating that nearly seventy per cent of alcohol sales in England, or some £23.7 billion, derive from those classed as 'harmful' drinkers, despite that group, who are described in industry circles as 'superconsumers', making up less than five per cent of the population (Sheron and Gilmore 2016). As with other forms of 'addictive' consumption, profits lie in excess. Furthermore, that excess is stratified. Although higher income groups regularly drink large amounts of alcohol, the negative health effects of heavy consumption tend to be concentrated amongst the poorest social groups, living in the most socio-economically deprived neighbourhoods – an imbalance described as the 'alcohol harm paradox' (Grittner et al. 2013).

Accordingly, the threat posed by the binge drinker has been presented as heavily classed and gendered. As in the portrayal of chaotic excess in the eighteenth century's Gin Lane, the figures spilling out of bars and rampaging along today's high streets are depicted as predominantly working class, and increasingly female. Like their predecessors, their public displays of drunkenness continue to be problematised as evidence of weak wills, irresponsible attitudes and lack of self-control. It was in this climate that the category of the 'ladette' emerged as a new kind of identity: a 'made up' person which, although largely a media construction, nevertheless served as a focus for widespread disapproval over the ostentatious drinking of mainly white working class women, whose behaviour was taken as a public flouting of ideals of 'feminine' behaviour and a signifier of more general irresponsibility and promiscuity (Skeggs 1997, 967; Griffin et al. 2009, 459). As with their historical predecessors, and similar to criticisms of smoking, current concerns around female alcohol consumption tend to be couched in medical-moral discourses that revolve around health risks to the woman and/or her child. In them, physiological differences between males and females are invoked as biological evidence that women's 'tolerance' to alcohol is lower than men's, their drinking inherently more harmful, and therefore women are more rightful objects of biomedical governance. The U.S. National Institute of Health articulates the position in its official publication *Alcohol: A Women's Health Issue*, writing that 'heavy drinking is much more risky for women than it is for men', and cautioning that some people should not drink at all, including, somewhat confusingly, 'women who may become pregnant' (NIH 2008, 2–3). Defined in this way, the stricture becomes, essentially, shorthand for young women in general. In this climate, the resurgence of concerns about Foetal Alcohol

Syndrome focuses risk on reproductive health in ways that recall eighteenth- and nineteenth-century discourses about inebriety, degeneracy and the decline of the nation. They work to stigmatise behaviour and mobilise morality around consumption and, particularly in the case of poor women, to surveil and monitor behaviour.

All of the medical, normative and penal discourses and practices that we have looked at so far work to recast alcohol as a risky, potentially life-threatening commodity. In turn, these are productive of a range of disciplinary measures that are directed towards those individuals who will not, or who cannot, 'drink responsibly', so governing disorderly bodies by regulating the spaces in which they move. Rather than 'attack[ing]' the issue of excess consumption 'from every angle', as promised in the government alcohol strategy, however, these measures are not even and tend to focus particularly on the drinking patterns and places of the poor, who are subject to extensive practices of surveillance as well as the biomedical governance of bodies. So, for example, along with CCTV surveillance in town centres and bars, a range of legislative measures were introduced in Britain around the turn of the millennium to monitor and curtail the free movement of drinkers. Similar to the creation of smoke-free zones, they also worked to demarcate 'alcoholic' from 'sober' spaces. For example, the Criminal Justice and Police Act 2001 allowed local authorities to establish 'Alcohol-Free Zones', with transgressions punishable by fines. Drink Banning Orders (DBOs), Anti-Social Behaviour Orders (ASBOs) and Dispersal Orders could be served for a number of reasons, from the catch-all 'anti-social behaviour' to urinating in public and carrying out graffiti. Punishments focused on curtailing offenders' freedom of movement by prohibiting them from drinking in public, buying alcohol or entering premises that served it and the vague but expansive 'spending time with people who are known troublemakers' (https://www.gov.uk/asbo). Most recently, plans for electronic tagging to monitor the alcohol consumption of individuals charged with drinking-related offences introduce an intensive new form of biomedical governance. The so-called 'booze bracelets' are modelled on American 'sobriety bracelets' and measure levels of alcohol in wearers' perspiration every thirty minutes, sending electronic signals back to probation officers via systems of GPS. Levels that exceed agreed amounts elicit police or probationary intervention.[12] Offenders can, of course, choose not to wear the tags – and face other penalties, such as jail or community services. Another 'tough choice' of neoliberalism which, in practice, often turns out to be no choice at all.

All of these measures work to surveil the consuming population and to demarcate intoxicating environments into respectable and controlled spaces, where Alcohol-Free Zones are the companion of No Smoking Areas. In so doing, they establish an ideological divide between 'responsible' and excessive consumers. They also render disorderly consumption increasingly visible, particularly when carried out by the lower classes. Whereas affluent groups tend to drink in private spaces, poorer ones spill out of bars and stagger around urban centres, their movements captured on CCTV, and their bodily exertions traced through tagging devices.

The moral panic of binge drinking highlights the contradictory pressures around alcohol and, indeed, around issues of intoxicating consumption more generally, in which increasing opportunities to get 'out of it' are matched by rising demands to consume responsibly: to maintain sobriety and reason in a 'controlled loss of control'. In such a climate, the 'binge drinker' is a symbol of respectable fears of intoxication. Such a figure – usually young, often female, mostly working class – drinks simply in order to get drunk. And in so doing, she flouts the self-control that is so crucial to neoliberal systems of governance in a very visible way.

End points

We can see from all this that the consumption of drugs has deeply contradictory aspects. On the one hand, the state of intoxication has long been regarded as a threat to the order of societies, especially when carried out by problematic social groups. But on the other hand, the promise of intoxication is also a lucrative feature of modern capitalism, where the trade in an ever-expanding variety of psychoactive substances is a profitable and widespread venture. Today, the political and economic drivers of neoliberalism not only facilitate but also actually encourage the spread of intoxicating environments. In them, the savvy consumer can order their legal highs online from the comfort of their living room while waiting for their taxi-couriered delivery of marijuana and popping their corporate-branded Ecstasy tablets. When they step outside, it is into an environment dense with bars and clubs selling cheap alcohol, open late. As a result of these intersections of technology and marketing with urban planning and policy, it has become increasingly easy to get 'out of it' in more situations, in more places, more often.

In this climate, the expansion of intoxicating environments is met by the shibboleths of responsibility and backed up by more overt forms of control. Today, the disciplinary approach of the 'war on drugs' is ceding to more complex processes of self-regulation and risk management, in which ideals of 'responsible consumption' work to produce a neoliberal taming of excess. These practices are not even, however, and are underscored by more disciplinary measures. In some ways, the similarities between new forms of neoliberal governance and the punitive approach exemplified by the 'war on drugs' are more revealing than the differences. Even governance that controls 'at a distance' by acting through freedom and choice is coercive and is deployed in ways that inscribe unequal relations of power. In practice, the consumption 'choices' of the poor, young people, women and ethnic minorities, as well as the spaces they consume in, like those of the nineteenth-century underclass, continue to be guided and disciplined by the hidden despotism of liberalism.

Throughout all this, the pleasures of intoxicating consumption continue to challenge the values of sobriety and productivity. The tropes of 'rational risk-taking', 'responsible drug use', 'controlled de-control' and so on may be useful ways of understanding the contradictory aspects of intoxicating consumption in neoliberal societies. However, the rationalist and functionalist assumptions underpinning such ideas also need to be recognised. Crucially, the activities they describe do not involve what Bataille would consider as 'genuine' excess or intoxication. They are not about the loss of the self or the undermining of sobriety, but rather allow a 'temporary and reversible slackening of the bonds of reason', as Van Ree (1997, 93) puts it. In other words, they produce catharsis so that the social structure can continue. And herein lies a contradiction, because, for many consumers, genuine intoxication resists such attempts at governance, with its very attraction lying in its unruliness and unpredictability (Yeomans and Cricher 2013, 311). The sheer exhilaration of being drunk, the camaraderie of nights in the pub, the sublime pleasures of cigarettes – these embodied, social and aesthetic pleasures transcend rationalist demands for reason, abstinence or health. For many, the rhetoric of 'responsible consumption' becomes meaningless after the second or third drink, when the whole point of drinking is to get drunk. Indeed, one of the youthful Ecstasy consumers in Shewan et al.'s study articulated the point, questioning his engagement in drug-taking sessions that were controlled and planned. He wondered about the authenticity of the experience, saying, 'Planned nights out can be boring. It's another routine, and I'm not convinced that's what drug use is supposed to be *like*, fundamentally. . . . That's not drug taking. You can use a bit of chaos in your life' (in Shewan et al. 2000, 447).

These issues of responsibility and excess, of place and pleasure and of class and gender that are wrapped up in shifting ideas about the consumption of intoxicating commodities work to complicate medical-normative discourses of addiction, and they destabilise the very concept of 'drug' itself. They also highlight the dualism of the *pharmakon* as something that can provide pleasure at the same that it delivers harm. In this, the pleasures of intoxication exemplify the ongoing dialectic between desire and repression that runs through consumer capitalism more generally, and in doing so, as Avital Ronell pointed out, make us question what it means to consume anything at all.

Notes

1 In the early years of the twentieth century, a series of Acts banned the consumption of a range of intoxicating substances. So, for example, The Pure Food and Drug Act (1906), The Smoking Opium Exclusion Act (1909), The Harrison Narcotic Act (1914), Narcotic Control Act (1956) and, in the United Kingdom, the wartime Defence of the Realm Act (DORA) of 1914 created the category of 'narcotics' as a forbidden substance: a foreign invader which must be prevented from crossing state lines, transforming large numbers of consumers into criminals in the process.
2 Craig Reinarman and Harry Levine (1989) outlined the trajectory of the 'crack crisis' in the United States, highlighting its political expediency in facilitating Republican efforts to reinforce law and order. They noted that when cocaine became 'downwardly mobile', moving into the ghettos and barrios of the black and Hispanic underclass, a range of politicised media discourses produced a 'crack scare' as responsible for much of the country's increasing social problems.
3 It should be pointed out that this thesis has been challenged, most notably by Shiner and Newburn (1999) who argue that Parker et al. overemphasise the extent of drug use amongst young people, and that the majority of the population still do not consume illegal drugs and do not consider them 'normal'. Despite this, it can still be reasonably claimed that the term is a useful description of a situation in which the consumption of illicit drugs is central to the leisure habits of large numbers of young people in the night-time economy. (Aldridge et al. 2011).
4 During the 1990s, Calvin Klein adopted what came to be criticised as a 'heroin chic' aesthetic, using moody, gaunt models such as Kate Moss and Jodie Kidd, whose extreme emaciation bore striking resemblance to the models of the anti-drugs 'heroin screws you up' posters of the 1980s.
5 So, for example, alcohol marketers can work to associate a brand with an environment, such as a nightclub, leaving explicit references to drunkenness to the user-generated material on Twitter feeds or non-official company Facebook pages, where photos of friends getting drunk and having fun at parties or on holiday do the companies' work for them (Nicholls 2012, 491).
6 As technologies of risk expand the potential for danger throughout the population, so every drug user becomes embraced within statistical calculations of harm and must come to regard themselves as possibly 'at risk'.
7 I argued in an earlier paper (Reith 2005) that intoxication through the consumption of drugs is a dramatic instance of edgework, which appears to be exemplified in the practices of many young people.
8 Toby Seddon draws attention to the contradiction implied in the very description of the provision described as 'Tough choices' within the British Drugs Act of 2005 and quotes the government policy that talks of drug users taking 'advantage of the opportunities for treatment and support that exist' (Home Office 2006, in Seddon 2009, 91) while actually describing practices of coercion.
9 The industry-mandated practice of smuggling, a multibillion-dollar business that fuels organised crime and makes tobacco the world's most widely smuggled legal commodity, has served only to reinforce its underground, illicit status.
10 Although ironically, the stigmatisation of smoking gives rise to new forms of sociality, especially when forced to huddle outside pubs and other public places, whereby smokers are united in their exclusion.
11 Interestingly, as Bancroft has noted, the social constructionist problematising of the concept of addiction that is routinely applied to addiction to drugs tends not to be extended to cigarettes, whose dangerous nature is generally regarded as a more privileged medical 'fact'.

12 The scheme has been piloted in London, whose mayor, Boris Johnson, presented it as a straightforward response to the problem of binge drinking, citing its 'impressive results' in the United States in 'steering binge drinkers away from repeated criminal behaviour' (*The Telegraph* 31 July 2014). Under the scheme, judges will be given powers to issue 'sobriety orders' mandating that offenders wear the tag for up to four months.

5
FOOD
Embodied consumption

> The political-economic contradictions of the neoliberal era are literally embodied.
> — *Guthman and DuPois (2006, 429)*

Introduction

Because food has an intimate association with the body, debates around its consumption link the material with the metaphorical in very visible ways. They highlight tensions between self-control and desire, asceticism and indulgence and body and identity, and in this, food can be seen as an area in which, as Guthman and DuPois note, the contradictions of consumption are quite literally embodied.

The food system that fuels the system of consumer capitalism produces a climate of over-abundance and excess as well as deeply contradictory attitudes to food and eating. On the one hand, the political and marketing strategies deployed by 'Big Food' generate a climate in which particular kinds of fast, 'junk' foods are cheap and widely available in larger sizes and in more places than ever before. But on the other hand, biomedical forms of knowledge increasingly talk of an 'epidemic' of obesity, of addiction to junk foods, of pathologies of eating, and point to the spread of 'obesogenic environments' that create risk, disease and premature death. Such overabundance also generates the requirement for ever higher levels of self-control in a climate in which the diet industry grows in parallel with the expansion of Big Food itself. Today, ideas about responsibility are returned to older notions of the will – that nineteenth-century ethical-medical hybrid – which is revived to act as a guide in a landscape of excess, and whose continual exercise becomes a sign of autonomous, controlled selfhood.

In such a climate, 'pathologies' of food and eating, such as anorexia, bulimia and obesity, have metaphorical significance about loss of control, unmanaged desire and unproductive bodies, played out in a landscape of fast food and Diet Coke. They also act as a form of governance, particularly of poor and ethnic minority groups and women, who are disproportionally subject to their normalising gaze.

To explore these issues, this chapter first focuses on the political-economic production of the food system of the Global North. It considers the commercial strategies of Big Food, from the creation of products that are deliberately engineered to encourage craving and desire, to the geo-spatial location of stores and the ergonomics of their interior design, that generate an environment of overabundance and excess. It then moves on to analyse the discourses that produce 'pathologies' of food and eating, arguing that biomedical and psychological forms of knowledge have translated political-economic issues of overabundance into problems of individual pathology, conceiving obesity as an epidemic of global proportions and food itself a source of addiction and mental disorder. The next section goes on to make the point that such understandings also act to make food and diet a means of biomedical governance, offering a range of individualised and commercially profitable solutions to the 'problems' of excess in ways that make the consumption of food a means of displaying citizenship. Furthermore, it is argued, the normalising gaze of these approaches is particularly directed towards the poor, ethnic minorities and women in ways that ultimately reveal the hidden despotism of neoliberalism. Finally, the chapter concludes by arguing that ideas about the consumption of food, and the bodies that result from it, can be viewed as cultural narratives that highlight the contradictions of both the industrial food system and the wider operation of consumer capitalism itself.

'Big Food': overabundance, excess and waste

The food industry that, quite literally, feeds the system of consumer capitalism is characterised by overabundance, excess and waste. In this, it exemplifies key features of neoliberalism, as well as highlighting contradictions within it, as we will see. The industry itself is supported by the state and driven by enormously powerful corporate interests – companies such as Nestlé, Heinz, Unilever and Philip Morris, collectively known as 'Big Food'. Their overriding aim, bluntly expressed by Marion Nestle, is to encourage people to 'eat more food, more often, in more places' (2002, xiv).

Producing excess

It is an aim that is facilitated by a number of strategies, ranging from the industrial organisation of farming and the influence of protectionist economic policies, to the techno-scientific engineering of ever-new products. It also includes tactics which Big Food has copied from the example of the tobacco industry, such as the lobbying and sponsorship of political, regulatory and academic bodies as well as heavy investment in marketing and public relations (Nestle 2002, 4). The result has been a proliferation of processed foods high in fat, sugar and salt and disproportionally consumed by poorer and ethnic minority social groups. Tellingly, the derogatory shorthand 'junk' that is generally used to describe them is also slang for heroin, an association that draws attention to the shifting status of these foods as they are increasingly reconceptualised in terms of addiction and risk.

The expansion of convenience and fast foods around the 1980s occurred at a very particular moment of political and social change. As we saw in Chapter 3, the neoliberal system of 'Walmart capitalism' oversaw a shift towards industries based on services and marketing as well as the reduced regulation of those industries. It also produced general decline in real wages amongst the middle classes and the poor, growing inequality and job insecurity and the requirement of many people to work long hours in 'McJobs' to make ends meet. In addition, increasing numbers of women entering the workforce in the last decades of the twentieth century[1] changed patterns of family life, with women spending less time preparing and cooking meals in the home (Smith et al. 2013). An economic system based on a low-wage, time-poor workforce helped to generate a market for food that was cheap, fast and convenient. And so, the emerging fast food system matched the accelerated pace of modernity by capitalising on time-poor consumers and emphasising 'freedom' from the drudgery of preparing food in an ever-expanding list of ready meals, snacks and burgers, all sold on their promise of immediate satisfaction and instant energy in ways that worked to make snacking and grazing ubiquitous.

Within this climate, neoliberal policies of reduced regulation and state support for business served to increase the political power of 'Big Food' itself. Agricultural subsidies and protectionist policies intended to support the farm sector and keep food cheap for consumers also work to make certain key commodities highly profitable and abundant. State subsidisation of the dairy industry, for example, has generated more produce than can be consumed, giving rise to what are described as 'lakes' of unwanted milk and 'mountains' of surplus cheese in both the United States and Europe (Moss 2014, 168). Meanwhile, sugar is the second most protected commodity in the world, with approximately one fifth of all agricultural support expended on it in ways that advantage the wealthy countries of the Global North at the expense of the producer countries of the South (Richardson 2015). Big Sugar has become an enormously powerful industry, contributing millions of dollars to political campaigns and, in return, influencing the highest levels of state power. In the United States, such connections ensure that the industry operates under essentially protectionist policies and manages to subvert labour laws (Richardson 2015).[2] And so, from its position at the centre of geopolitical colonial exploitation in the eighteenth century, the domination of Big Sugar continues today, fuelled by a labour force of low-paid, often immigrant and underage workers. As a result, the low cost of sugar has made it ubiquitous. As a flavourer and preservative, it is now included in some eighty per cent of processed foods in a pattern that has seen consumption double over the past thirty years (Lustig 2012).

Meanwhile, various food corporations have been highly successful in attempts to co-opt or subvert the authority of regulatory bodies and expert organisations in a process described by Nestle (2002) as regulatory capture. This means that the industry often operates effectively virtually without government oversight, working instead within such voluntary frameworks as 'pledges' or 'responsibility deals', rather than mandatory legislation that would reduce production and marketing. The involvement of the state in the business of food in these ways has contributed to the production of overabundance, excess and waste. It is in this context that some writers have even gone so far as to argue that excess is actually an integral part of the industrial food system itself. In this sense, getting rid of food in various ways – through food dumps, waste disposal, even food aid is, as Guthman and DuPois put it, 'as central to capitalist accumulation as is producing and eating it' (2006, 442).

Along with these political-economic strategies, the food industry's drive to encourage consumers to 'eat more' involves the targeted marketing of new products in larger sizes and the perfection of the elusive qualities of 'taste' – the area in which the category of food, through the alchemy of science, is moved more closely towards that of drugs. These strategies are the focus of the next section.

The manufacture of desire: craving and bliss

The investigative journalist Michael Moss spent three years documenting the techniques deployed by Big Food to increase consumption, and his findings *Salt, Sugar, Fat* (2014), are the eponymous title of his best-selling book. The subtitle, *How the Food Giants Hooked Us*, makes unambiguous reference to the role of addiction in this process. As well as drawing out the political and economic conditions for the growth of Big Food, Moss documented the drivers of 'taste': the process whereby food is engineered in ways that work, essentially, to manipulate desire. In this process, combinations of sugar, fat and salt, along with optimal consistency – or 'mouthfeel', as the food technologists rather unappetisingly call it – are synthesised to create the perfect taste, and so deliver maximum pleasure. This is the production of the state known in industry circles as 'the bliss point', described by Moss as 'the defining facet of consumer craving' (2014, 30). Its elusive qualities are the key drivers of industry attempts to generate desire or craving in new, ever more appealing food products – a quest which mobilises a range of techno-scientific forms of knowledge and expertise. Moss recounts, for instance, how Howard Moskowitz, a food engineer with a background in military research, was employed by major food companies to produce a marketable answer to the question 'How do you get people to crave?' In the quest for an answer, Moskowitz spearheaded the craft of 'optimisation', in which complex statistical algorithms were used to organise consumer responses to myriad variations of tastes, textures, colours and smells. Fuelling the search for the bliss point still further was the molecular manipulation of key ingredients in ways that increased their intensity by, for example, refining sugar to multiply its sweetness two hundred-fold and engineering the shape of salt into a fine powder to 'hit the taste buds faster and harder' (Moss 2014, xxvi). Moss's deployment of the imagery of drugs is deliberate here, and he makes the connection between food and addiction explicit in numerous parts of his book, not least when describing the effect of these engineered products. As he puts it, 'If sugar is the methamphetamine of processed food ingredients, with its high-speed, blunt assault on our brains, then fat is the opiate, a smooth operator whose effects are less obvious but no less powerful' (2014, 148).

The significance of these commercial-scientific practices is two-fold. Not only do they start to blur the distinction between food and drug, and between eating and craving, but also they aim to quantify the experience of pleasure, and so turn the intangible quality of desire into a knowable and manipulable source of profit.

Marketing junk

Both the marketing and consumption of the foods produced in this way has a demographic and geographic gradient: one that, perhaps not surprisingly, maps on to the socio-spatial distribution of obesity. The food industry invests in sophisticated, multimillion dollar campaigns and 'pinpoint psychological targeting' (Moss 2014, xxv) to market products towards their most profitable demographics: generally poor and low-income, ethnic minority consumers as well as children and young people (Grier and Kumanyika 2008). African American youth, for example, see eighty to ninety per cent more ads for sugary drinks than white children (Harris et al. 2011), and McDonald's is increasingly basing its marketing strategies on minority groups, whom it regards as trendsetters for white America. Together, such groups are subject to far greater exposure to 'junk food' advertising, across a wide range of media, as well as within their everyday environment. Most recently, their increasing mobilisation of social media such as Facebook, Twitter and Snapchat signals the move of Big Food into virtual space in an attempt to extend their market reach to children and young people: a process described by Freeman et al. (2014) as the marketing of 'digital junk'.

At the terrestrial level, the general retreat of the neoliberal state from public life has created a space into which food companies – and, crucially, their revenues – have moved. In these loosely regulated, generally low-income areas, sponsorship and franchising deals are used to enhance brand visibility and build up customer loyalty by linking burgers, snacks and fizzy drinks with fashion, music and sports. In the United States in particular, as Eric Schlosser (2001) has pointed out, the profits from junk foods provide a welcome source of revenue for schools who face declining support for education. Indeed, under-resourced schools can sign deals with food companies for free materials, such as, for example, *The Story of Coca-Cola*, a reading exercise that also serves as a form of marketing which aims to build brand recognition for life.

Coca-Cola's marketing strategy – known as a 'ubiquity strategy' – is summed up in the directive to 'put the product within arm's reach of desire' (in Moss 2014). Coke's arms have a social gradient, however, reaching out particularly extensively to the poorest people, living in the poorest areas. It is a distribution that invokes the Pareto Principle, whereby eighty per cent of the world's soda is consumed by twenty per cent of the population (Moss 2014). It is this twenty per cent towards whom marketing efforts are focused most intensively. Coke's goal, as bluntly expressed by one of their executives, is 'how [to] drive more ounces [of soda] into more bodies more often' (in Moss 2014, 110). One way has been through 'super-sizing' – increasing portion sizes for very little extra cost: a practice that heavily subsidised sugar makes extremely cheap, and that has worked to increase profits, as well as consumers' waistlines, across the fast food industry more widely.[3] In its super-sized cans, per capita consumption of Coke increased dramatically, with sales rising more than four-fold between 1980 and 1997. Tellingly, as Moss reveals, the company refers to its customers not as consumers but as 'heavy users', or people with a 'habit', in similar language to that deployed by the alcohol industry, as we saw in the previous chapter, to describe its excessive 'superconsumers': the five per cent who provide its greatest profits.

The social gradient in the marketing and consumption of fast food is also characterised by a geo-spatial distribution, which means that the excesses of consumption are inscribed into the landscape of food in very visible ways. Since the 1980s, trends in urban design and public planning, as well as the marketing of the food industry itself, have worked to make low-income neighbourhoods subject to the increased presence of Big Food. As well as higher concentrations of fast food outlets themselves, poor urban spaces are frequently served by convenience or corner stores selling what nutritionists describe as cheap 'energy-dense nutrient-poor' (EDNP) products (Powell et al. 2007). This is often the only kind of food available in neighbourhoods that lack access to healthy, affordable alternatives, resulting in the labelling of such areas as food deserts, or 'toxic' environments (Brownell 2004). Packed with convenience foods and confectionary, the design of these stores, although it may look haphazard, is anything but. Layout is guided by the insights of ergonomic research which have produced what are known as 'shopper density maps' of so-called hot spots which are used to plan the placement of particular types of products or special offers. These exercises suggest that individuals tend to enter the shop from the right and move towards the back, leaving 'dead zones' for consumption in the middle of the store (Moss 2014, 112). And so, the layout of merchandise in these stores follows a similar pattern, with cheap, easily 'grabbable' soda, crisps and sweets near the door, and staples such as bread and tinned foods towards the back. Here, then, particular forms of psy-ec knowledge are deployed, within specific geographical contexts, in ways that ultimately work to translate shopper movements into profit, producing store layouts that are specifically designed to stimulate the consumption of products packed with sugar and fat.

The food system that drives consumer culture, then, is one founded on overproduction and excess. Its features – from lobbying, sponsorship and regulatory capture, to the geo-spatial location of stores, the ergonomics of their interior design, and the techno-scientific creation of products that are deliberately engineered to encourage craving and bliss – generate a climate in which cheap, energy-dense food is available in greater varieties, in more places and in larger quantities than ever before. Like the spread of intoxicating environments that we reviewed in the previous chapter, such a system also contributes to an expansion of medical discourses about obesity as well as a spread of entire environments characterised as 'obesogenic'. Such medicalised understandings of the excesses of the food system are the subject of the next section.

Obesity, addiction, risk

The global march of the overabundant food system has also produced a number of what could be called 'collateral realities'. Most significantly, biomedical and psy forms of knowledge have translated political-economic issues of overabundance and excess into problems of individual pathology, conceiving obesity as an epidemic of global proportions and food itself a source of addiction and mental disorder. It is argued here that such medicalised understandings are underwritten by a range of normative and cultural assumptions that act to make food and diet a means of governance; a point that will be developed throughout the chapter.

Over the last thirty years, various commentators have argued, in increasingly hyperbolic terms, that a combination of plentiful fatty, sugary foods with sedentary 'Western' lifestyles has led to an epidemic of obesity, which is threatening the health of individuals and the productivity of nations alike, not only in the Western world, but also in developing countries. As Western foods, and the ideas and cultures that drive them, spread to the Global South, so too do ideas about 'pathologies of eating' such as obesity. Fernand Braudel (1979) wrote that 'the success of a food is the success of a culture', explaining that when a society became powerful, it introduced or imposed its cultural preferences, including its eating habits, on others. And, in the extraordinary expansion of companies like McDonald's, we can see the global march of the ideology of neoliberal consumer capitalism, the ambitions of both for world dominance articulated in the marketing logo: 'One world, one taste'.[4]

Between the end of the 1970s and 2011, the percentage of obese adults more than doubled, in what Schrecker and Bambra (2015) have described as a 'neoliberal epidemic'. In 2000, the World Health Organization announced that, for the first time, the number of overweight people worldwide equalled those who were underfed. The scales balanced at 1.2 billion on either side, triggering the depiction of what they described as an epidemic of 'globesity' as a 'chronic disease' and threat to world health (WHO 2007, 2). Public health discourses frame obesity as a risk to both individual health (as a 'disease' in its own right as well as a risk factor for further illness such as diabetes, heart disease and cancer) and, through lost productivity and costs to medical services, to the well-being of the social and economic fabric too. In such a framing, we can see the 'destructive' nature of consumption counterposed to the rational and orderly values of production in a manner that recalls long-standing historical dualisms. In 2014, the head of the National Health Service in England, Simon Stevens, announced that 'obesity is the new smoking' in terms of economic health costs, likening it to 'a slow-motion car crash in terms of avoidable illness and rising healthcare costs' that could undermine the very sustainability of the NHS (in Triggle 2014). Such alarmist statements reflect a growing consensus that, as Sander

Gilman put it, 'the war against obesity' had replaced the 'war against tobacco' (Gilman 2008, 15), with food joining alcohol and tobacco in what Kirsten Bell (2011) described as public health's 'axis of evil'.

By and large, public health understandings of obesity are produced through calculations of Body Mass Index (BMI) that divide weight by height to produce estimates of 'normal' and 'excess' body weight. Such medico-actuarial technologies conceive the body as a kind of machine for processing food and define the problem of obesity as one of imbalance between energy in and energy out (Jones et al. 2007).[5] These imbalances, when mapped across populations, have a demographic gradient, with excess weight inversely associated with low socio-economic status, particularly amongst women and ethnic minority groups. It is also correlated with geo-spatial locations, with poor neighbourhoods having higher concentrations of obesity in ways that map on to social inequalities (Cummins and MacIntyre 2006). Here, the focus of public health has increasingly been towards entire 'obesogenic environments' that are characterised by a range of factors that contribute to high consumption of energy-dense foods and sedentary lifestyles (Swinburn and Figger 2002). These are the 'toxic environments' (Brownell 2004) that we saw in the previous section: the landscape of processed foods, fast food joints and inner city convenience stores that map onto the social relations of race and class that obesity distribution itself is associated with.

That obesity is both a medical crisis and an epidemic, has become virtually a shibboleth of public health understanding and, indeed, of much lay 'common sense' knowledge. We turn now to look more closely at how these kinds of understandings of food consumption are produced, before going on to explore the ways that they act as a form of biopolitical governance in consumer societies.

Addiction and mental disorder: food and neurochemical selfhood

The issue of excess food consumption is increasingly understood through the forms of knowledge produced by neuroscience and the psy sciences that frame personhood in terms of what Nikolas Rose calls 'neurochemical selfhood'. These, in turn, are situated in alliances between powerful medical-commercial interest groups, amongst them the pharmaceutical industry, or 'Big Pharma', as well as the diet industry and, especially in the United States, medical insurance companies. Such forms of knowledge and power conceive issues of overabundance and excess as problems of individual consumption and offer up equally individualised solutions.

The revised version of the *DSM-5* presents disordered relations with food as a psychiatric condition which, although ostensibly defined by medical criteria, are actually produced through a range of normative, cultural and experiential factors. The manual is expansive in its production of new food and eating disorders, including the newly established category of 'binge eating disorder' (BED), which is classified as 'recurring episodes of eating significantly more food in a short period of time than most people would eat under similar circumstances' (APA 2013). Those with BED may feel out of control; eat 'too quickly', even when not hungry; may experience feelings of 'guilt, embarrassment or disgust'; and may eat alone to hide their behaviour. As we saw in Chapter 3, although claiming to be based on 'objective' principles, the diagnostic criteria utilised by the *DSM* are, in fact, shifting and subjective. Here, the focus on eating 'too quickly', alone, in ways that are 'different' to other – presumably more conventional – patterns of behaviour highlight the culturally relative underpinnings of the BED classification, with its emphasis on social conventions and normative ideas about appropriate portion size, whereas the emphasis on affective states such as embarrassment and disgust highlight the subjective dimensions of assessment. Even the director of the *DSM-5*'s working group on eating disorders, Timothy Walsh, admitted the criteria were subjective, and that distinguishing a 'binge' from a large meal was not, as he put it, 'a sharp line in the sand' (in Gever 2010). The definitions of anorexia and bulimia nervosa are similarly inflected with cultural and normative judgements. Although the *DSM* characterises anorexia in terms of 'severe weight loss' as well as unquantifiable criteria such as 'distorted body image' and a 'pathological fear of becoming fat', it bases its diagnosis of bulimia on assessments about the eating of 'unusually large' amounts of food, followed by 'inappropriate behaviour' such as self-induced vomiting, use of laxatives, fasting or 'excessive' exercising to avoid weight gain (APA 2013).

In the framing of these behaviours as 'psychiatric' conditions, we can see the elision of medicine with ethics as well as the production of new types of consumers: a range of 'made up' people, constituted through their problematic relations with food. The authority of the psy sciences, upon which these new types rest, are, in turn, backed up by neuroscientific forms of knowledge, which we turn to in the next section.

Food addiction: this is your brain on sugar

The revisions to the diagnostic criteria of *DSM-5* were influenced by the broader epistemic climate generated by neurochemistry, genetics and brain imaging, which, as we saw earlier, produced new understandings of the material basis of behaviour. In them, obesity is conceived as an outcome of a form of addiction – an addiction to food – and explained with reference to brain functioning. These kinds of accounts began to emerge in the 1980s, at the very time when political-economic shifts were generating the conditions for the enormous growth of the mass food industry – and were assisted by the development of brain scanning and imaging technologies.

In such accounts, certain types of foods – particularly 'junk' foods high in fat, sugar and salt – described as 'highly palatable' or 'refined' – are argued to act like drugs, in susceptible individuals, where they generate a state of addiction. This state invokes physiological mechanisms that will be familiar from Chapter 3 – the activation of neural pathways in the brain, such as the pleasure centre and reward system, as well as the involvement of various genetic markers and neurochemicals that are responsible for craving and desire. In the magic tunnel of the fMRI scanner, it is suggested that the sight, taste and smell of certain foods 'light up' the same regions of the brain as those of conventional narcotics, travelling along the same neurological pathways to reach the brain's pleasure zone, where they generate intense feelings of euphoria. Once there, the chemistry of these 'highly palatable' foods continues to act like a drug, generating feedback loops of reward and withdrawal that constitute an addictive 'state' (Fraser et al. 2014, 204) and changing the structure of the brain in ways that change eating patterns themselves. Individuals are thus driven by pleasure seeking, loss of control, craving and the need for ever-greater amounts of the food in question, as their brain circuitry is 'hijacked' by addiction. The dramatic imagery of NIDA's iconic 'this is your brain on drugs' is now joined by equally striking images of brains illuminated by sugary, fatty, caffeinated snacks and, in the 'expansive mode' that we saw in Chapter 3, draws an ever-greater variety of foods into its fold. Chocolate, pizza, chips and, most recently, cheese – described by one doctor as a form of 'dairy crack' (in Millward 2015) for its overwhelming of the brain's pleasure centre – are here reconfigured as toxic agents of addiction (Schulte et al. 2015).

As we have seen, there is an elective affinity between these kinds of understandings of the self, pleasure and desire and the interests of capital. In this sense, the food industry itself mines neuroscientific knowledge about food addiction as part of its aim to manufacture and sell the bliss point. Recently, a number of the largest companies have invested heavily in research in their search for the material substrate of desire. Unilever, for example, hosts a $3 billion operation involving brain scanning equipment to examine how customers react to foods, which the company hopes will tell them more about customer tastes and preferences than focus groups. The words of their chief researcher, Francis McGlone, interviewed by Michael Moss, articulate the aims of the venture and give clear expression to the reductionist principles guiding it, as well as highlighting the companies' conception of the location of desire. McGlone stated, 'There is not a lot to be gained by asking people why they like something because they don't bloody know'. And so he looked to neuroimaging instead, explaining, 'I'd gotten into imaging because it's a good way to sort of bypass the mouth, if you like, so you can see just what the neural processes are underpinning a behaviour' (in Moss 2014, 150). 'Bypassing the mouth' also bypasses the social and political economy of food: a diversion that neuroscientific forms of knowledge take on a large scale when accounting for the excesses of consumption in neoliberal capitalism. The criticisms of neuroscientific accounts of addiction that we discussed in Chapter 3 also apply to this particular arena of 'addiction attribution', of course. The reduction of the pleasures of food and eating – complex, socially embedded practices – to neurochemical processes simplifies context and disregards the influence of a wide range of social factors in producing the behaviours being examined as well as in framing understanding of them. Precisely by *not* 'bypassing the mouth', extensive social science research has illuminated the role of culture and desire in the embodied, sensuous pleasures of food and eating (e.g. Mennell 1993; Beardsworth 1997). Even the Big Mac – icon of all that is wrong with fast food – is more than its nutritional and corporate content, as Daniel Miller's (2008) nuanced exploration of the role of its 'truly happy meals' in everyday family rituals, has shown.

Nevertheless, neuroscientific perspectives tend to present not only food and eating, but also consumers themselves, in a very different light. Such forms of knowledge have been deployed in ways that 'reveal' differences not only in the 'addictive' potential of certain foods, but also in the brains of the individuals who consume them. In this vein, European scientists used fMRI technologies to examine the brains of 'normal' and overweight people when exposed to images of food and suggested that food craving may be 'hard-wired' into the brain of overweight individuals (European College of Neuropsychopharmacology 2015). Similar techniques were used to argue for the physical differences in the brains of anorexic and obese women, whose reward circuits were apparently sensitised and desensitised, respectively (Frank et al. 2012). As well as evoking Peele's criticism of brain scanning as 'high tech phrenology', it can be argued that such techniques produce new types of 'neurochemical personhood'. In them, not only are individuals' eating habits revealed through the shape of their bodies – fat or thin, obese or 'normal' – but are also physically inscribed in their brains, where they are regarded as determinants of behaviour.[6]

It is specific substances that have been the primary focus of this kind of neuroscientific attention, however, with caffeine and sugar of particular interest. These 'drug foods' of the eighteenth century are now key ingredients of twenty-first century diets, where they are increasingly being reformulated as addictive, intoxicating substances. Under biochemical scrutiny, the 'very evil and dangerous effects' of coffee that so exorcised Charles II have been located within its molecular structure, with 'caffeine intoxication' now listed as a condition in the World Health Organization's *International Statistical Classification of Diseases and Related Health Problems (ICD-10)* and 'caffeine use disorder' defined as a 'condition requiring further study' in *DSM-5* (APA 2013). Other research has moved it closer to the lexicon of addiction, citing its biological effects in terms of dependence and craving as similar to 'other drugs of dependence' (Meredith et al. 2013).

Sugar, in particular, has been subject to concentrated attention for its 'addictive' effects on the neural pathways – a feature made explicit by Lenoir et al. (2007) in the title of their article, 'Intense Sweetness Surpasses Cocaine Reward'. In it, they argued that the consumption of sugar affects 'reward pathways' in the brain by raising dopamine levels, so that those who eat excessive amounts develop cravings and need to consume increasing quantities to feel the same 'high'. In another study, Australian researchers extrapolated from neural circuits in mice to suggest that the drug Champix, commonly prescribed to wean smokers off nicotine, could also reduce sugar cravings by modulating the release of this dopamine (Shariff et al. 2016). In an interview, lead researcher Masroor Shariff argued that 'like *other drugs of abuse*, withdrawal from chronic sucrose exposure can result in an imbalance of dopamine levels and be as difficult as going cold turkey from them' (in *The Telegraph*, 13 April 2016; italics added). This sugar-mice experiment is replete with elisions between mice and people, and exposure and eating, in its merging of sugar into the category of drugs. It also highlights understandings of neurochemical selfhood as something that is formed at the molecular level, particularly through processes that go on in the brain. Corresponding to medicalised understandings of food consumption that we have seen in this chapter, such forms of knowledge are based on ideas about embodied personhood as something that can be acted on through similarly medicalised interventions.

These neurochemical forms of knowledge have also been key drivers behind the repositioning of public perceptions of sugar, which has increasingly been characterised as a toxic substance, closer in nature to drugs than to food. Hence the title of John Yudkin's *Pure, White and Deadly* (1972) deliberately evokes the symbolic properties of cocaine to highlight what he regards as the deadly health impacts of sugar. His treatise influenced the endocrinologist Robert Lustig, whose polemic *Fat Chance: The Bitter Truth About Sugar* (2012) similarly demonised sugar, describing it in hybrid scientific-ethical terminology as both toxic and poisonous as well as 'evil'. He explicitly compared it to drugs such as cocaine, heroin, alcohol and tobacco, writing that soda acts as a 'fructose delivery system', similar to cigarettes' delivery of nicotine, and describing sugary drinks as the 'alcohol of childhood'. Although biomedical forms of knowledge themselves do not produce such hyperbole, what they do provide is a language with particular claims to authority in which to express it. It is within such narratives that Kathy, whom we met in the Introduction, with her six litre a day Coke habit, situated her cautionary tale of addiction, warning us to be aware just 'how quickly this sort of habit can ruin your life'. They have also inspired health advocacy groups such as *Action on Sugar* as well as public health proposals for sugar to be taxed and labelled with health warnings. In 2015, the World Health Organization recommended halving levels of sugar consumption while calls to regulate consumption through taxation have been gaining traction since the 'twinkie tax' idea was first proposed by Julie Brownell in 2009. In 2016, Britain proposed to tax sugary drinks, joining a list of countries, including France, Australia, Hungary, Finland and Mexico, that already impose taxes on products with high levels of added sugar (Public Health England 2015).

Although such proposals have so far been unevenly enacted, having met fierce resistance from industry, their power may prove to be as much symbolic as material. What they have achieved is to highlight the increasingly problematic status of sugar, whose public image shifts ever closer to the category of drugs. And in this regard, the trajectory of sugar is instructive. It is a 'social life' that has been intimately entwined with relations of power and domination. At the start of our story, it was a status symbol with curative, medicinal powers in the lives of the wealthy, later a commodity with a key role in eighteenth-century colonial domination and then a kind of sweet fuel for the workers of the industrial revolution. From playing a central role in geopolitical relations of colonial power and industrial productivity, sugar is now a central ingredient in the profits of the twenty-first century food system. Indeed, products that are packed with sugar (as well as fat, caffeine and salt) and scientifically engineered to deliver pleasure are akin to mildly psychoactive substances. These foods provide an experience that is typical of consumer culture itself: pleasurable and yet transient, consumed quickly and so requiring constant repetition. In this, today's 'junk foods' have some similarities with their eighteenth-century predecessors: the 'drug foods' that provided energy and pleasure to the workers of the colonial and industrial eras. Both fuelled low-paid workers, and both have been subject to critical discourses based on normative-medical concerns about heath and productivity. Today, medicalised forms of knowledge have reconceived the dangers of sugar in particular, and junk food in general, in terms of the risks of addiction and obesity, and located them largely in the diets (and brains) of the poor, who are their biggest consumers.

The governance of consuming bodies

The medicalised forms of knowledge that understandings of the 'problem' of obesity rest on have also provided a range of equally medicalised – and commercially profitable – solutions, ranging from surgery and drugs to diet and various 'practices of the self'. These understandings also act as a form of biopolitical governance that works to control the consumption, bodies and behaviour of the population. Through these, the consumption of food becomes a means of displaying selfhood and exercising citizenship in neoliberal societies.

Such governance is the focus of this section. First, however, it is helpful to take a slight detour, away from medicalised understandings, to briefly consider how it is that food – and the bodies that result from eating it – have come to have significance as sites of governance at all.

Bodies in culture

Despite the hegemony of current medicalised understandings of obesity, it has long been recognised that bodies are far more than simply machines for processing food Because food is part of the self, dietary choices are full of political as well as personal significance. It is within this tradition that alternative perspectives that cast food and body shape as metaphors for wider cultural meanings have flourished. Building on Pierre Bourdieu's (1984) insights that bodies are markers of social capital, numerous writers have argued that food and body shapes have discursive as well as material meanings. In this tradition, Susan Bordo's (1993) classic account of the political economy of the body, *Unbearable Weight: Feminism, Western Culture and the Body*, has argued that throughout history, changing body ideals have been embedded in shifting socio-economic relations and associated with ideas about productivity and control. In cultures where food is cheap and abundant, the slender body ideal is the one with the most 'cultural capital' and is associated with higher socio-economic status and economic success. What Levenstein (1993) describes as this apparent 'paradox of plenty' is made possible, Bordo explains, in a culture of abundance: when there is so much food to eat that refusal becomes a personal choice, rather than something that is imposed by necessity. She draws aesthetics back to political economy by arguing that the needs of capital are best served by streamlined body forms, which, in turn, are read as signs of producer efficiency. Thus, in a culture of overabundance, slim body ideals are also symbols of refinement, status and the civilised restraint of appetite.

It is in this context that food and body image have wider cultural significance as sites of self-governance as well as metaphors for broader cultural meanings. To a greater or lesser extent, these forms of governance ultimately espouse neoliberal ideals of 'biocitizenship' (Rose and Novas 2005) that emphasise the responsibility of the individual for their health and well-being and their duty to take charge of their own bodies and regulate their consumption of food through appropriate 'care of the self'. They are supported in this by the medical-industrial complex that comprises Big Pharma and Big Food, as well as the diet and medical insurance industries, which provide a range of commodified solutions to the problem of obesity. These, in turn, are embedded in neoliberal relations of power, or what has been called the 'biopolitical economy' (Pitts Taylor 2010), in which the shrinking of the welfare state is matched by the increasing privatisation of healthcare and the redefinition of patients as consumers. All of this is underlined by the normalising logic of public health and backed up by more coercive measures that demonstrate the 'hidden despotism' of neoliberalism. These forms of governance are the focus of the rest of this section.

Bodies and brains

Medicalised understandings of excess food consumption produce interventions that act on the bodies and brains of the obese through surgery and drugs, in what can be seen as acts of symbolic – and sometimes real, material – violence. And because obesity has a social gradient, such acts are largely directed against the poor, women and ethnic minorities. So, for example, the discipline of bariatric medicine works to modify the obese body through surgical procedures such as jaw wiring and stomach clamping, whereas 'Big Pharma' aims to reform its neurological processes via medications like appetite suppressants. Surgical procedures such as gastric bypass, in which the stomach and intestines are severed and re-sewn and internal organs rearranged, in order to dramatically restrict the body's ability to consume food, has been described by British surgeon Christopher Pring as 'a mutilating operation' (in Williams 2015). The cutting away of bodily excess is also a gendered and racialised procedure, concentrated amongst black and ethnic minority women (Birkmeyer and Gu 2012). Overall, approximately eighty five per cent of bariatric patients are women (Santry et al. 2005). Through such radical biomedical technologies that limit stomach capacity to tiny teaspoonfulls of liquid, obese individuals are essentially reduced to non-consuming subjects for the rest of their lives.

Obese bodies can also be drugged. A variety of pharmacological interventions aims to reduce excess through acting on physiological or neurological processes, with drugs that reduce the appetite or suppress the absorption of fats. Many of these, particularly those involving ephedrines, such as Ephedra products, act like conventional amphetamine-type drugs or 'uppers' (although when produced by the commercial-pharmaceutical complex, prescribed by medical 'experts' and consumed for the 'legitimate' purpose of losing weight, are framed as a licit and, indeed, responsible form of consumption). Although frequently subject to health concerns and banned, such psychoactive commodities are, nevertheless, hugely profitable and are frequently consumed 'off label' in ways in which the licit and illicit markets merge. And it is a highly lucrative form of merging: some two billion doses of Ephedra products were consumed in the United States in 1999, generating sales of $900 million (Nestle 2002, 283). Similar profitability has accompanied the more general extension of drugs to treat increasing forms of food addiction. It has been suggested, for example, that Champix, the smoking cessation drug that researchers believe could also be used to relieve sugar cravings, may represent a 'novel new treatment strategy to tackle the obesity epidemic' (Shariff, in *The Telegraph*, 13 April 2016). If it were to materialise, this would also be a highly profitable strategy for Pfizer, who owns the drug, as well as a highly individualised one whereby the excesses of one form of consumption are balanced out through the consumption of something else, in a modulation that goes on at the level of the individual. In such an application, consumption of Champix would be used to offset consumption of sugar, with the drug itself acting as a solution to excess: in the words of Shariff, as a 'tool that a person can use to control their weight gain' (in *The Telegraph*, 13 April 2016).

The weight reduction industry itself operates a similar logic to this, but on a larger scale, and often alongside the food industry, with which it is frequently conjoined. In the United States, the market in dietary advice and products was valued at around $60 billion in 2015 (*The U.S. Weight Loss Market* 2015) and is often owned, at least in part, by the same food giants that generate the problems it exists to counter in the first place. For example, Slimfast is owned by Unilever, and Weightwatchers was bought by the food giant Heinz. These companies offer a range of diet solutions to the problem of overabundance and work to subvert health concerns around obesity in typical neoliberal style by offering more choice: low-fat spreads, low-calorie Coke and McDonald's salads, which exist alongside full-fat, high sugar, mainstream products in an immensely profitable parallel market of line extension and diet products. This kind of offsetting has been described by Courtwright (2001) as a form of 'problem profits': commodified solutions to the problems that are generated by the system of consumer capitalism itself.

The production of what Nestle (2002) calls 'techno products' – foods that do not act like foods and that blur drug/food distinctions – are a kind of problem profits that have been integral to the food industry's development of dietary products. Sugar and fat substitutes such as Splenda and Olestra, added to biscuits, crisps, yoghurts and cakes, are engineered to pass right through the body; consumed but not absorbed, in ways that encourage even greater quantities of consumption. After all, if one bag of crisps contains only half the fat it used to, now it is possible to consume twice as much – a logic that has seen portion sizes of 'low fat' options actually increase (Moss 2014). Olestra, in particular, is not only not digested, but also actually interferes with the absorption of other nutrients as well as causing a range of side effects such as abdominal cramps and diahorrhea. Perhaps just as significantly, this plethora of diet foods has transformed the nature of some substances altogether – from butter to 'spreads' and from sugar to 'sweetener'. Like the blurred distinctions between drug foods in the eighteenth century, today the separation between food and chemical 'other' is again indistinct in commodities that start to problematise the very concept of 'food' itself.

This blurring of products is matched by an equally blurred division of boundaries between the food, diet and tobacco industries that produce them. The very strategy of 'line extension' itself is one that Big Food learned from Big Tobacco, in a relationship that began in the 1980s when Philip Morris acquired General Foods and Kraft, making it the largest food company, as well as the largest tobacco company, in the world. The resultant commercial giant redeployed tobacco industry expertise around new marketing strategies to deal with public health concerns around junk food, as well in the creation of low-fat, low-calorie products, that were modelled on lessons learned from smoking, particularly from Philip Morris's introduction of filter cigarettes as a 'healthy alternative' designed to offset public concerns about smoking. Influence flows in the other direction, too. In their efforts to formulate a low-nicotine cigarette, Philip Morris is currently adapting the technologies used by General Foods to remove caffeine from coffee to attempt to take nicotine out of tobacco (Moss 2014, 197). The production and marketing of e-cigarettes by Big Tobacco can be seen to represent a similar strategic sleight of hand. The corporate interdependence expressed in these relationships between the food and tobacco industries also highlights the blurred boundaries between the marketing of 'addictive' commodities (like cigarettes) and 'conventional' ones (like foods) in a process that destabilises the distinctions between ideas about addiction and practices of consumption.

In many respects, these medical-commercial 'solutions' to the problems of overabundance are the ideal commodities, in that, as Guthman puts it, they 'allow markets, but not necessarily waistlines, to expand' (2011, 181). And, indeed, the diet industry itself is the perfect market, as Schwartz (1986) points out, insofar as it is self-generating, infinitely expansive, predicated on failure and with a guaranteed clientele. Ironically, then, as a condition produced by the excesses of consumption, obesity is a profitable and infinitely expansive business in its own right.

The normalising logic of public health

Public health discourses around healthy eating and body weight act as a technology of governance by categorising a variety of body shapes into a medical-normative binary between a weight that is 'normal' or 'ideal' counterposed to one that is 'overweight' or 'obese' and at risk from a range of health problems. Calculations of BMI, which are integral to such distinctions, exemplify this. Described by Guthman (2011) as 'needlessly abstruse', its measurements, like the guidelines on alcohol units for responsible drinking, are shifting and relative and fail to account for variables that that could affect optimal weights for different people. In this way, it operates a normalising logic that equates 'thin-ness' with 'health', and which is used to cajole or stigmatise those who fail to measure up to its standards. Furthermore, the changing techniques used in the measurements of BMI mean that supposedly 'scientific' distinctions between normal and overweight can be subject to commercial influence and political expediency. This was illustrated in 1998, when the International Obesity Task Force, an organisation funded by pharmaceutical companies, produced a report for the World Health Organization making the controversial recommendation to lower the cut-off point for overweight from a BMI of 27 to 25. Although the reports' authors denied being influenced by the drug companies that funded them, as the investigative journalist Jacques Peretti noted, 'there's no doubt that, overnight, [the] report reclassified millions of people as overweight and massively expanded the customer base for the weight loss industry' (2013). This, along with the definition of obesity as an 'epidemic', were significant for the industry in terms of, as one insider put it, 'changing the market perception' of obesity, and so opening the way for drugs companies to provide 'the magic bullet' to 'cure' it (in Peretti 2013). These kinds of intersections of knowledge and influence that go on within the industrial-medical complex work to define and redefine notions of normal body weight, 'making up' (or, perhaps more accurately, 'slimming down') new types of neurochemical selves as they do so.

Commercial influence aside, critical scholars have noted that the practices and discourses of public health itself are part of a normalising project of governance which can actually work to stigmatise and reinforce social divisions based on class, gender and ethnicity (e.g. Lupton 1995;

Bell et al. 2011; Guthman 2011). Its focus on the commodities involved in the 'axis of evil' underline this, where it has been noted that proposals to discourage, for example, the consumption of sugar through taxation, like proposals for minimum pricing for alcohol, would act, in effect, as a regressive form of taxation, targeting the poorest, who eat proportionally more of such foods, at least partly because they are cheap and, by extension, whose consumption would, therefore, be most quickly curtailed if they became expensive.

Although public health campaigns have had some success in realigning perceptions of 'healthy' and unhealthy foods, especially around sugar, their efforts to alter the wider environment in which food is made available, have been less so. Up against the interests of the food industry, attempts to influence the population's eating habits have tended to invoke neoliberal strategies of information provision and 'nudges', such as 'traffic light' systems of labelling and guidelines for healthy eating, to encourage consumers to take responsibility for their own food choices – individualised strategies that largely bypass the wider structural production of overabundance and excess.

Technologies of the self: 'discipline is liberation'

In neoliberal societies, where the requirement for self-control is ever present, the task of governing the consumption of food is one that goes deep into the individual and is particularly focused on attempts to shape the embodied subjectivities of consumers themselves. It is here that ideas about personal responsibility and willpower increasingly come to the fore in calls for an ongoing 'care of the self'. Such a commitment works to regulate diet and produce a suitably disciplined body, not only for personal reward, but also out of a sense of social obligation – to avoid being a burden on public resources and an inefficient member of society. The fit, healthy bodies that result are regarded as visible signs of rational and responsible (bio)citizenship, whereas the fat ones that fail to comply are taken as evidence of deficient reason, weak willpower or failed morality. Here, the key message of the political-economic food system – 'eat more!' – is countered by the equally strident demand of neoliberal ideals of health – 'eat less!'

The ideology of diet and exercise is the primary means of meeting this demand, not only in terms of weight loss, but also as a means of controlling desire more generally. It is in this sense that Hillel Schwartz has described the diet as 'a supreme form for the manipulation of desire' (1986, 328). As he points out, dieting is not only an industry in itself, but also the ideology of constant weight loss feeds into the more general dynamic of capitalist ideology and expansion. Ironically, as bodies shrink, they consume more – diet foods and devices, new clothes to accommodate changing body shapes – all fuelled by the quest for the 'idealised self' and based on the hope that reshaping the external body will also transform the inner self. The dieter is constantly renewing herself by reducing herself through engagement in commodity culture. As Kim Chernin (2009) has pointed out, although metaphors of feminism are couched in terms of the expansion of consciousness, the widening of horizons and the increasing of opportunities – in effect, the expansion of the self – those of dieting – and of popular culture more broadly – are of reducing, of limiting, of shrinking and losing – of minimising the self in the drive to be a size 0: to literally take up as little space, to be as small as it is possible to be. In such a climate, fat is quite literally a feminist issue.

Self-governance requires not only a slender body, but also a toned one that displays evidence of its owner's willpower and discipline through being 'worked on'. Schwartz has highlighted the metaphorical dimensions of these material practices, writing that the culture of capitalism itself demands 'producer bodies' that are fit and efficient: 'The streamlining of the workplace demands a streamlining of the human body. . . . [it] cannot abide loose flesh or unbalanced forms' (1986, 328). The message from the classic weight loss guide of the 1980s, *Jane Fonda's Workout Book* – 'discipline is liberation!' – brings the puritanical valorisation of self-denial up to date, reframed as the neoliberal ideal of government through freedom.

The recent emergence of the quantified self movement – an ideology that merges technology with the ideology of healthism – takes such ideals one (quantified) step further. Using wearable technologies, such as wristbands, or devices attached to clothes and bodies, advocates (or 'self-trackers') record and measure the minutiae of their daily exertions – steps taken, stairs climbed, sleeping patterns, their consumption of caffeine or alcohol – as well as extensive biometric information, from heart rate, oxygen and insulin levels, to calories burned and BMI, in order to improve wellness and, ultimately, productivity through a continual process of self-surveillance. Such technologies take the instrumental rationality that conceives bodies as consuming machines to its logical conclusion, as well as generating profitable new forms of consumption themselves, in the shape of devices such as Fitbit, Apple watches, and various accelerometers and apps that link with smartphones.

All of these strategies work to produce a consuming self as an object of governance: a docile body to be worked on and improved through a continual process of self-surveillance. Crucially, diet and exercise are not temporary options; rather, they must become permanent routines, integrated into an entire lifestyle based on the pursuit of health and well-being and the ongoing monitoring of desire (Keane 2002). The pressure that these strategies exert is gentle but pervasive: as constant as the Fitbit on the wearers' wrist. The healthism that lies behind these modern forms of governance can be seen as a reframing of puritanical struggles between the sins of bodily desire against the virtues of asceticism, played out against a backdrop of fast food, super-sizing and Diet Coke. In them, we return to the idea of the will – that nineteenth-century ethical-medical hybrid – which is revived today to act as a guide in a landscape of excess, and whose successful exercise is taken as a sign of autonomous, controlled selfhood, proudly displayed in the fit and healthy body. In this instrumental-normative approach to food, we can see the legacy of Cheyne's system of 'diatetick management', in which the control of personal consumption is a secular virtue as well as a route to health.

The hidden despotism of food

As we have seen so far, the carefully managed consumption of food, and the streamlined bodies that result, are today regarded as outward signs of inner worth: visible evidence of willpower and self-control, and so, ultimately, a demonstration of responsible biocitizenship. However, those who are unwilling, or unable, to govern their consumption in this way make up the stigmatised underclass of the obese. Like the unruly alcohol consumers we saw in the previous chapter, these people are increasingly subject to punitive debates over who 'deserves' healthcare and benefits in ways that reveal the hidden despotism of neoliberalism.

Underlying the framing of obesity as a failure of personal morality are economic concerns about lost productivity and the burden on healthcare: concerns that are evident in the continual calculations of how much obesity costs the health service, the community, the taxpayer: silently framed as the healthy, and hence, deserving, majority. A recent high-profile report from global consultancy firm McKinsey and Company estimated that obesity cost the world economy two trillion dollars every year and, at a cost of £47 billion to the United Kingdom, came to the conclusion that it amounted to a greater economic burden than war and terrorism (Dobbs et al. 2014). In a review of the British welfare system carried out in this climate of calculative economic anxiety, Prime Minister David Cameron announced that overweight people, along with addicts and alcoholics, would have their benefits reduced or ended altogether if they refused to lose weight or seek help for the excesses of their consumption. The proposals, which would effectively end welfare support for those deemed too fat to work, were presented in the neoliberal language of opportunity and entrepreneurialism, with Cameron stating, 'Our One Nation approach is about giving everyone the opportunity to improve their lives and for some that means dealing with those underlying health issues first and foremost' (in *The Telegraph*, 28 July 2015).

Insofar as the poor are blamed for their own lack of willpower, they have become part of an 'undeserving' constituency that stands outside the rest of consumer society. These kinds of debates are part of what Bell describes as the increasingly aggressive approach by public health policy towards its 'axis of evil', especially in terms of women and childrearing. Although women who smoke and drink during pregnancy have been accused of harming their foetus, childhood obesity is presented as a form of child neglect or abuse, and mothers the rightful targets of social intervention. In such increasingly punitive approaches, we see an aspect of what Cederstrom and Spicer (2015) have called the 'hidden brutality of libertarianism' for those who do not use consumption to shape their bodies into socially productive forms. It is part of what they call the 'Wellness Syndrome': a normative technology that undermines political engagement through its focus on individual responsibility. In effect, because individuals are responsible for their own well-being, they are to be blamed when things go wrong. I would argue further that all the surgery, the pills, the diets and the paraphernalia of technologies like Fitbit is equally a feature of such 'hidden brutality': forms of governance that work to shape bodies, brains and inner states in accordance with ever more stringent neoliberal ideals of selfhood.

What is perhaps most striking at the end of this discussion about governance is that despite the location of its target in economic and political systems, the 'War against Obesity' has primarily been a medical-pharmacological one, waged within – or perhaps against – the body of the individual consumer: through surgery, drugs and 'nudges', and backed up by punitive policies that punish the poor for their consumption choices. Those who 'let themselves go' and cannot, or will not, control their weight may well be suffering from a disease or an addiction and be part of a global epidemic. But they are also blameworthy. And in this, the consumption of food is a site in which medical 'facts' elide aesthetic and normative judgements, and the overweight are framed as greedy, weak-willed and thus lacking 'biological citizenship'.

Metaphorical bodies

As we noted earlier in the chapter, despite the dominance of medicalised understandings of excess food consumption, both food and bodies are invested with metaphorical meanings that express wider tensions within consumer capitalism. To a greater extent than other forms of consumption, food demonstrates control – or lack of it – in very visible ways. A number of scholars have written eloquently on the symbolic meanings of obesity, anorexia and bulimia as cultural conditions that link individual bodies with the body politic. As we saw earlier, as Guthman and DuPois put it: 'The global political-economic contradictions of the neoliberal era are literally embodied' (Guthman and DuPois 2006, 429). In these kinds of readings, medicalised understandings of excess food consumption in general and obesity in particular are translated into cultural narratives that speak of wider social concerns around issues of free will, control and the limits of consumption. It is to these we now turn.

Obesity: excessive bodies

For Susan Bordo, anorexia and obesity represent the binaries of consumer capitalism. In a climate of overabundance and excess, these conditions act both as symbols, as well as material embodiments, of the paradoxical nature of consumption. In an environment in which individuals are encouraged to demand instant gratification, and at the same time are surrounded by a cornucopia of plentiful, cheap foods, the corpulent body is a very visible sign of unchecked desire, of indulgence made real. The overweight individual, she argues, symbolises the dominance of the 'consumer self' in its 'extreme capacity to capitulate to desire' (Bordo 1993, 201). Here, obesity stands as a visceral embodiment of loss of control. The obese person has failed to control their urges – has 'let themselves go' – in a state in which unconstrained appetites and unlimited desires have defeated willpower and reason. Such a loss of control transforms and threatens to overwhelm the self and acts as a visual reminder of the ever-present possibility of succumbing to consumption altogether.

If, as was noted earlier, part of the project of the self can be conceived as a 'taking in' or 'filling up' with good things, then, by extension, the self can also be filled up *too* much, to the extent that it is overwhelmed and spills over. The rolls of fat on the obese person are a striking sign that such a body has been 'filled up' too much and signals a breakdown of bodily boundaries. The obese individual has failed to separate their body from the object of their desire – food – and so has been overtaken by it. The consequence is a dissolution of boundaries: between hunger and desire, between the self and the world, between reason and irrationality. The word 'obesity' itself comes from the Latin *obedere*, 'to eat up, to devour' (OED 2003), a meaning which can be applied to both the actions of the consumer on their food, but also reversed as a description of the effect food can have on the consumer, in terms of something that can overwhelm their body, their will and their very identity. This returns us to the literal meanings of consumption – 'to use up, to destroy' – as well as to ideas about addiction. As in the framing of addiction as a rejection of neoliberal ideals of consumer sovereignty, so obesity can be cast as a state that undermines ideals of reason and responsibility, in this case, in highly visible ways. Whereas the thin, 'civilised' body displays its owners' willpower and self-control, the 'grotesque', fat one is stigmatised for its visible loss of control and its repudiation of biological citizenship.

Such associations are not new. We can recall from Chapter 1 the ways in which eighteenth-century associations of excess consumption and individual overindulgence were produced within medical-ethical discourses of diet. It was in this period that George Cheyne's system of *diatetick management* articulated fears of consumption overwhelming the individual body, at the same time that the critique of luxury was expressing mercantile concerns about the influx of foreign commodities overwhelming the economic realm. Today, in an era of deregulated consumer capitalism, continued reference to the unproductive aspects of obesity and the social and economic costs of the condition articulate wider neoliberal concerns about economic productivity and immigration, elided in concerns over health and addiction as well as a valorisation of thin body ideals and the willpower required to achieve them. This linking of individual bodies with the wider body politic has been consistently gendered. Although the concept of luxury was feminised as an enervating force that destroyed rational 'masculine' values, feminist writers today have noted the continued construction of female desire as a disruptive force, with expressions such as 'man-eater' articulating ideas about voracious sexuality, particularly, as in this instance, in the intersections between women and food. Female appetites are portrayed, then, as 'hungering, voracious, all-needing, and all-wanting' (Bordo 1993, 160) and as such necessitate control by the individual as well as the social body. Failures of control are rendered visible in fat female bodies, which are particularly stigmatised as lazy, immoral and irresponsible. Samantha Murray, an activist-academic, described this kind of normative judgement that frequently underlies medical concern in *The (Fat) Female Body* (2008). In it, she wrote of herself:

> You see me as a high risk candidate for diabetes, gall bladder disease, hypertension and heart attack. At a deeper level, you may see a lazy woman without willpower, a sedentary being, with questionable hygiene. You see a woman who will not help herself, a woman out of control, a woman of unmanaged desires and gluttonous obsessions.
>
> *(Murray 2008, 2)*

Its inverse associations with social class and ethnicity also make obesity a means of discriminating against particular groups of people while eliding the source of that stigma, as in Murray's quote, in concerns over health. As such, Bordo has characterised the current age as one of 'fat phobia', directed against what is essentially a stigmatised underclass. Given the levels of 'fat phobia' in the culture that produces it, it is perhaps not entirely surprising that the *DSM-5* defines anorexia as a 'pathological fear of becoming fat'. Such barely concealed discrimination is an expression of long-standing disgust and fear over the habits and tastes of poor people, where 'junk' food is the corollary of 'trash' culture. Lacking refinement and 'taste', junk food can be read as the embodiment of lower class culture in general, rendered visible through excess flesh. It is 'empty' and 'vacuous'[7] and fails to deliver nutrition to the body in the same way that 'trash' culture fails to provide sustenance to the mind. This stands in contrast to the other end of the food-class spectrum, where what is described as healthy or 'real' food lies. This is the produce found in artisan markets, upscale restaurants and organic delicatessens that celebrates the richness of natural ingredients in ways that distance it – in terms of aesthetics as well as the social class of those who eat it – from processed food. Here, food is 'slow' not fast, 'real' not junk.[8] Significantly, this is also the food of the affluent who have both the time and the resources to prepare it as well as the cultural capital to consider the exercise worthwhile in the first place.

Anorexia: regulated bodies

If obese bodies can be read as signs of disorder and indulgence, anorexic ones tell a different story. Theirs is a narrative of excessive control in what amounts to a kind of triumph of the will over consumption itself. Surrounded by imprecations to consume, the anorexic body stands emaciated and wasting away. It is an image captured evocatively in John Sours's (1980) description of anorexia as 'starving to death in a sea of objects'. Although for Bordo, obesity represents the consumer self in control and the 'extreme capacity to capitulate to desire', anorexia is its opposite: the producer self in control, as she puts it: 'An extreme development of the capacity for self denial and repression of desire'. Both conditions, she says, are rooted in the same consumer culture construction of desire as overwhelming and overtaking the self (Bordo 1993, 201).

Since its emergence as a 'hysterical' syndrome within nineteenth-century psychoanalysis, and through its twenty-first century incarnation in the psy sciences as a mental disorder, the condition of anorexia amongst young, mainly middle class women has been of interest to feminists, who have explained it in terms of women's lack of control in patriarchal societies. In them, struggles around autonomy and desire are materially and symbolically played out, through the conduit of consumption, within women's bodies (Bordo 1993; MacSween 1993). In this vein, Morag MacSween has described anorexia as 'a disease of desire' (1993, 201) which represents a central contradiction in that although women must *be* 'desirable' as the passive objects of others' desires, they must not themselves 'desire' too much. The excessively desiring – or obese – subject, as we have just seen, is cast as voracious, out of control and all consuming. But for the anorexic, such desire is something to be overcome, and appetite is the enemy. As Bordo puts it, 'Appetite is the chaos which makes discipline so necessary' (1993, 194). In this formulation, we can again see a reframing of the luxury debates in which (feminised) desire was equated with chaos, with the power of uncontrolled consumption to undermine both the individual and the body politic. By controlling desire, and with it, bodily size, anorexics achieve a state of control over themselves – and so the world – more broadly. Through the subjection of appetite, autonomy replaces dependency and control overcomes powerlessness. In such a framing, the cultural condition of anorexia both reflects wider social values of body management and self-surveillance and also extends them to their logical, if extreme, conclusion.[9] As such, it reflects a culture that exists in what Campos (2004) calls a permanent state of 'anorexic ideation'.

In some ways, the excesses of the anorexic converge with the cultural figure of the addict that we saw in Chapter 3. As Irvine Welsh's Renton put it, 'Choose us, choose life, choose . . . junk food. . . . well I chose not to choose life'. Surrounded by overabundance, junk and choice, like Renton, the anorexic chooses not to choose, and so eats nothing at all.

Bulimia: wasteful bodies

In these kinds of interpretations, the cycles of bingeing, purging and waste that characterise the condition of bulimia have been framed as a dynamic that extends beyond food to embrace the political economy of consumer capitalism itself (Bordo 1993; Guthman 2011; Campos 2004). Here, the demand is to give in to consumption while at the same time rejecting the excess body weight that comes with it. As Helen Keane (2002) put it, it is a case of quite literally having your cake and eating it too.

In bingeing, we see the expression of a hunger for more than just burgers, but one that taps into what Colin Campbell described as the 'spirit of modern consumerism' itself: a constant hunger for the new – new commodities, new selves, and immediate gratification – in a stream of goods and experiences that are designed to generate a state of constant desire without, however, delivering satisfaction. The purge that follows is the flip side of this insatiability: the need to get back in control – 'of bodies, food, selves' (Bordo 1993, 201), and the discarding of what has been consumed as new items replace them. This is a visceral enactment of Barbara Kruger's graphic image: 'You want it, You buy it, You forget it'.

The waste that is inherent in the cycle links the individual's relation with food to the wider political economy of consumerism. As we have seen, overproduction is built in to the system of consumer capitalism which is characterised by disposable fashions, throwaway packaging and the excess production of cheap foods. Just as quickly as novelties fill the shelves, the discarded goods that have failed to meet expectations fill the garbage bins. As Bauman put it, consumerism is 'an economics of waste and excess' (2007, 48). While the lakes of excess milk and mountains of unwanted cheese of the modern food system are testimony to this political economy of overabundance, at the level of the individual, the bulimic's relation to food is similarly one of pure waste, graphically rendered in the vomiting or use of laxatives to expel unwanted food. Divorced from the material and social roles of satisfying hunger or providing pleasure, here the very notion of food itself is problematised: reconceived as matter which simply passes through the body. It is this logic that capitalism has captured in the creation of techno products such as Olestra: 'non-foods' that do not sustain, but act as conduits to continued consumption.

And so, food becomes a site for some of the central contradictions of consumer capitalism: the ongoing historical tension between the work ethic and the consumption ethic, between giving in and letting go, between 'just do it' and 'just say no'. In the 'pathologies' of addiction, obesity, anorexia and bulimia, the strains that are produced by a system of overabundance and excess are translated into individual problems and resolved at the level of the body (MacSween 1993, 239).

End points

The food system that drives consumer capitalism is one founded on overproduction and excess. Like the spread of intoxicating environments that we reviewed in the previous chapter, such a system also contributes to the spread of entire environments characterised as 'obesogenic' as well as an expansion of medical discourses about obesity and addiction that act as a form of biopolitical governance.

These forms of knowledge work to individualise political-economic issues of excess by framing the problems of food consumption, broadly conceived, as a distinct physiological syndrome as well as a form of mental disorder. Although the target of the 'war against obesity' is located in political-economic systems, the struggles have been waged primarily at the level of the bodies, brains and subjectivities of individual consumers themselves. Within these discourses, the framing of certain foods, such as sugar, as risky or addictive continues the problematic trajectory of the 'drug foods' of the eighteenth century, although today reconceived as agents of obesity in the diets and brains of, by and large, the poorest sectors of the population. Such medicalised understandings once again blur the distinctions between drug and food, and they also produce dichotomous thinking around 'good' and 'bad' or 'healthy' and 'junk' foods, which embodies the dualism of the *pharmakon* in ways that are similar to drugs.

And, because 'we are what we eat' literally, as well as figuratively, what is chosen and what is rejected – 'real' or 'junk' food – is part of a self-presentation that is interpreted as sign of biocitizenship and controlled selfhood. In such a climate, food and body shape are invested with wider metaphorical meanings, in which ideas about obesity and addiction represent fears of loss of control, unmanaged desire and unproductive bodies, and in which the consumption of food is full of significance at both the level of individual subjectivity as well as political economy.

Notes

1 For example, in 1900 only twenty-one per cent of the U.S. labour force was female. By 1999, it was nearly sixty per cent (Smith et al. 2013).

2 Abbott has described the art of lobbying itself as one of sugar's 'enduring legacies' and the model adopted by many other special interests.
3 And in this sense, as Guthman and DuPois and others have pointed out super-sized portions of 'energy-dense' products actually provide value for money, in terms of the calories they provide and the energy they generate. In their words, it is 'more pleasure for less money' (2006, 441).
4 A phrase whose totalitarian connotations somewhat undermine the ideology of consumer freedom and choice that drives its success.
5 As the U.K. Government's Foresight Report into *Tackling Obesities: Future Choices* explained it, 'The marked rise in obesity levels amongst the British population is directly due to an increasing imbalance between calories consumed and those expended' (Jones et al. 2007, 1).
6 While noting the materialist implications of such perspectives, it should also be acknowledged that these kinds of understandings can also be actively adopted by individuals themselves. Groups like Overeaters Anonymous and Food Addicts Anonymous (strap line, 'Recovering together one day at a time from the biochemical disease of food addiction'), for example, mobilise some of the ideas about 'addict identities' that we saw in Chapter 3 and reconfigure ideas about food addiction in ways that produce new forms of solidarity.
7 Tellingly, even Guthman and DuPois's critique of the political economy of food is marked by a turn to the normative when they talk of 'vacuous' foods and the 'nutritional disaster of the Big Mac' (Guthman and DuPois 2006, 435).
8 It is worth noting, however, that these indulgences of the affluent are, nevertheless, mediated by ideals of moderation and balance, and the delights of food itself valorised through its association with the virtues of health.
9 However, although normative levels of self-control are valued, too much (as well as too little) are regarded as pathological. As Helen Keane points out: 'If control and exercise of the will are taken to extremes they can be interpreted as lack of these very qualities' (2002, 115).

6

GAMBLING

Dematerialised consumption

> No society has ever been quite so addictive as . . . [America], which did not invent gambling, to be sure, but which did invent compulsive consumption.
> – *Fredric Jameson (2004, 52)*

Introduction

As Jameson noted in his essay 'The Politics of Utopia', gambling is a type of consumption that is aligned with compulsion. It is also a practice that is illustrative of wider trends in capitalism, and he goes on, 'late capitalism has at least brought the epistemological benefit of revealing the ultimate structure of the commodity to be addiction itself (or, if you prefer, has produced the very concept of addiction in all its metaphysical richness)' (2004, 52). His general points refer to themes that recur throughout this book as a whole, but in this chapter, they will be explored with particular reference to gambling, which, it is argued, can be seen as a unique form of dematerialised consumption.

Over the course of the late twentieth and early twenty-first centuries, gambling was transformed from a stigmatised, highly regulated activity into a massive, global industry, with deep ties to state power. In this trajectory, capitalist restructuring and technological innovations – particularly with respect to financial and communication technologies – revolutionised the ways that games of chance could be played and marketed and, by extension, the ways that they could be experienced by millions of consumers around the globe. Consequently, commercial gambling has become a site of intensified consumption, with games that act as almost perfect vehicles for capital accumulation. They are dispersed throughout increasingly *aleatory* environments, in which gambling is more ubiquitous, more pervasive and its imagery more widespread than ever before.

Alongside this, however, it has also become the site of a new form of pathology. Neuroscientific and psychological forms of knowledge have positioned it as a behavioural addiction that is based on impulsive and irrational cognitions. As a result, along with other twenty-first century forms of excess, such as binge drinking and obesity, we now have a population (or, more accurately, segments of populations) classified as disordered or 'pathological' gamblers.

This chapter critically reviews the conditions that have created this situation. To begin, it examines the expansion of a global gambling industry and its relation to the neoliberal state. It also considers the convergence between the operation of commercial gambling with the wider system of finance capitalism in which it is embedded. It then moves on to explore the role of technology in the acceleration of the gambling economy, with respect to mobile, social and machine-based games in particular. Here, it is argued that intersections between technology, industry and the state are generating increasingly intensified forms of gambling and driving the spread of aleatory environments. The following section then moves on to document the development of biomedical discourses of 'disordered' gambling that have accompanied this expansion and that present excessive gambling as a cognitive deficit, founded on irrationality and loss of control. It argues that such a focus on individual risk and pathology works as a form of governance and also detracts attention from the wider structural conditions that promote aleatory environments in the first place. The next section critiques these medicalised understandings by parsing the cultural and normative assumptions that underlie them. It suggests that their focus on the apparent economic irrationality of gambling in terms of its waste of time and money actually works to highlight some of the contradictions of gambling as a form of dematerialised consumption, whose logic, in turn, reflects features of the wider system of financial capitalism itself.

The gambling state

The emergence of a global gambling industry throughout the 1970s and 1980s can be seen as a microcosm of a number of the trends we have reviewed already, particularly the deregulatory and privatising tendencies of neoliberal consumer capitalism, innovations in technology and the globalisation of financial institutions. These are aspects of the techno economic system of informational capitalism that Manuel Castells (1996) talks about; the post-industrial economy that generates increasingly immaterial forms of production, where materially unproductive services have become the largest, fastest growing sector of Western economies. In Naomi Klein's words, this represents a move towards a 'divestment of the world of things' (1999, 4), in which companies concentrate less on producing goods than on marketing and branding them, focusing on their most profitable, and materially intangible, assets in the process.

The expansion of a global gambling industry can be seen as an exemplary instance of this shift. It is a business that does not produce tangible goods but rather markets intensified experiences, creating profits from the pure circulation and extraction of money from players. In this, it is an archetypal form of dematerialised consumption. In this respect, gambling can also be said to have some convergence with the wider system of finance capital, which is based not on the production of goods or services, but on speculation on the future value of money itself. In the nineteenth century, Marx drew out the similarities between gambling and capitalism when he described the operation of stock markets in which no commodities were produced. Rather than investing money in capital such as goods or services to create profits (the formula M–C–M′), in stock markets, money was simply speculated in order to make more money, shortening the formula to M–M′. It was this, Marx wrote, that gave bankers and speculators, like gamblers, their character of 'swindler and prophet' (1977, 572). Although the logic is intensified, the new global economy of finance capital works in similar ways, trading on speculation without creating material goods or services. In financial products that are separated from their material or economic base we can see the divorce of exchange value from the production of use values (Hilferding 1981) and the emergence of a new kind of economy based not on the production of goods or services but on speculation on the future value of money itself (Jameson 1997; Nealon 2002). In this global economy, financial practices such as hedging, spread betting, arbitrage and derivatives trading have increasingly been described as a form of gambling or 'casino capitalism' (Strange 1986). Indeed, Jameson argues that the future of capitalism is based on this gambling logic, no longer residing 'in the factories and the spaces of . . . production, but on the floor of the stock market . . . in the form of speculation itself' (1997, 251). Although enacted in different ways, Marx's formula of M-M' can be said to drive both the logic of gambling (for the industry, at least, if not players) and the system of finance capitalism itself.[1]

Into this system, two features have increased the expediency of gambling for states. On the one hand, neoliberal policies of low taxation have created a revenue vacuum into which gambling profits appear as an attractive political solution to cash-strapped states. On the other, state-sponsored games of chance encourage consumers to engage in gambling on a large scale while deregulated lending and cheap credit enable them to access the finances to do so, forestalling debt in the future for the pleasures of consumption in the present. And so, as governments liberalise regulations and markets expand, commercial gambling has proliferated. Since the 1970s in particular, the gambling industry has undergone a period of dramatic deregulation, with a loosening of legal restrictions on promotion and expansion resulting in the massive proliferation of commercial gambling as a global enterprise. Governments have systematically legalised increasingly intensive, or 'hard' forms of gambling, beginning with lotteries and moving on to casinos, sports betting and machines, on a vast scale, as sources of both state revenue and commercial profit. At the same time, new information and telecommunications technologies have launched gambling into cyberspace and onto smartphones and social media networks, breaking down national boundaries and posing complex regulatory challenges as they do so (Reith 2013).[2]

These trends drive the global spread of capital in the 'spatial fix' that Harvey (2006) talked of. In the competition for new markets, companies and manufacturers continually update and refine their products to 'fit' national gambling habits and colonise emergent markets in, for example, the former Eastern European communist bloc as well as the developing countries of South East Asia and Africa. In post-Maoist China, for example, the historical association of gambling with individualism and capitalism has given way to a more open market in which leisure and pleasure have been redefined as legitimate expressions of wealth and success (Paules 2010), and in which gambling is part of a growing transnational leisure economy.

This global drive is a highly profitable one, and the economic utility of what Balzac described as an 'essentially taxable passion' (1977, 21) is enormous. It has been noted that commercial gambling is a highly successful 'extractive industry' (Adams 2007), with companies extracting vast profits from players, and federal and national governments, in turn, extracting revenues from companies through various forms of taxation.[3] In the financial year 2013, expenditure on gambling (i.e. amount wagered minus payouts for winnings) was approximately $440 billion, ranking the industry roughly equivalent in size with the global pharmaceutical industry. Internationally, consumers spend more on gambling than they do on alcohol and tobacco combined (Adams 2007). In the United States alone, expenditure increased from $10 billion to $50 billion between 1982 and 1997, as the size of the industry increased ten-fold (NRC 1999).[4]

In this shifting trajectory, we can see the transformation of gambling from a source of disruption into a source of profit and the commodification of chance itself as the ultimate twenty-first century product. The shift is clearly articulated in the annual brochure of the Las Vegas casino Circus Circus, which states that just like any shop, 'the casino is an entertainment merchant. It's just that we happen to merchandise playtime to our customers rather than goods' (in Spanier 1992, 101).[5] Casinos – and, indeed, the gambling industry in general – are in the business of selling experiences – dreams, hopes, thrills and escape – rather than products, making it a high-stakes player in what has been described as 'the experience economy' (Pine and Gilmore 1999). Along with industries based on, for example, fast food, fashion and credit, it is a business that explicitly celebrates an ethic of consumption, urging players to spend, to indulge in pleasure and to fulfil their desires while nevertheless keeping fulfilment – winning – constantly out of reach. In this convergence of commerce with chance, the state-sponsored fantasy of the big win turns the ethos of production and accumulation on its head, advocating the benefits of massive, unearned wealth over the satisfaction of modest gains, in a shift that reflects not only the transcendence of the work ethic but also the promotion and celebration of a new kind of 'consumption ethic'. The values of risk-taking, hedonism and instant gratification are promoted in lottery advertisements that urge consumers to live for the present: 'forget it all for an instant' (U.K. scratchcard); to reject work: 'work is nothing but heart attack-inducing drudgery' (Massachusetts lottery); to embrace risk: 'lotto – the biggest risk of becoming a millionaire' (Netherlands lottery); and to dream of a life of leisure: 'the freedom to do what you want to do, year after year' (Queensland Golden Casket), all for a simple purchase: 'all you need is a dollar and a dream' (New York lottery). Appeals to the democracy of chance have particular resonance in the context of the wider inequities of neoliberalism. In gambling, anyone can be lucky; bountiful state lotteries do not discriminate, and the downtrodden McWorker has as much chance of winning as the Ivy League lawyer. As the U.K. lottery slogan puts it, 'It could be YOU!'

Many states now gain considerable revenues from the profits of commercial gambling, some of which are used to fund services such as education, community services and healthcare, especially in the United States and Australasia as well as various European countries (Goodman 1995; Livingstone and Adams 2010). Proceeds from lotteries have long been used for what are euphemistically referred to as such 'good causes', whereas revenues from machines are increasingly dispersed in ways that create entire constituencies, including voluntary organisations and retailers, who depend on the existence of gambling for jobs and livelihoods. In Australia, for example, approximately ten per cent of state tax revenue depends on profits from machines (Productivity Commission 2010). In 2014, the U.S. casino and casino games industry contributed $38 billion in taxes, and employed 1.7 million people (Oxford Economics 2014). As states become increasingly involved in what Robert Goodman (1995) calls 'the gambling business', the activity itself comes to be deeply embedded in the power structures of Western nations, a relationship that Markham and Young describe as the industry-state gambling complex of 'Big Gambling' (2015, 1).

Although gambling is regulated in similar ways to alcohol, tobacco and food, governments are deeply conflicted in their regulatory roles, given their dependence on the revenue it supplies (Livingstone and Adams 2010; Orford 2011). In this, the symbiotic relationship between the gambling industry and its regulators can be compared with the 'regulatory capture' of the food regulator by the food industry (Nestle 2002). As Markham and Francis put it, 'Big Gambling uses its enormous political power to accelerate deregulation, expand its remit and resist public health reforms' (2015, 2). As we saw in the previous chapter, subsidies, promotions and the use of the revenues of fast food concessions in schools and town centres create not only easy availability of particular foods, but also enduring fiscal relationships between communities, policymakers and individuals (Schlosser 2001). Patterns around gambling are similar in many ways, with, for example, sponsorship and advertising by corporations such as Paddy Power, Ladbrokes and Bet365 becoming increasingly visible and ubiquitous, especially around sports. Indeed, some commentators have described the overtaking of the sports experience with the increasingly visible sponsorship of games, teams and events as 'the gamblification of sports' (Thomas et al. 2011). As a part of this trend, liberalising legislation has also facilitated the proliferation of advertising across print, billboard and broadcast media. As a result, the iconography of Big Gambling increasingly features on billboards and magazines as well as on public transport and pops up in the commercial breaks in the Saturday night film. After the implementation of the 2005 Gambling Act in Britain, for example, gambling advertisements on television screens increased by six hundred per cent (Ofcom 2013).[6] In Australia, the amount of money spent on advertising betting rose by one hundred and sixty per cent between 2011 and 2015, making gambling the fastest growing category of advertising (AdNews 2016).

As the neoliberal state retreats from public life, so gambling capital advances, filling public spaces, as well as the revenue gap, left behind with the imagery of games of chance. The following section explores this trend in more detail.

Intensified consumption and the spread of aleatory environments

Within this climate, intersections between technology, marketing and capital work to both intensify the experience of gambling and drive it deeper into the spaces of everyday life. Such intensification is typical of wider trends within late capitalism. We saw in Chapter 3 how new forms of consumption are increasingly based on dematerialised experiences rather than the consumption of tangible commodities and on accelerated types of 'turbo' (Schor 2008) or 'hyper' (Ritzer 1993) consumption. Big Gambling exemplifies this. It has harnessed technological and financial systems to generate games that are increasingly fast and repetitive and that circulate money in accelerated cycles of loss. These trends are particularly encapsulated in electronic gaming machines (EGMs) as well as by the recent ascendance of mobile and social forms of gambling which are the focus of this section.

Manuel Castells (1996) pointed out that technology always develops in relation with the state and that capitalism itself is characterised by 'its relentless expansion, always trying to overcome the limits of time and space' (Castells 1996, 101). In gambling technology, we can see a highly successful exemplar of this, for the industry has harnessed technology in the interests of capital. As the anthropologist Natasha Dow Schull puts it, the gaming industry 'has established itself as an engine for experimentation and innovation with emergent digital capabilities producing military-grade surveillance and networks, sophisticated systems of accounting and sleek gaming machinery' (Schull 2005, 66). The largest and most lucrative sector of the gambling industry is EGMs, which account for some seventy to eighty-five per cent of their profits (Fahrenkopf 2004). Requiring no staffing and minimal maintenance, they produce pure profit as what has been described as 'almost perfect vehicle[s] for capital accumulation' (Young 2011). More colloquially, they are simply known as 'cash machines in reverse'.

Schull (2012) has documented the tactics used by industry to create machines that are manufactured for the extraction of profit, or what she describes as 'addiction by design'. In this respect, Big Gambling, like Big Food, mobilises marketing, design and technology in a concentrated effort to intensify consumption. Every aspect of casino architecture, ergonomics and ambience is crafted to encourage individuals to play on machines and to keep them gambling for as long as possible in order to maximise what is known in industry circles as 'time on device'. From the moment individuals walk in the door of a venue, a range of features work on them to generate particular visual perspectives and affective states. Low ceilings, narrow aisles and curving passageways gently direct them towards machines in a carefully constructed atmosphere in which optimal levels of sound, lighting, colour, temperature and even odour are calibrated to generate an ambient climate that both energises and soothes players, encouraging them to focus on the machines in front of them and extend playing time for the maximum possible duration. Once seated, the ergonomics of machines themselves work to 'engineer experience', creating a seamless, uninterrupted flow in which nothing distracts the player from exclusive focus on their device. Adjustable screens and stools, arm rests and optimally placed buttons ensure a close fit between the body of the gambler and the body of the machine while service features provide assistance at the touch of a button and the use of cards and tokens releases play from the interruption of coin or note insertion. As well as making financial loss invisible, these features accelerate gambling and generate hypnotic states in which, for players, the outside world ceases to exist (Schull 2012, 64). Indeed, many gamblers remain immobile for hours, never leaving their seats to eat, drink or use the bathroom, hypnotised by the rhythm of the machine in front of them.

Deep inside machines, the design of games themselves are carefully calibrated, utilising all the expertise of psychological research and ergonomic insight, to extend 'time on device'. High-resolution imagery and sound, state-of-the-art animation and player-centric features, as well as games that adjust to players' movements and even begin to anticipate their desires, encourage their hosts to 'play to extinction' – the point where their funds run out. Games are calibrated to generate 'near misses' (Reid 1986): the illusion that a winning sequence has almost come up, recently described as the more nuanced 'losses disguised as wins' (Dixon et al. 2010), which encourages the experience of always 'almost winning', so prolonging consumption and encouraging maximum expenditure. These kinds of sophisticated psychological features have been described as exploiting a form of 'operant conditioning', after the experiments of B.F. Skinner, in which rats were conditioned to repeat the same actions over and over again, in the hope of receiving random rewards (Skinner 2004). Experts in the field of the psy sciences have extended this observation to argue that gamblers in a situation of constant uncertainty appear programmed to continue playing until forced to stop by the erosion of their bankroll.

These digital and financial technologies are guided by sophisticated psy-ec forms of knowledge and deployed by the industry to produce maximum profit: in the words of Steve Wynn, the Las Vegas casino magnate, the casino floor is 'strictly a receptacle, a cash register' (2016). They also work to intensify the experience of gambling and produce distinctive subjective states that have been described by players and researchers alike as the experience of 'the zone' (Reith 1999; Livingstone 2005; Schull 2012). The zone is an affective, trance-like condition in which gamblers' surroundings, the passage of time, the value of money and even their sense of self are dissolved by the immersion in intensive play. Like the kind of peak experience described by Czikszentmihalyi (1990) as 'flow', gamblers in the zone are fully focused on the here and now, in hypnotic rhythms of play. Schull's respondents described it in various ways, evoking nineteenth-century terminology of hypnosis as well as contemporary references to computer processing and television viewing. One said, 'you're in a trance, you're on autopilot', another, 'the zone is like a magnet, it just pulls you in and holds you there' and a clinician who treated problem gamblers said of his patients, 'they talk about climbing into the screen and getting lost' (in Schull 2012, 19). For many players, it is this 'world dissolving state of subjective suspension and affective calm' (in Schull 2012, 19), rather than the chance of winning money, that becomes an end in itself. Indeed, given that winning can (temporarily at least) stop play, and therefore disrupt the zone, for some players, winning can actually come to be regarded as an unwelcome distraction and money itself become devalued as simply 'the currency of chance' (Reith 1999, 144). It is here that the abstract or dematerialised qualities of gambling become clearer, because in this state, even money – or rather, its representations, in credit, chips or virtual currencies – is devalued and becomes a counter in a game, the medium of play, rather than an end in itself (Reith 1999, 143–145).

Mobile and social: the new gambling landscape

The recent adoption of mobile and social technologies by Big Gambling has extended these trends even further, generating entire environments in which gambling is ever more pervasive and accessible. As we saw in Chapter 3, these technologies intensify consumption and extend its reach, 'to the most remote places and the deepest pores of the world' (van Dijk 2012, 57) while also making it more intimate: driving it into the psyche of the individual through the smartphone in their pocket. In the embrace of such powerful new media, games of chance have become highly potent products.

In the past few years, all sectors of the industry have invested in systems that enable remote playing on smartphones and tablets, through wireless, cable and satellite networks, facilitating wagering on distant events, such as sports and racing, and speeding up the financial transactions between players and games. At the time of writing, mobile is the fastest growing sector in the industry, overtaking desktop as the most popular way to play online (Juniper Research 2014). The games played in this way exemplify the conditions described by Giddens (1991) of 'disembedding' and acceleration, noted earlier – the overcoming of space and time – because gambling technology creates a vast, global stage in which gamblers can bet, along with countless, anonymous others, on the outcomes of distant games.[7] In the embrace of the gambling industry, geolocational and data tracking technologies, interlinked with personalised marketing, and allied to the power of social networks like Facebook and Twitter, have made gambling more ubiquitous, more pervasive and more intensive, and has made gamblers themselves, in Aideen Shortt's (2014) words, 'always on'. Mobile devices and extensive cellular networks have released gambling from the physical confines of the casino or the betting shop and facilitated its spread throughout the daily rhythms and spaces of everyday life.

In their analysis of what they call the 'new frontier' of mobile and social gambling, Cesar Albarres Torres and Gerard Goggin describe how the 24/7 availability of online gambling has been extended still further by smartphones: devices that are characterised by 'ubiquity, personalisation, and sociability' and that work to encourage 'intensive real-time gameplay' (2014, 103). In this new digital landscape, it is now possible to gamble during the morning commute, in the supermarket queue or from the comfort of the sofa – television remote in one hand, smartphone-casino in the other. As Torres and Goggin put it, 'The player does not *go to the casino*, but *carries the casino around in their pocket*' (2014, 103).

Into this digital landscape, mobile marketing that is delivered directly to individuals' smartphone and based on extensive knowledge of their betting history and preferences, makes advertising more personalised and more effective, tailoring messages that let players know, for example, when a game is about to start, and updating them on changing odds in real time. This kind of direct marketing on the device on which individuals also bet is also more potent, shortening the gap between the desire to play and the means to do so. The somewhat understated advice from the marketing consultants Bullet Business to their corporate customers notes that 'reaching a customer on the device where they can instantly take action is a very powerful tool' (Bullet Business 2013) while alluding to the possibilities for impulsive – and, therefore, profitable – action.

Geolocational apps embedded in smartphones assist in these kinds of marketing efforts and can be used to send promotions to gamblers as they move around their environment, targeting them when they are physically nearby particular venues: a strategy known in industry circles as 'acquisition efforts' (Shortt 2013).

In this new landscape, social media is being increasingly operationalised by gambling corporations as a key site for social or viral marketing efforts to encourage gambling and recruit new players to Facebook games like Bingo Friendzy and Zynga Poker. To this end, 'likes', leaderboards and bonuses act to incentivise players and expand and monetise play, whereas Twitter feeds and 'seeded' conversations aim to extend brand awareness into the social space of players. It is an approach that is exemplified by the online betting company Paddy Power, whose controversial tweets are designed to attract notoriety, publicity – and, therefore, bets. Its deliberately provocative advertisement for betting on the Oscar Pistorius murder trial, for example ['bet he walks'], drew the largest number of complaints of all time in Britain (ASA 2014). Such tweets are part of a wider social media strategy, however, in which deliberately 'mischievous or irreverent' commentaries on current affairs are used to embed more serious tweets designed to update followers about the latest odds, games and special offers, and are presented in a way in which calls to take action, to place bets, are, as one online commentator put it, 'cleverly camouflaged so as not to alienate, but to further engage. The perfect approach to selling on Twitter' (Bermingham 2014).

The recent ascendance of 'social gaming', which is unregulated and based on free-to-play or 'freemium' models, complicates ideas about money in this new gambling landscape. Games that utilise virtual currencies or microtransactions, and that are based on intangibles such as virtual, in-game items, 'skins' or 'lives' rather than cash, have begun to erode distinctions between 'real money' gambling and social 'gaming', disrupting the very notion of value itself. Money that is already devalued in gambling is further problematised in social games that can involve, for example, the use of real cash to purchase virtual currencies to play games that return only virtual currency, or 'rewards' such as extended playing time or higher levels of play or, even, amongst some bingo players, the use of real money to buy virtual cups of tea. The popular mobile game Candy Crush, for example, highlights some of these issues around the blurring of ideas of money and value as well as the problematising of notions of addiction. Although it is not a gambling game and is based on the freemium model, the game makes an estimated $800,000 a day from players buying 'lives' and boosters that help them climb to higher levels of the game, and it is worth some $7.1 billion (Smith 2014). It has come to stand as a kind of cultural shorthand for 'addictive' gaming, with developers and players alike celebrating its compulsive qualities. Indeed, some of its users' tweets read like those of any self-help group:

> **@MariaHo**: My name is Maria and I am a Candy Crush Addict and it has cost me more money than I would care to admit
>
> **@HeyChrisA**: My attitude to Candy Crush is like a former drug addict. I don't judge people playing it, I want to help them stop
>
> *(#CandyCrushAddiction. 22 January 2014)*

A recent seminar paper by the mobile gaming developer *SOOMLA* (2014) entitled 'Addictive Games: Getting Users to Dream about Virtual Goods' articulates such blurred boundaries, challenging the very concept of value and making us question the role of money itself in this new, constantly shifting landscape of gambling. The 'virtual goods' of these socially networked games highlight the general absence of any kind of physical product that is at the heart of all gambling transactions, although the notion they might be 'addictive' points to the distinctive subjective experience of this kind of dematerialised consumption.

As with the embrace of e-cigarettes and diet foods by the food and tobacco industries, many sectors of the gambling industry are becoming involved with social gaming in ways that are intended to introduce brand awareness and 'soften up' the market ahead of anticipated legalisation of online gambling 'proper', or alternatively, to reduce competition, in different jurisdictions (with all the criticisms of 'gateway' activity that this involves). In this sense, social gaming can perhaps be regarded as yet another in an increasing line of simulacra: commodities and practices that, like e-cigarettes, or 'non-foods' such as Olestra, act as representations, or copies, of more mainstream products, but with key agents removed. Whether gaming without money, vaping without smoke or eating without digesting, such practices highlight not only the adaptability of capital, but also the shifting regulatory and normative currents that problematise ideas about addictive consumption itself.

Together, the new technologies and commercial strategies reviewed here work to intensify gambling, producing games that, like EGMs, are perfect vehicles for capital accumulation. They also make gambling a form of surveillance. Financial, personal and biometric information is gathered through gamblers' interaction with their machines and mobile devices – as one industry insider put it, tracking 'every click of the mouse' (author, personal communication, 29 June 2011) – amassing vast amounts of 'big data' that work to surveil betting behaviour and target marketing to individuals, not just at a time but also at a place, when they are most receptive to inducements to gamble.

Such technologies generate what Deleuze (1995) would call environments of 'continuous control' that stimulate desire, encourage play or, in industry terms, increase 'time on device'. In this, they go far beyond the panopticon-style design of casinos, with their ubiquitous cameras and security, to create networks of surveillance across a range of 'gambling spaces', which, due to the extended mobility of mobile and social gambling, can, in reality, be potentially *any* space.

These trends in marketing and technology bring what I would describe as 'turbo charged' features to gambling. Guided by geolocational software and personalised marketing, mobile and financial technologies disembed gambling from the constraints of time and place, so that individuals can play almost literally anywhere, day or night, on games that are more pervasive than ever before. This is the most recent manifestation of a trend towards the dispersal of games throughout the spaces and communities of everyday life. In the 1990s, the terms 'McGambling' (Goodman 1995) or 'convenience' gambling (NGISC 1999) were used to describe the ways in which gambling was becoming increasingly ubiquitous throughout non-gambling spaces. Today, however, intersections between technology and the deregulatory neoliberal state have accelerated these trends, driving intensified forms of mobile, social and machine-based gambling deeper into public spaces. From the proliferation of betting shops in British high streets and the dispersal of 'pokies' throughout suburban Australia, and from the increasing ubiquity of mobile devices to the general visual creep of gambling sponsorship and advertising, games of chance have become pervasive features of the modern consumer landscape. This is a move towards the generation of what I would describe as 'aleatory environments', after the Latin, *alea*, for 'gambling'. Within them, both the products and imagery of gambling have colonised public space, becoming part of the fabric of everyday life and taking over entire neighbourhoods, as well as the interior space of the individuals who inhabit them.

Poor gamblers

Aleatory environments may be ubiquitous, but their effects are generally concentrated in particular areas. Despite its global nature, gambling is characterised by unequal socio-economic and geographic patterns of consumption. It is the most vulnerable in society, living in the poorest neighbourhoods, who spend – and lose – the highest relative amounts of income on gambling. Similarly, gambling opportunities and venues tend to be concentrated amongst low-income and ethnic minority groups and communities (Rintoul et al. 2012; Doran and Young 2010). For instance, in Australia, where states derive substantial revenues from gambling, the greater the socio-economic disadvantage of a municipality, the higher its numbers of gaming machines, with residents of the most deprived areas in a region spending almost double the state's average on them (Marshall and Baker 2001). American research has also found that excess gambling is strongly associated with neighbourhood disadvantage (Welte et al. 2004), with similar spatial patterns characterising the newly liberalised, post-Gambling Act regime in Great Britain (Wardle et al. 2012), where betting shops are increasingly opening in poor neighbourhoods, with pawn shops and money lenders following closely behind them. These inequalities of lost wealth are complicated by the interdependent relation between the state and the gambling industry, resulting in a situation in which commercial gambling effectively becomes another regressive form of taxation (Clotfelter and Cook 1989).

Ironically, it is those who feel they have most to gain from the possibility of a gambling win who, in reality, lose the most. As Livingstone and Woolley (2007) have pointed out, the EGM industry's most problematic consumers are their best customers. This kind of pattern characterises the uneven social and spatial distribution of other 'addictive' or problematic types of consumption, particularly, as we saw in the last two chapters, food, alcohol and smoking, where profits lie in the excesses of a minority of consumers: with the 'superconsumers' of alcohol and the 'heavy users' of Coke. Similarly, researchers from various jurisdictions have estimated that between half and three quarters of the revenue from machines derives from a minority of problem players, who make up only between one and two per cent of the population (Williams and Wood 2004; Productivity Commission 2010). As with the case of alcohol consumption, this distribution demonstrates the operation of the harm paradox, whereby poorer social groups suffer greater ill-effects from gambling involvement, despite engaging in similar or even lower levels of play than their wealthier counterparts. Like 'poor smokers', then, poor gamblers are situated at the bottom of the social pyramid, and, as with obesogenic environments, aleatory ones tend to reflect wider geo-spatial patterns of inequality. There are structural drivers behind such patterns. Many of the strategies deployed by Big Gambling – from the geo-spatial location of games and the ergonomics of casino layout, to the creation of machines and games that are deliberately designed to intensify consumption – are similar in many ways to those of Big Food, with its manufacture of products that generate craving and its careful geo-spatial targeting of stores. The techno-scientific generation of 'the bliss point' has its counterpart in the engineering of 'the zone'. In both cases, psy-ec forms of knowledge work to produce environments and commodities that generate specific subjective states based on ongoing desire, and which, in turn, work to generate profit.

In the next section, we turn to look at some of the ways that the impacts of these broad structural trends have been reconfigured as individual problems through medicalised discourses of addiction and risk.

The neurobiology of chance: risky technologies and addiction

Despite its proliferation in a climate of intensified consumerism and economic liberalisation, the explanations for the 'excesses' of gambling that emerged in the 1980s, and that continue to be influential today, were framed within a reductive epistemology of disorder and disease. Bio-psy forms of knowledge produced the syndrome of 'compulsive gambling', as it was first known, in 1980, when it was introduced into the *DSM-III* as an impulse control disorder. Along with binge drinking and 'binge eating disorders', we can see this as the constitution of yet another social 'type': part of the process described by Foucault (1976) whereby the observation and classification of behaviour makes new types of subject increasingly visible and so 'real'.

With the production of pathological gambling as a psychiatric disorder came a proliferation of interest in the subject, accompanied by a range of medical, legal, academic and treatment professionals, as well as lay groups and formal organisations, all with their own conception of and interest in 'the problem' (Volberg 2001). Various explanations for the syndrome were proposed, many of which simply tended to 'explain' it in terms of a description of the features that characterised it. Whereas psychological research focused on what appeared to be the fundamental impulsivity and irrationality of gamblers, biomedical research attempted to locate biochemical and neurological causes of the disorder, and public health perspectives utilised a variety of approaches to estimate the prevalence of problems and calculate patterns of risk across populations. All of this resulted in a somewhat 'messy' overlapping of discourses that configured problem and pathological gambling in a range of different ways: as a mental disorder, a physiological syndrome or sometimes a (calculable) combination of all of these things, expressed as factors of 'risk'.

This new gambling subject proved capricious, however, and was reclassified three times over the next two decades, shifting from 'compulsive' to 'pathological' to 'disordered' gambling, as attention moved from the mind to the body of the afflicted individual and began to focus on its similarities with substance dependency and addiction (APA 1980, 1987, 1994, 2013). From the *DSM*, a variety of diagnostic screens flourished,[8] all acting to construct the categories of 'recreational', 'risky' and 'excessive' gambling out of a quantifiable checklist of symptoms, organised loosely around ideas about loss of control and irrationality. In this perspective, increases in commercial gambling have been linked with increases in pathology, manifest through largely social problems such as familial breakdown, lost productivity, financial problems and even suicide, all of which are particularly acute amongst the poorest and most vulnerable social groups. It is in this context that various stakeholders have talked about an 'epidemic' of gambling, newly conceived as a public health problem as well as a disease agent and cause of social disorder. So, for example, the U.S.-based organisation Stop Predatory Gambling described gambling as 'one of the biggest public health issues in America today' (in Meyer 2014), whereas others, such as the Public Health Advocacy Institute, compared it explicitly to tobacco, citing Jahiel and Babor's (2007) concept of the 'industrial epidemic' to describe the promotion of gambling as 'a product that is also a disease agent'. They stated that 'legalised casino gambling causes devastating effects on the public's health' and that electronic gambling machines 'are designed to addict their customers in a way that is similar to how the tobacco industry formulates its cigarettes to be addictive by manipulating their nicotine levels and other ingredients' (PHAI 2014).

In these discourses, gambling has joined alcohol, tobacco and obesity in what Bell (2011) described as public health's 'axis of evil'. Alongside this 'unholy trinity', it has become another form of consumption whose excesses can be reframed through new kinds of techno-scientific understanding. And, as with the others, particular kinds of normative and cultural assumptions lie behind such forms of knowledge. It is to both of these that we now turn.

Neuroscience: the ghost in the (gambling) machine

A considerable amount of psychological and neurocognitive research effort has been expended on examination of what is regarded as the fundamental irrationality of gamblers. The *DSM* classifies these as 'disorders in thinking', in which long-term negative consequences are ignored in the pursuit of immediate gratification and behaviour is driven by impulsivity and risk-taking as well as a range of 'irrational' traits. Such traits include 'biased evaluations of outcomes' (Gilovich 1983), notions of 'near misses' (Reid 1986) and 'illusions of control' (Langer 1975), which describe gamblers' tendency to overestimate their influence in games of chance, attribute losses to external factors, hold out unjustified optimism in the likelihood of winning, misperceive patterns in random events and trust mysterious, influential forces such as 'luck' (Wagenaar 1988).

Neuroscience has been invoked to demonstrate the physiological basis of some of these features, with a range of studies investigating their material basis in the hidden crevices of players' synapses and the firing of neurochemical circuitry. To this end, researchers have utilised MRI technology in an attempt to identify the physiological profiles of subjects' brains (Breiter et al. 2001; Potenza et al. 2003), whereas substances such as noradrenalin and serotonin have been associated with impulsive disorders and craving. In brain imaging studies, the so-called cognitive deficits involved in misperceptions about one's chances of winning, such as seeing patterns in random events, believing that a win is more likely after a series of losses, and the tendency of 'near misses' to encourage further play, have been explained with reference to a hyperactive insula (Clark et al. 2014). The exact mechanisms through which this region of the brain exerts its influence remain mysterious, however, with researchers simply stating that it makes gamblers 'more susceptible to errors in thinking' and 'impaired decision-making' (Hewig et al. 2010; Tanabe et al. 2007). In a narrative that will be familiar by now, such studies suggest that gambling activates the reward system in much the same way that a drug does with brains 'lighting up' in fMRI scanners when exposed to images – usually via a video screen – of gambling wins. Biological markers, cognitive deficits and genetic vulnerabilities have been proposed as explanations for cravings, withdrawals and highs and for 'irrational thinking' as well as for arguments about the hereditary basis of the disorder (Potenza et al. 2003; van Holst et al. 2010).

In these kinds of inquiry, gambling is sometimes positioned as almost a 'pure' case of addiction. With no substance to act as intermediary, it can be argued that the 'cause' of pathology must be directly located within the individual themselves. Schull (2015) described the way that such discourses are interpreted, stating that, amongst neuroscientists, 'gambling and these "process addictions" are being taken as a pure form of addiction because they show us a direct window into the chemical changes happening in the brain'.

Such powerful narratives of addiction raise questions about free will and responsibility, and they can also generate new forms of identity amongst those who identify with the distinctive version of selfhood that they generate. The Gamblers Anonymous fellowship, for example, like other twelve-step models, advocate the disease status of addiction, stating in their handbook that 'compulsive gambling is an illness, progressive in its nature, which can never be cured, but can be arrested' (Gamblers Anonymous, n.d.). 'Pathological gamblers' do not exist only in clinics and diagnostic screens, then, but also as real players who actively identify themselves as such and adopt the language of medicine to articulate and, in some cases, lend authority to their condition. In previous research I conducted with members of Gamblers Anonymous, one woman articulated the segueing of medicalised discourses of addiction with her sense of self, describing Gamblers Anonymous meetings as a 'medicine' for her illness: 'I do what's good for me and this [attending meetings] is good for me. I take medicines for illnesses and this [gambling] is an illness so this is my medicine' (in Reith and Dobbie 2012, 384).

In these kinds of approaches, we can see a narrative of the pathological gambler as a distinct 'type' of individual, whose actions are primarily reducible to physiological processes located deep in their body but beyond their conscious control.

DSM-5 *and the risky subject*

These neuroscientific forms of knowledge underpinned a reconceptualisation of gambling in the revised version of the psychiatric manual *DSM-5*. The updated version renamed 'pathological' as 'disordered' gambling, shifting it from the category of 'impulse control disorder' to that of 'substance related and addictive disorder', so aligning it more closely with drug addiction 'proper'. At the same time, the threshold for diagnosis was reduced from five to four criteria, so widening the diagnostic net (APA 2013). As with the general criteria for addiction and also for the specific pathologies of food and eating that we saw in Chapters 3 and 5, those for gambling disorder are based on a range of socially relative, subjective and normative judgements. As listed in the *DSM*, they include preoccupation with gambling, spending increasing amounts of money to feel the same level of excitement, making unsuccessful attempts to cut down, feeling restless or irritable when trying to control play, gambling when feeling distressed, chasing losses, lying to conceal the extent of one's losses, risking social relationships through gambling and relying on others to help with financial problems caused by gambling (APA 2013).

These criteria (as well as those of the many other clinical screens) are based on individuals' subjective assessments about their motivations and moods, including evaluation of states such as preoccupation, excitement and loss of control. Meanwhile, the indirect effects of excess, as with substance use, are measured in terms of negative feelings, such as guilt, anxiety and depression that derive from spoiled relationships, unsatisfactory jobs, financial worries and general existential ennui (Keane 2002). The screens are, however, remarkably silent on the issue of what is, after all, the medium and the signifier of both gambling and problem gambling – money. Attitudes and behaviour relating to money, such as borrowing, stealing or lying about it, as well as chasing losses, are judged more important than the actual amounts of money wagered or lost (far less money lost relative to income). It is not money – in an absolute or relative sense – that is important here, but rather *loss of control* of money that acts as a measure of pathology. And in this sense, the definition of problematic gambling becomes potentially limitless: when evaluation of one's own subjective feelings about wins and losses is the criteria of pathology, anyone can experience problems, and the distinction between normal and problematic behaviour starts to collapse.

A number of gambling screens have been incorporated into prevalence surveys in ways that work to quantify the number of disordered gamblers, as well as those 'at risk' from addiction, across populations. Such an approach works to establish a bio-politics of the gambling population, monitoring their demographics, their mental health and their relationships with other problematic forms of consumption, such as smoking and drinking, in a mass of quantifiable data. Although the numbers of those defined as 'at risk' are low (typically only one to two per cent of the population), because the status of risk is established through endorsement of only one or two diagnostic criteria, the assessment of potential or probable problems has the effect of drawing much larger numbers of people in the therapeutic 'gaze' of the screens. And so, despite the concentration of harms amongst disadvantaged groups and poor neighbourhoods, this emphasis on 'at risk' status, along with the focus on subjective assessments, means that the disorder fans out across the population, incorporating increasing numbers of the middle class in its spread. Easy access to credit and technology mean that gambling-related embezzlement and bankruptcy are becoming familiar narratives of middle class downfall. The case of Scott Stevens, the Ohio businessman whose gambling-motivated suicide illustrated the dangerous potential of consumption in the Introduction of this book, is a case in point. Stevens, who embezzled more than $7 million dollars from his employer and gambled away his children's college fund before killing himself, was thoroughly 'respectable'. Media coverage of the case consistently drew attention to his status as a husband and father, his position as community leader and church-goer, his well-paid, responsible job. We are told that 'the respected business executive, married father of three daughters, community leader, and company Chief Financial Officer was *well-acquainted with the value of money*' (*The State Journal* 2014, italics added). As his widow's attorney put it, 'if it [gambling addiction] can happen to a guy as smart as he was, it can happen to anybody' (Terry Noffsinger, in Meyer 2014).

In the case of gambling, then, an increasing focus on risk does not appear to 'dissolve' the subject of addiction, as has sometimes been argued (Castel 1991), but could, in fact, be argued to actually expand the remit of addiction itself, which now spreads to include swathes of the otherwise rational majority. If it could happen to Scott Stevens, it can happen to anyone. Put another way – it could be YOU!

Governing risk

Medicalised discourses of addiction and risk have gained considerable authority in recent years. Here, they act as a form of governance in ways that detract attention from the wider political economy of gambling to focus on the actions, and particularly the cognitions, of individual players themselves (Reith 2013, 2014). Such governance is the focus of this section.

As the gambling industry is liberalised and ever more areas of public life expand into 'aleatory environments', requirements for self-control go deeper into individual players themselves. Now that roulette machines have moved into the high street and mobile technologies have turned smartphones into pocket casinos, gamblers are exhorted to inform themselves about risk, manage their money responsibly and 'when the fun stops, stop' as the industry-body Senet Group strap line tells them. These demands for control aim mainly to reform the cognitive 'errors' that are regarded as the root of excessive behaviour and work on a number of levels: pharmacological and therapeutic as well as through a mobilisation of ideas about responsibility, all of which are interconnected.

At one level, medicalised discourses of gambling addiction hold out solutions to reform the disordered individuals they produce. As 'neurochemical selves' (Rose 2004), gamblers are subject to pharmacological interventions, including drugs such as lithium and SSRIs that attempt to rewire the faulty reasoning of their brains. Most recently, clinicians have introduced the opiate antagonist naltrexone as a treatment for gambling disorder. Normally used to dull the euphoria and cravings generated by opiates such as heroin, it has been argued that it will similarly disrupt the pleasure circuits and so dampen the excitement involved in gambling (Grant and Kim 2006). In a similar way that the deployment of methadone is conceived as a 'technocratic magic bullet' (Bourgois 2000, 176) that will neutralise desire in heroin users, it is hoped that naltrexone will work to chemically negate the impulsive irrationality of gamblers. In this, naltrexone, along with all the other drugs utilised to treat excessive gambling, can be regarded as a form of biomedical governance whose aim is to return subjects to sober, and especially rational, subjectivity.

By and large, however, the governance of the gambling population is enacted mainly through the 'responsibilitisation' of players themselves. To a large extent, such efforts to shape behaviour work at the cognitive level and attempt to reform the 'irrational cognitions' that underlie excess playing. To this end, for example, therapy focuses on cognitive restructuring to modify expectations of gambling and enhance understanding of odds and to develop decision-making strategies to foster control over excessive expenditures of time and money. The psy sciences are deeply embedded in this governmental project and have generated an army of specialist gambling counsellors and therapists – Rose's (1999) 'engineers of the human soul' – who provide treatment that aims to reform the irrational drives and, therefore, the aberrant behaviour of players. The promise held out by such therapeutic interventions, as Rose explains, is 'not of curing pathology, but of reshaping subjectivity' (Rose 1999, xxxi). This is a deeper aim, one that goes to the heart – or, rather, the mind – of the individual and attempts to reform their cognitive processes in ways that align with dominant neoliberal ideals about the value of money and the relation between work and reward – issues we will return to in the next section.

We can see a discursive convergence between these types of cognitive therapy and the strategies of public health, whose aims to educate players are embedded in libertarian assumptions that decisions about whether and how much to gamble should be largely left to the individual and also that informed choice will result in rational and, therefore, responsible behaviour manifest in limited spending. A range of individualised 'responsible gambling strategies' coalesce around this broad theme, all of which focus on the individual player as both the source of – and solution to – the problem. In recent years, gambling corporations have embraced this 'responsibility agenda', declaring their commitment to responsible practice at the same time that they produce and market increasingly intensified games of chance. Meanwhile, the tropes of 'responsible gambling' themselves have been accompanied by a semantic shift from 'gambling' to 'gaming'; a sleight of hand that seeks to elide connotations of loss and realign commercial gambling with softer, more innocent pastimes. And so, corporations sign up to 'social responsibility' with a range of measures, such as signage on venues and advertisements alerting players to the potential risks involved in 'gaming', 'self-exclusion' programmes enabling them to ban themselves from gambling venues (because venues themselves are not legally obliged to do so) and 'pre-commitment' schemes that allow individuals to set their own limits for expenditure before they play. The same technologies that have facilitated the spread of mobile and social forms of gambling are also being invoked in the responsibility agenda. In particular, a range of online tools and apps are currently joining 'individual awareness' strategies, often developed in tandem with gambling companies themselves, as a means of tracking player behaviour in ways that highlight problematic or risky patterns. The aim is for the internalisation of the 'therapeutic gaze' by players themselves, so that individuals who gamble too much can engage in an ongoing process of introspection, continually monitoring their behaviour for signs of irrationality or excess, presumably as a first step towards changing their ways. The normalising gaze of these therapeutic strategies is evident in a system called BetCheck, an online tool designed by the Ontario Responsible Gambling Council that allows the individual to compare their expenditure of time and money with that of 'the average player', so situating them within a continuum of 'normal' play, out of which their 'risk profile' can be identified. The advertisement states: 'BetCheck – your responsible gambling safety check – [is a computerised] tool that allows [you] to compare [your] gambling habits with the "typical gambler"'. Visitors assess their gambling for example, considering time and money spent and level of risk for problematic gambling (Responsible Gambling Council 2015a). And so, out of a mass of data, standards of 'responsible' and 'average' versus 'excessive' or 'risky' play are produced and players invited to situate themselves – in order to better govern themselves – within the continuum.

Ultimately, these discourses of (ir)responsibility and disorder suit the aims of Big Gambling. The idea that the deficiencies of a small proportion of 'disordered' gamblers, rather than, say, the properties of the object (the gambling product) or the wider ecology (the political and regulatory environment) it is made available in, shifts the focus away from structural and political issues and towards individuals in a way that supports existing power structures. The focus of this kind of governance is bluntly underlined by the Victorian Gaming Machine Industry, when it warns those who play its machines: 'When you're playing a poker machine, the only thing you can control is *you*' (VGMI 2004).

Rage against the machine

However, there is also another trend at work here. Despite the tendency for medicalised forms of knowledge to detract attention from the wider gambling environment, the insights they generate can also be mobilised in ways that draw attention to the role of the products generated by the gambling industry itself. This emergent, critical trend joins more established community based and political forms of resistance. For example, in Australia, a single-ticket politician, Nick Xenophon, won popular support on his 'no pokies' policy, whereas in Britain, the Campaign for Fairer Gambling agitates for policy change towards machines. Elsewhere, local residents and grassroots groups campaign against the expansion of gambling in their neighbourhoods. Such popular resistance has also penetrated popular culture, with the Australian band The Whitlams composing 'Blow up the Pokies' as an anthem to resistance.

It is in this tradition that critical voices have appropriated popular readings of neuroimaging to argue for the addictive nature of machines, known colloquially as the 'crack cocaine of gambling', and to resist their spread throughout communities.

For instance, in a test case in Australia, a legal firm together with the new organisation Alliance for Gambling Reform are planning to use consumer laws to argue pokie machine operators engage in 'misleading and deceptive conduct'. In particular, the lights, graphics and sounds that disguise losses as wins and act to reinforce behaviour are the focus of critical legal attention. Jacob Varghese, leading the case for Maurice Blackburn lawyers, invoked science to back up the case, stating that 'what is coming more and more to light through neuroscience is that players are helpless because of the design of the machines' (Varghese 2015). A recent documentary about Australian gambling machines, *Pokie Nation*, underlined such claims, mixing metaphors from neuroscience as well as nineteenth-century ideas about mesmerism to describe how gamblers get 'hooked, hypnotised and hijacked by Australia's electronic morphine' (*ABC News* 2015). Here, it is the interaction of individual biochemistry with a powerful commodity, in this case, a machine, that undermines agency and produces addiction. As Tim Costello, an anti-gambling campaigner, put it: 'People who get addicted to gambling are doing exactly what the machines have designed them to do' (Costello in ABC News, 2017, 2). These kinds of discourse begin to move ideas about addiction beyond the individual to incorporate the role of capital. Like neuroscientific studies of food addiction, medicalised understandings of gambling converge with commercial understandings of the 'bottom line'. The 'bliss point' has its counterpart in 'the zone' – the neurological foundation of desire, as well as the location of profit. What makes fast food so tasty is similar to what makes machine gambling so appealing, and both underscore the ability of consumption to undermine volition and destroy reason. This kind of configuration evokes aspects of earlier critical discourses of the power of consumption, recalling, in some ways, for example, the eighteenth century's concern with dangerous products, and the nineteenth's focus on the wills of susceptible individuals, re-formed here in news ways around the power of twenty-first century capital.

However, in making such arguments, proponents also deny gamblers agency. In these discourses, players are like Pavlov's dogs or Skinner's rats: unable to resist the conditioned response of the sound of bells or coins, 'helpless' because of the way machines act on the brain. This kind of intersection of technology with neurology undermines agency and leads the gambler away from rational action, beyond autonomous subjectivity. Ultimately, the kind of subject produced by the bio-psy forms of knowledge that we have reviewed here appears as an individual driven by a restless desire for novelty and excitement, prey to irrational beliefs and lured into 'the zone' by forces that are beyond their control. It is telling that this apparently helpless, irrational creature appeared at precisely the point when the gambling industry began its global expansion in the 1980s: collateral damage from the deregulatory, competitive climate that also produced an epidemic of obesity at around the same time.

Dematerialised consumption and the disorders of chance

At this point, it is instructive to pull back a little and to look more closely at the ways in which ideas about disordered gambling are produced within this epistemological climate. In particular, this section sets out to parse the criteria of the diagnostic tools which 'make up' the figure of the problematic gambler. In doing this, the argument here is that medicalised understandings of gambling not only draw attention to some of the contradictions of consumption, but also work to highlight convergences between commercial gambling and the wider operation of finance capitalism itself.

Like the neuroscientific and psychological forms of knowledge that diagnose addiction in other areas, the gambling screens are replete with normative judgements about productivity, rationality and self-control. Within them, the disordered gambler emerges as a subject who undermines these ideals. Elsewhere (Reith 2013), I have argued that in this, we can see a continuation of puritanical criticisms about the waste of time and money involved in gambling that were widespread throughout the eighteenth and nineteenth centuries but given new emphasis in an era of neoliberal capitalism in which controlled consumption is valorised as a means of affirming the self and demonstrating responsible citizenship.

The primary theme running through neurocognitive and psychological narratives of gambling disorder is one of irrationality. In them, excessive behaviour is positioned as a problem of deficient reason, based on a range of cognitive errors. As one analysis put it, it is a case of 'faulty or irrelevant incoming information . . . producing erroneous behavioural output' (Zangeneh and Haydon 2004, 3). This is the key flaw that is argued to underscore all the other problems that gamblers have, from their impulsive relationship with time and money to their irresponsible attitude toward family and work. It should be clear from much of the previous discussion in this chapter how many of these 'irrational' beliefs, especially those relating to 'luck' and near misses, are actively encouraged by the industry-state complex of Big Gambling itself. Indeed, the deliberate construction of such beliefs are a core element of the marketing of games of chance – 'it could be you!' as the British National Lottery advertisement promises, and 'it almost was you!', as machines everywhere suggest.

Money is central to these narratives of cognitive deficiency. The way it is perceived and handled and, of course, particularly the way that it is lost, is taken as prima facie evidence of irrationality. After all, who would willingly 'throw good money after bad' in games where there is no hope of winning? The ways that money is used in gambling counters ideas about the rational, productive allocation of resources, expressed in a terminology that reflects normative disapproval. Gambling money is rarely simply 'spent', as it is in other forms of consumption, but is rather 'lost', 'wasted', 'squandered' or 'thrown away' in destructive cycles of loss. In this ratio-centric perspective, money spent on games is money that could be spent on more socially productive and material forms of consumption such as household bills, children's clothes or family holidays. Viviana Zelizer highlights this kind of framing when she uses gambling as a negative example of the uses of money, writing, 'When we earmark money for our child's college fund, we are affirming our parental relationship with that child. On the other hand, by gambling the money away we would seriously undermine that connection' (2011, 90). The hours and days spent on the Internet, in the casino or playing the slot machine is time taken from families, workplaces or engagement in community activities – in other words, time and money that would be better spent on more 'worthwhile' – ostensibly more middle class – pursuits. These kinds of normative judgements about the waste of money, as well as time, involved in gambling are particularly acute when the gamblers in question happen to be poor. The moral panic that developed around the proposals for the 2005 British Gambling Act serves as a case in point. A media uproar was spearheaded by the tabloid newspaper *The Daily Mail*, which started a 'kill the casino bill' campaign against the 'squalid', 'trashy', 'wasteful' activity (1 October 2004), whereas other broadsheets focused on the misery and poverty of the 'pitiful victims' (*The Times* 22 October 2004) or expressed patrician disdain at the 'vast and irreversible cultural change' mass gambling would bring about (Toynbee 2004). Running as a leitmotif through these discourses, from all sides of the political spectrum, however, was a barely concealed disgust towards the pleasures and consumption of the working classes more generally.[9]

These accounts of both financial loss and cognitive deficiency reviewed so far are based on increasingly discredited assumptions about 'the rational economic actor', in which individuals are conceived as utility maximisers, acting from perfect knowledge in ways that are consistent with achieving satisfaction. In these, gambling emerges as a kind of economic behaviour with negative expected value (i.e. gamblers can expect to lose), and so is regarded as antithetical to the self-interest of rational consumers. Indeed, the urge for instant gratification and lack of self-control that depictions of disordered gambling are based on represent the antithesis of ideas about decision-making and forward thinking that responsible subjectivity is supposedly based on, and it is these that the various therapeutic and pharmacological interventions seek to correct. However, as we have seen, the intensity of the zone obliterates this ideal of calculative rationality, and for many players, money is *not*, in fact, the primary goal of gambling. Motives for playing are almost as varied as games themselves and include, amongst other things, the quest for 'action' or excitement (Goffman 1972), the formation of social relationships (Malaby 2003), the display of status and prestige (Geertz 1973) and the affirmation of a sense of self (Reith 1999) as well as, alternatively, the loss of one's self in the zone (Schull 2012). In all of these, although money might be central to involvement in a game, it is not the aim of play itself. Although representing the supreme measure of value in the world outside, for many gamblers, money is simply the medium of play – the price of entry to 'the zone'. The top poker player, 'Chip' Reese, articulated this peculiar devaluation, saying,

> Money means nothing. If you really cared about it you wouldn't be able to sit down at a poker table and bluff off $50,000. If I thought about what that could buy me, I wouldn't be a good player. You treat chips like play money and don't think about it til it's over.
> *(in Alvarez 1991, 42)*

Here, money is simply a counter in a game – quite literally, when cash is converted into shiny coloured chips or virtual currencies in social networks – playthings that are the currency of chance. It is dissociated from material consumption – as Reese put it – '*If I thought about what that could buy me*, I wouldn't be a good player' – and prized not as an end in itself, but for its ability to allow continued consumption in repeated play, to prolong the experience of total immersion in the zone.[10] The inveterate gambler, Fyodor Dostoevsky, who would be diagnosed as 'disordered' in the latest edition of the *DSM*, expressed such indifference towards money when he proclaimed that 'the main thing is the play itself: I swear that greed for money has nothing to do with it' (Dostoevsky 1914, 119). As Baudrillard recognised, quite simply, 'the secret of gambling is that money does not exist as value' (1983, 86).

The desire for intense experience rather than profit in gambling contradicts ideas about the utilitarian value of money, and it also undermines neoliberal ideas about the creative potential of money for building up self-identity and reinforcing social relationships. Money is the great facilitator of the sovereign consumer: the medium of self-sufficiency, self-expression and social cohesion, to be handled with the appropriate attitudes of responsibility and respect – all of which is undermined by the disordered gambler's insouciant approach to playing *with* rather than *for* it. Underlying such accounts is the issue of excessive consumption through the misuse of money – or, rather, lack of money: money spent inappropriately, money spent on the 'wrong' things. In place of the consumption of material goods, the conspicuous consumption – or, perhaps more accurately, conspicuous loss – involved in gambling is a dramatic instance of what Bataille (1985) described as 'unproductive expenditure'. In his essay *Visions of Excess*, Bataille specifically described gambling as such an expenditure: a form of pure consumption that wastes or squanders wealth in an inversion of the values of 'bourgeois' rationality and economic utilitarianism. The anthropologist Clifford Geertz's (1973) notion of 'deep play' also encapsulates these kinds of non-utilitarian expenditures. Characterised by highly charged, high-stakes gambling, such practices challenge ideas about the rational accumulation of wealth and the very notion of pecuniary value itself while demonstrating players' distance from economic utility in games that are played for their own sake or for social rewards.

Today, such unproductive expenditures are institutionalised in a vast global industry, and it is here that some of the broader relations between commercial gambling and more general economic processes become clearer. Jeffrey Nealon has recently used ideas about non-productive expenditures to describe the economy of Las Vegas as a site which, as he puts it, produces 'intensities', described as 'hypnotic states of excess, loss and expenditure', so making it a 'privileged site in the emergence of the newest American economy' (2002, 79).

It is at this point that we can return to some of the considerations outlined at the beginning of this chapter where we noted the convergence between the dematerialised nature of gambling and the wider operation of finance capital. Both share the logic of Marx's formula M-M′ in which money is part of materially unproductive cycles or, in Nealon's words, is 'directly intensified – made greater or smaller – rather than being transformed' (2002, 79). This, in turn, brings us back to Jameson's observation that late capitalism has revealed 'the ultimate structure of the commodity to be addiction itself (or, if you prefer, has produced the very concept of addiction in all its metaphysical richness)' (2004, 52). Gambling unravels some of the meanings of this statement, because it is based on what can perhaps be seen as the ultimate commodity. Marx has already pointed to the 'mysterious qualities' of the commodity (1976 [1867], 163), whose value lies in an abstraction, namely, exchange. This 'metaphysical nicety' is especially the case in gambling, where the source of value lies not in a physical product but in the continual turnover of money, endlessly repeated, in order to continue play itself. It is through this dynamic that the industry derives profit, since players' losses are its gains. The wider system of finance capital itself is similarly abstract, trading on speculation without the creation of tangible goods or services. And so the dissociation from material consumption that takes place in games of chance is mirrored by the divorce of value from material production in the wider economy.

In all of this, then, gambling can be said to represent a unique form of dematerialised consumption that is based on the pure circulation of money and that exemplifies the intensified logic at the heart of late modern capitalist societies.

End points

The expansion of Big Gambling has been embedded in the techno economic systems of late capitalism and driven by deep and multiple ties to state and federal governments. As a result of intersections between states and capital with technology, contemporary societies have become saturated by opportunities to risk money on high-tech, high-speed games of chance in what are effectively aleatory environments of intensive consumption. The spread of these environments, as well as their associated discourses of pathology, have some similarities with the expansion of the obesogenic and intoxicating environments we saw in the last two chapters. Common across all is the engineering of desire in particular kinds of subjective states: 'the zone' in gambling is matched by the 'bliss point' in food.

And, as in those cases, despite the existence of broad structural features that drive the expansion of intensified consumption, we find a familiar focus on the individual as the source of the problems that result. Bio-psy narratives of addiction and disorder interweave with ideologies of responsibility in familiar ways here, although focusing particularly on the mind and rationality of the individual gambler, where the root of the problem is perceived to lie. The devaluation of money that is commonplace in gambling undermines ideals about both rationality and value, and it is this feature that underscores medicalised critiques of the activity as a fundamentally irrational type of consumption. In this framework, the governance of 'irrational' subjects is operationalised largely at the cognitive level: through therapy, as well as drugs, that attempt to restructure the 'faulty' mental processes behind excessive behaviour, and so restore rational, autonomous selfhood.

In a broader sense, this devaluation of money also challenges basic tenets of neoliberalism itself. Rather than the consumption of material goods with which to realise and express the self, the endless repetition of dematerialised consumption in diminishing cycles of loss that is involved in gambling appears as not only wasteful but also supremely insubstantial – contributing nothing to the 'narrative of the self' in which sovereign consumers are supposed to be engaged. In a way, this peculiar form of consumption appears as the consumption of nothing at all.

Notes

1 Despite these convergences, we need to also be mindful of the significant differences between commercial gambling and the broader economic system of 'casino capitalism'. Each is governed by different practices and cultures as well as different types of 'player', acting towards different ends (cf. Cassidy 2009). Furthermore, the gambling industry deals in the sale of risk, where the rules of games are fixed and the probabilities of winning are determined in advance, meaning that the 'price' of gambling is – theoretically – knowable. On the other hand, the system of international finance is based on what can be better described as a form of radical uncertainty, where their sheer complexity means that the price of transactions can be impossible to calculate.
2 Gambling corporations are organised in a similar way to other publicly owned and traded companies, utilising the principles – identified by Ritzer (1993) as 'McDonaldisation' – of calculability and control, through harnessing technology to facilitate mass production of continually updated products, standardisation of prices and odds and investment in market research and advertising strategies to identify and target new markets.
3 Although profitability varies by sector, some – particularly free-standing EGMs which require no staffing and minimal maintenance – are especially lucrative and produce almost pure profit (Young 2011).
4 Similar expansion can be found elsewhere, with Gross Gambling Yield (the amount retained by industry after payments, but minus operational costs) in Great Britain now exceeding £13.6 billion (Gambling Commission 2016) and annual expenditures in Australia of AU$ 19 billion (Productivity Commission 2010).
5 Lotteries exemplify this trend: with their links to public services and 'good causes', they attract language the rest of the industry can only dream of, with patrons described as 'playing', 'participating' or enjoying a 'flutter' – but rarely 'gambling' proper.
6 The number of gambling advertisements increased from 234,000 per year in 2007 to 1.39 million in 2012, with adults viewing approximately six hundred and thirty and under-16s exposed to an average of two hundred and eleven each (Ofcom 2013).
7 They also exemplify what Marc Auge calls 'non-places': the transient spaces of supermodernity that are characterised by pure circulation and consumption. Auge identified gambling as such a space, writing of places in which 'the habitué of supermarkets, slot machines and credit cards communicates wordlessly, through gestures, with an abstract, unmediated commerce' (1995, 63).
8 For example, the South Oaks Gambling Screen (SOGS), the Canadian Problem Gambling Index (CPGI) and the Problem Gambling Severity Index (PGSI), amongst others.
9 At the same time, frequent reference was made to the 'American' companies who were the perceived benefactors of British players' losses. Such a portrait of a foreign invader undermining productivity and corrupting youth is a key narrative around the consumption habits of the poor.
10 Even the *DSM-IV* admitted that 'most individuals with pathological gambling say that they are seeking "action" (an aroused, euphoric state) even more than money' (APA 1994, 616).

AFTERWORD

In a climate of drug wars, obesity epidemics, binge drinking and disordered gambling, consumption is a battleground over ideas about excess, responsibility and risk. New addictions and behavioural disorders appear all the time and lie on the borderlands between morality and medicine.

As we have seen throughout this book, these are only some of the latest expressions of enduring tensions around consumption – the descendants of ideas about *ludomania* and inebriety, of diseases of the will and luxurious excess – given specific form in a system of neoliberal capitalism. From the vantage point of today, it is clear that consumption has always been regarded as problematic. Although it is integral to ideas about selfhood and social status, 'excessive' consumption – especially when carried out by marginalised social groups – has historically been viewed as a potential threat to the social order. This ambivalence is reflected in the semantics of the term itself, whose medicalised connotations of waste and destruction also have some convergence with the idea of addiction as enslavement.

This book has attempted to show how these kinds of ideas about consumption and addiction are inter-related, both as they change over time and in the ways that they are played out across different practices of consumption. It has suggested that ideas about 'addictive consumption', broadly defined, are entwined with processes of imperialism, industrialisation and globalisation in ways that articulate wider concerns about Western ideals of control, productivity and reason.

The shifting problem of consumption

Understandings of 'the problem of consumption' itself are variable and shifting and, like all forms of knowledge, are embedded in their wider socio-economic environment. As Christopher Lasch put it, 'Every era develops its own peculiar forms of pathology, which express in exaggerated form, its underlying character structure' (1979, 41). Tracing these shifting understandings through three historical eras has suggested that, ironically, as consumerism has expanded, explanations for its excesses have become narrower, moving from ideas about dangerous commodities, to defective individual wills, and finally to the neurological circuitry of brains and the inner workings of the psyche. Running throughout all these diverse formulations, however, is the expression of long-running themes in Western thought, which are concerned with the control of 'irrational' excess and desire by the rational, civilising force of society and, in particular, with the tension between autonomy and dependence in both the individual as well as the body politic.

The idea of consumption as a fearful, disruptive force with the power to enslave the individual and the nation emerged with birth of consumer society itself. As we saw in Chapter 1, the first expression of large-scale consumerism in the eighteenth century was met with alarm. As they trickled down the social hierarchy, the criticisms of luxurious excess that were directed at the commodities of colonial commerce expressed mercantile fears about economic dependence, particularly the threat of foreign goods to productivity and their unleashing of newly imagined desires. Concerns about the effects of this emerging materialism were articulated in metaphors of enslavement and dependence in particular ways in which women were positioned as conduits for forbidden desire and dangerous sexuality. Hence, Mandeville's claim that luxury 'effeminates and enervates the People' and criticisms of the emasculating effects of coffee as a 'eunuch's drink': a gendered discourse on the dangers of consumption that persists into the present day.

The medicalising of consumption as a form of economic behaviour also appeared throughout the early modern period, with the pathologising of imported commodities as 'noxious' invaders and bearers of 'epidemical disease': an image of consumption overwhelming both the individual and the social body. In this convergence of physical and economic health, we can see the forerunners of what would come to be an enduring understanding of the problems of consumption in the language of medicine and particularly the idea of excess as a specific kind of disease: whether of the will, in the nineteenth century, or of the brain, in contemporary neuroscience.

Fears about compromised autonomy continued into the nineteenth century, when the epistemological climate of industrial modernity saw a shift in the location of the problem of consumption. Away from exogenous explanations that framed pathology in terms of an invasion of external agents, in a period in which self-control became increasingly important to nation states, ideas about excess moved inwards, in endogenous accounts that focused on pathologies within the individual themselves. In this climate of economic liberalism, the idea of addiction as a disease of the Will was a moral-medical hybrid that expressed the idea of compromised wills too weak to withstand the 'insatiable and bottomless abyss' of desire generated by commodity culture.

Such concerns continued to be gendered, with conditions such as degeneracy or kleptomania reflecting wider anxieties about women's changing status in the nineteenth century as well as Britain's shifting economic position on the global stage. These narratives continued historical dualisms between dependence and autonomy, counterposing the restraint of the will to the disorder of desire, and producing the cultural figure of 'the addict' as an individual who had failed to manage the new relations required by modernity and, rather than being enriched by consumption, was enslaved by it: hence, Thomas Trotter's statement that Britain 'had degenerated into a nation of slaves'.

Today, a globalised system of neoliberal capitalism has spread consumption further around the world and deeper into the interior space of the individual than ever before. Within such a climate, explanations for the excesses of consumption are moving still deeper into the individual, where new forms of neuroscientific knowledge have shifted understandings of addiction from a disease of the will to a disease of the brain as well as a disorder of the psyche.

Throughout the second part of the book, we have noted a convergence between the political economy of neoliberalism with the epistemological climate of neuroscience. A system that generates increasingly intensified forms of consumption, as well as strict demands for self-control, has also produced a proliferation of ideas about addiction. It is no coincidence that, during the 1980s, at the very time when consumption was expanding and intensifying, gambling was being defined as a pathology, the obesity epidemic was underway, the drug wars were raging and myriad forms of consumption were being declared as newly 'addictive'. This was the era of the defective consumer – the pathological gambler, the binge eater, the shopaholic – new identities who were collateral damage of the competitive, deregulatory climate they were made up in. This pathologising trend continues to expand the potential of addiction to an ever-increasing roll call of commodities and experiences, as well as to wider swathes of the population, in tandem with the exponential growth of consumerism itself.

A pathologised version of the desire that is so central to consumer capitalism lies at the heart of these medicalised understandings, which frame the excesses of consumption in terms of a neurobiological 'hijacking' of the brain and a psychological loss of control. It is a narrative that evokes the 'insatiable and bottomless abyss' of the nineteenth century, 'revealed' today through brain scans and diagnostic screens. This is an understanding of addiction which, like ideas about diseases of the will, acts as a metaphor for wider cultural anxieties, in particular those that relate to the proliferation of consumption in neoliberal capitalism and the complex ideologies of freedom, responsibility and choice that guide behaviour within it. The gendering of irresponsible or 'incorrectly' enacted consumption is continued here, where concerns about the effects of excess – particularly of psychoactive commodities – are tied up with concerns about women's sexuality, their reproductive capacities, and their economic position.

As we have seen in the case studies in the second part of the book, the general idea of the overwhelming of individual autonomy by irrational, destructive excess is operationalised in different contexts of consumption. In this sense, it is not the case that the ideas of each historical moment that we looked at in the first section are confined to their particular era, fading into insignificance when it passes. Rather, notions of luxurious excess, compromised willpower and the power of particular commodities linger on, where they continue to influence understandings about the problems of consumption today. And so, the state of intoxication through the consumption of drugs, for example, can be read as an image of the sober, 'civilised' body overtaken by chaotic forces in a condition that undermines ideals of productivity and rational autonomous subjectivity. Meanwhile, the tensions of consumer capitalism are quite literally embodied in food, which acts as a site for the reframing of puritanical struggles between bodily desire and asceticism. Within it, the state of obesity is cast as a physical sign of appetites that have overwhelmed the self, with anorexia representing a triumph of the will over the materiality of the body. And in gambling, what is perceived as the 'irrational' waste of money challenges ideals about reason and value, in a dematerialised activity that appears to undermine the very basis of consumer sovereignty itself.

In different ways, each of these understandings of consumption calls into question the values of reason, productivity and self-control and, in doing so, highlights the contradictory pressures of neoliberal consumer capitalism.

Running as a leitmotif throughout the distinctive historical moments and the case studies of consumption that we considered in Parts One and Two is a concern with the power of uncontrolled consumption to destroy both the individual and the social body, to undermine autonomy and willpower, to 'hijack' reason and erode morality. Each formation links personal consumption with wider socio-economic concerns; with imperial, industrial and neoliberal structures of power, and the gendered, ethnic and class-based relations within them. In different ways, then, these shifting understandings of the problems of consumption can be read as expressions of long-running concerns about loss of control: a condition that hovers around the boundaries of Cartesian dualism: part physical disease, part mental disorder, and located in the hybrid zone between the body and the mind. All share a concern about the dangers of Desire that is uncontrolled by the state, the will, the mind or the chemistry of the brain and produce a disturbing image of the personal and social destruction it leaves in its wake. Such concerns return us to the original, negative meanings of consumption, *consumere* – 'to make away with, to devour, waste, destroy' (OED 2003) – as well as to the root of addiction itself, from *addictus*, where it designated a kind of enslavement – 'to devote, make over; to surrender, to enslave' (OLD 2012).

These ideas about consumption and addiction also articulate an ongoing contradiction within the system of consumer capitalism: namely, that at the same time it produces excess and desire, it also demands self-control and restraint.

The contradictions of consumer capitalism

Although the concepts of excess, desire and waste have long troubled classical economics and notions of rational utilitarian action, as we have repeatedly seen throughout this book, they are also central drivers of consumer capitalism itself. Recognition of the economic value of luxury in the eighteenth century marked the beginning of a transformation of ideas about the value of 'excess' in political economy, and its role in the nineteenth-century social hierarchy was noted by Veblen, in his statement that 'in order to be reputable, it must be wasteful' (1912, 77). Throughout the second part of the book, we have seen how overproduction and waste are increasingly important in the system of neoliberal capitalism which, as Bauman put it, is nothing less than 'an economics of waste and excess' (2007, 48). And, indeed, the issue of waste has been a constant theme throughout our case studies – from the pure financial waste involved in gambling and the graphic bodily waste expelled in bulimia to the psychic state of getting 'wasted' in intoxicating consumption.

The political and economic drivers of neoliberalism encourage the production of whole environments of excess, in what Scott Vrecko calls a 'landscape of temptation and excess' (2010, 559). These are operationalised in different ways in what have been described as intoxicating, obesogenic and aleatory environments, in which psychoactive commodities, cheap, energy-dense foods and commercial gambling are increasingly available and pervasive throughout both local, terrestrial neighbourhoods as well as digital social spaces.

These drivers also produce particular forms of subjectivity. So, for example, the techno-scientific creation of products that are designed to encourage people to 'eat more' generate the experience of the 'bliss point', whereas the engineering of gambling machines to encourage players to extend 'time on device' create 'the zone'. It is here that we saw the convergence between the interests of capital and the epistemology of neuroscience: between commercial understandings of the 'bottom line' and medicalised understandings of addiction, which has seen the food and gambling industries mine neuroscientific knowledge about addiction as part of their aim to manufacture more habit-forming products. The 'bliss point' has its counterpart in 'the zone': the neurological basis of desire, as well as the location of profit.

The result of these commercial, political and scientific trends has been both an intensification and an expansion of consumption which has now come to permeate the rhythms of everyday life, as well as the interior spaces of individuals, more profoundly than ever before.

At the same time, however, as we have repeatedly seen, just as consumption becomes increasingly intensive, so demands for individual self-control become more urgent. The same political-economic drivers that encourage excess also produce new forms of governance to contain them. This is part of a long-running imperative to subjugate desire and the unruly pleasures of the body to the civilising force of society. Today, the enduring historical tension between excess and control and between desire and will is continued in the pairing of ideologies of freedom and responsibility. In this, libertarian ideals about individual freedom, embodied in the figure of the 'responsible sovereign consumer', can be seen as the corollary of the deregulation of markets and the global expansion of mass consumption.

This emerges as the central contradiction of consumer capitalism whereby subjects are required to consume, desire and spend in order to demonstrate responsible citizenship – but not too much. The seductions of the market must be countered by the restraint of sovereign individuals, who are urged to tame excess, to reduce waste and to limit desire. As Sedgewick put it, it is the demand for 'just do it!' coupled with 'just say no!' – to which we might add 'eat more' alongside 'eat less' and 'it could be you!' countered with 'gamble responsibly'. These tensions run through the case studies, where food can be framed as a source of health and biocitizenship as well as of illness and embodied excess, gambling can serve both as a recreational engagement with chance as well as an act of irrational financial destruction, and where the celebratory, but also destructive, potential of intoxicating commodities represents the dualism of the *pharmakon*.

It is in this sense that Guthman and Du Pois's claim about the contradictory aspects of the food system can be applied to the system of consumer capitalism more generally. In the same way that, as they put it, neoliberalism 'encourages (over) eating at the same time that neoliberal notions of discipline vilify it' (2006, 437), so the cultural and political systems of neoliberalism encourage (excess) consumption across a range of practices at the same time they criticise it. And, because this is a normative venture, those who fail to control their behaviour are presented as flawed consumers: an addicted or irresponsible minority who is lacking willpower, self-control or responsibility and is, therefore, also blameworthy. In this, the individualising focus of ideologies of responsibility and addiction act as a discursive sleight of hand that diverts attention from the wider body politic and towards the (defective) body of the individual consumer, who is cast as both the source of the problem as well as the solution.

Such perspectives encourage interventions that work at the level of the individual. So despite the economic and political factors involved in the production of whole environments of excess, the target of battles against it, particularly in medical and policy 'wars' against drugs, tobacco, obesity and gambling, still tends to be largely focused on individual consumers: their bodies and cognitive processes as well as their brains and innermost subjective states. Drawing on debates around public health in the second part of the book we saw how today, sumptuary and disciplinary forms of control are ceding to governance that works at the level of individual subjectivity, where the shibboleths of responsibility are invoked to produce self-governing consumers. This is operationalised in different ways across different forms of consumption. So, for example, the embodied excesses of food are governed through the ongoing care of the self, in which diet, exercise and continual self-monitoring become part of the formation of biological citizenship. In gambling, the governance of 'irrational' subjects is operationalised largely at the cognitive level: through therapy, as well as drugs, that attempt to restructure the 'faulty' mental processes behind excessive behaviour, and so restore rational selfhood. Meanwhile, intoxicating forms of consumption have been incorporated into ideals of self-management, involving the ongoing monitoring of the self to produce a neoliberal kind of 'responsible intoxication'.

Behind such normative forms of persuasion, however, lies the hidden despotism of liberalism: a range of disciplinary and legislative measures that effect more direct forms of control in attempts to enforce the values of sobriety, reason and productivity amongst those who cannot, or will not, control themselves. In their disproportionate scrutiny of the poor, ethnic minorities and women, such measures – from the governance of space to the disciplining of bodies; and from sobriety bracelets to No Smoking Zones – continue the long-standing focus of the 'gaze' of ideas about problematic consumption on marginalised groups, whose problematic pleasures have historically been a source of fear and disgust as well as paternalistic concern, and subject to a range of disciplinary and normative measures to control them.

Trajectories of excess

This critical gaze has also directed the trajectories of various commodities themselves, which continually shift over time in response to changing social relations. Following their trajectories throughout this book has been a journey that reveals the geopolitics of consumption, and it also highlights the social divisions that are both reflected and reinforced in ideas about excess. We have seen, for instance, that many of the commodities involved in discourses of addictive consumption have had complex trajectories, moving in and out of commodity status, between respectability and deviance, and from licit to illicit. Such movement is embedded in shifting relations of power and tied up with status politics: with the social and economic capital of some groups as well as the lack of influence of others. In this context, the public health and philanthropic movements, new forms of scientific knowledge and the shifting habits of the middle classes, amongst other things, have all contributed to the acceptability – or otherwise – of a range of commodities and practices of consumption over time. As well as highlighting the ambivalence of notions of problematic consumption, such fluidity has also thrown into sharp relief the ways that such ideas act as a form of governance.

So during the mercantile period, it was not simply the overseas origin of the colonial commodities but their downwards trajectory through the social hierarchy that was cause for alarm. In this climate, discourses around 'luxurious excess' played a similar role to sumptuary regulations, acting as a form of normative governance that was directed largely towards the poor and emergent 'middling' groups in criticisms of the 'debauched', 'evil' or 'seditious' consumption of commodities such as tea, coffee, tobacco and alcohol. Such invective, however, was also backed up with disciplinary forms of control in a range of statutes that attempted to restrict consumption and impose the values of productivity, sobriety and moderation amongst the population: for example, in the banning of tobacco consumption amongst the poor in a number of European states, German laws outlawing coffee, English ones limiting the consumption of gin and in the prohibition of gambling games and the taxing of dice and cards.

These practices, and the meanings of the commodities they were directed against, were ambivalent, however, and were tied up with the social capital of specific groups of consumers. So at the same time that they were being denounced for their threat to moral and economic well-being, when consumed by different actors, in different contexts, the very same commodities were also regarded as important symbols of the increasing power of the bourgeoisie. Rather than a source of 'epidemical disease' when consumed by 'the very poorest Housewife', when poured by women in the bourgeois parlour, tea was a mark of respectability. Likewise with the consumption of coffee and tobacco, which were variously positioned as emasculating wastages of time or money, or as features of a symbolic male universe of sobriety and productivity.

Nineteenth-century ideas about diseases of the will also tended to focus on the consumption of Victorian 'troublemakers' – especially the urban working classes, women and ethnic minorities – in a 'stratification of the will' that reflected the stratification of industrial society itself. Accordingly, the Victorian era was littered with a range of medical and juridical projects that attempted to instil the values of self-control and reason amongst the consuming population. As a part of this, we saw, for example, how the temperance and public health movements looked upon consumption as an ethical conflict between self-restraint and excess: a battle that was reflected in the trajectory of opium which, over the course of the century, shifted from mass consumption as a panacea of the people to a highly regulated substance and symbol of medical authority.

Today, the shifting trajectories of various commodities continue to reflect and reinforce relations of power and domination. In the second part of the book, considering the changing status of some of the eighteenth century's 'drug foods' through the lens of public health drew attention to the tactics of Big Business in the production and marketing of risky commodities. At the same time, it also highlighted a critical ongoing focus on the consumption and pleasures of marginalised social groups. Now, however, their threat is articulated in discourses of addiction and risk and located largely in individual diets, bodies and brains. During the last decades of the twentieth century, the new public health's 'axis of evil' has found new enemies, with the war on drugs expanding to embrace new battles in the field of consumption. From narcotics, it shifted to tobacco, then to foods like sugar in the war against obesity, and most recently, to gambling. These forms of consumption continue to reflect a socio-geographical gradient, being disproportionally consumed by the poorest social groups, living in the poorest neighbourhoods. At the same time, we have also seen how this gradient of excess produces profits, which are extracted from the 'superconsumers' of alcohol, the 'heavy users' of Coke and the gamblers who 'play to extinction' – the excessive consumers who, in industry terms, are also the best customers.

Although not denying the very real problems correlated with smoking, excessive drinking, gambling and obesity, it is, nevertheless the case that many of the battles against them are, in effect, directed more at their (poor, marginalized) consumers than at the systems that produce them, and are articulated in normative language that, as Kirsten Bell has noted bears a 'striking resemblance' to Victorian criticisms (2011, 3). We saw in Chapter 2 how the Vice Society, for example, claimed to 'extend the happiness and comforts of the poor by checking their destructive excesses' (p. 49): a paternalistic aim that also recalls Nietzsche's authoritarian assertion that 'excess is a reproach only against those who have no right to it' (1987, 124). The ethical battle between self-restraint and excess continues in this normative-medical universe today, where today, 'junk' food is framed as the corollary of trash culture, machine gambling as wasteful and irrational, the excesses of binge drinking as disorderly and unfeminine and smoking as a 'dirty' and selfish habit.

Shifting assemblages of power continually realign practices of consumption over time, and the social gradient of these shifts persists today, with the trajectories of acceptability closely aligned with the social capital of consumers. So, for example, as we saw in Chapter 4, the association of Ecstasy with suburban middle class youth contributed to the increasing acceptability of ideas about its managed consumption as a relatively harmless leisure option. Likewise, advocacy from 'respectable' professional and medical organisations has driven the juridical and normative repositioning of cannabis as a benign, medically beneficial substance and encouraged its development as commercial industry. On the other hand, the denormalisation of tobacco and practices of 'binge drinking' has been intimately related to their associations with lower status groups. Despite the undeniable harms of tobacco, there is also a normative aspect to its trajectory that is symbiotically associated with the lack of social capital of those who consume it. As smoking has moved down the social hierarchy and into the poor countries of the Global South, it has become increasingly stigmatised, with current criticisms of the 'disgusting' and polluting nature of smoke recalling nineteenth-century fears of the 'contagious miasma' of the urban underclass as well as King James I's invective against the 'blacke stinking fumes' of tobacco.

Meanwhile, the trajectories of many other intoxicating commodities are in a state of flux, with a range of scientific and regulatory as well as commercial factors working to blur the boundaries between licit/illicit and acceptable/addictive consumption. What we described as these *simulacra* act as representations of mainstream commodities but with key properties removed. So, for example, the production of diet foods that are consumed but not absorbed transforms the nature of some commodities altogether – from food to chemical 'other' – in ways that recall the blurred distinctions between the drug foods of the eighteenth century. Meanwhile, vaping has emerged as a practice that separates the material act of smoking from the harmful substances at its core, so providing a simulacrum of smoking itself, while 'social gaming' based on intangibles such as virtual items, 'skins' or 'lives' rather than cash disrupts distinctions between gambling and gaming, problematising the very notion of value as it does so.

Such practices highlight the dichotomous ability of consumer capitalism to provide commodified solutions to the very excess it produces, in a commercial sleight of hand that destabilises distinctions between ideas about addiction and practices of consumption. Vaping without smoking, eating without digesting, gambling without money – these are practices that represent emerging frontiers in consumption, and that, to paraphrase Avital Ronell, make us question what it means to consume anything at all.

The shifting trajectories of the commodities involved in discourses of addictive consumption trouble absolutist ideas about addiction, which, when considered over time and across different contexts, emerges as a fluctuating relationship rather than a fixed set of practices or an inherent property of things. Such a broad perspective highlights the complex social relations involved in changing ideas about consumption, addiction and legitimacy which, as we have seen, obscure relations of power and authority as well as normative judgements about productivity and properly managed desire. In this, they return us to Marx's observations on the commodity itself which, he noted, embodies social relations and values like a 'social hieroglyphic' (1976, 163). The commodities that are tied up in trajectories of addictive consumption similarly conceal social relationships 'like a hieroglyphic', their cultural biographies in constant flux as they weave their way through history.

Problematic pleasures

Before leaving this discussion of addictive consumption, we should sound a note of caution. We need to be careful, in considerations of issues such as pleasure, excess and desire, to avoid the implications of a kind of Frankfurt School-type 'manipulationism', whereby demand and desire are simply reduced to the manipulations of the market, and to be wary of accounts that regard consumption as a direct form of domination: a means of 'engineering consent' (Bernays 1947) or an 'opium of the people' that narcotises dissent and induces passivity. At times, Courtwright's historical analysis veers towards this perspective, as do books about the consumption of popular drugs with titles such as *Drugging the Poor* (Singer 2008). As Don Slater (1997) has noted, consumers are frequently presented in terms of a simplistic dualism: either as 'cultural dupes' of the system or, alternatively, as 'heroes' who resist it. However, the complexities of actual consumer behaviour, lived out in particular economic and historical contexts, transcend such schematic accounts. As we have seen, it is not the case that the political-economic structures of capitalism simply 'impose' the state of desire on unwilling consumers. Rather, as Colin Campbell has pointed out, the existence of 'modern autonomous desire' exists independently of consumer capitalism's efforts to generate, encourage or otherwise exploit it (although, of course, as we have seen, such vigorous efforts do go on). Although it is undoubtedly the case that certain forms of what we have termed 'addictive consumption' are linked to structures of domination, the relationships are complex and are not always driven by straightforward, top-down manipulation. Rather, they are fuelled by intersections with consumer desire and agency: with ideas about taste and pleasure, expressions of identity and formations of the self which express, amongst other things, resistance to both the normalising logic of discourses of addiction and to the governance of consumption. Although deeper consideration of these issues is outwith the scope of this book, we can recognise that these are contested fields, subject to agency and active reworking by individuals in number of ways. And so, alongside the undoubted manipulations of modern capitalism is the counterbalance of agency and desire: an ebb and flow of influence that drives the system of consumerism in complex, sometimes unpredictable ways.

These considerations also bring us to issues of desire and pleasure, particularly to the problematic types of pleasures that, as we have seen, are associated with marginalised social groups. The absence of pleasure that has been noted in the literature on drugs (e.g. O'Malley and Valverde 2004) is even more notable by its absence in accounts of addictive consumption more generally. Although not the main focus of this book, we have, nevertheless, noted throughout it that the commodities and practices of 'addictive consumptions' act as conduits of pleasure and desire in a range of ways. From the camaraderie of nights in the pub to the sheer exhilaration of being 'out of it', from the sublime consolations of smoking to the comfort of food, from the anticipation of betting to the escapism involved in the hours spent feeding coins into a machine – these are pursuits that transcend rationalist accounts of responsible action and autonomous subjectivity. The sensuous, social pleasures involved with the embodied practices of drinking, smoking and eating, as well as the dematerialised thrills of gambling, can be celebratory and social as well as deeply fulfilling for the individual. The pleasures of these, and many other kinds of consumption, resist ideals of productivity, sobriety, moderation or self-control. This is consumption that goes beyond health, beyond reason, returning us to Bataille's notion of the importance of unproductive expenditures, excess and waste in economic life. Such ideas problematise concepts about 'rational' economic action as well as neoliberal ideals of autonomous subjectivity. Indeed, Bataille's alternative framework describes features of the structure and experience of consumption elsewhere described as addictive or pathological and discussed in terms of 'luxurious excess' and insatiable desire. In these alternative readings, consumption is subject neither to the rules of scarcity, nor to 'rational' restraint; it has no deeper purpose or utility and is simply pursued as an end in itself.

The continued existence of excess, in different historical formations, and across various practices of consumption challenges long-standing tendencies to pathologise certain types of behaviour. Rather than a troublesome aberration, excess now starts to appear as an inherent feature of the system of consumer capitalism itself. In this reading, obese bodies, pathological gamblers, binge drinkers and unrepentant smokers, amongst others, emerge as cultural figures that are formed in the shadow of ideas about reason and productivity, where they act as both material as well as symbolic counters to the ideology of responsible, controlled consumption itself.

Consideration of such alternative perspectives on excess may be especially timely in a climate in which ideas about addiction are in expansive mode. As we have seen, the spread of a global system of mass consumerism, as well as the development of particular ways of thinking about excess within it, has generated an environment in which long-standing fears about the power of consumerism to undermine autonomy and reason are flourishing. In this permissive climate, the idea of addiction is coming to embrace an increasing variety of commodities and behaviours, as well as wider sectors of the population, who are increasingly regarded as, or who feel themselves to be, at risk from the threat of excessive desire and loss of control. These are the people like Denise, Scott and Kathy, with their problems with shopping and gambling and Coke. But although their problems are certainly unique, situated within the system of neoliberal consumer capitalism and framed in neuroscientific discourses of pathology, they are also part of a much longer standing tradition of concerns about the destructive effects of materialism.

Despite their historical flux and cultural variation, running throughout ideas about the enslavement of foreign commodities, the overwhelming of weak wills and the hijacking of brains are continuing tensions around control and excess that are interwoven with the very development of capitalist modernity itself.

BIBLIOGRAPHY

Abbott, E. (2011) *Sugar: A Bittersweet History*. London and New York: The Overlook Press.
ABC News (2015) *Pokie Nation*. 21 October 2015. At: http://mobile.abc.net.au/news/2015-10-20/pokie-nation-documentary-highlights-australia-gambling-addiction/6856878
Abelson, E. (1989) *When Ladies Go A-Thieving: Middle Class Shoplifters in the Victorian Department Store*. Oxford: Oxford University Press.
Adams, P. (2007) *Gambling, Freedom and Democracy*. New York: Routledge.
AdNews (2016) 'Gambling ads: Place your bets'. *AdNews*. 1 July 2016. At: www.adnews.com.au/news/gambling-ads-place-your-bets
Advertising Standards Association (ASA) (2014) At: www.asa.org.uk/Rulings/Adjudications/2014/3/Paddy-Power-plc/SHP_ADJ_261396.aspx#.VxSlr3gnSfQ
Agrawal, A., Verweij, K.J., Gillespie, N.A., Heath, A.C., Lessov-Schlaggar, C.N., Martin, N.G., Nelson, E.C., Slutske, W.S., Whitfield, J.B. and Lynskey, M.T. (2012) 'The genetics of addiction-a translational perspective'. *Translational Psychiatry* 2, e140.
Alcoholics Anonymous (2001) *The Big Book: The Story of How Many Thousands of Men and Women Have Recovered From Alcoholism*, 4th Edition. New York: Alcoholics Anonymous World Services Inc. At: www.aa.org/assets/en_US/alcoholics-anonymous/b-1-alcoholics-anonymous (accessed 9 October 2016).
Alvarez, A. (1991) *The Biggest Game in Town*. England: Oldcastle Books.
Aldridge, J., Measham, F. and Williams, L. (2011) *Illegal Leisure Revisited: Changing Patterns of Alcohol and Drug Use in Adolescents and Young Adults*. London: Routledge.
Alexander, B., Beyerstein, B.L., Hadaway, P.F. and Coambes, R.B. (1981) 'Effects of early and later colony housing on oral ingestion of morphine in rats'. *Psychopharmacology, Biochemistry and Behavior* 58: 175–179.
American Psychiatric Association (1980) *Diagnostic and Statistical Manual of Mental Disorders*. (DSM-III), 3rd Edition. Washington, DC: American Psychiatric Association.
American Psychiatric Association (1987) *Diagnostic and Statistical Manual of Mental Disorders*. (DSM-III-R), 3rd Edition: Revised. Washington, DC: American Psychiatric Association.
American Psychiatric Association (1994) *Diagnostic and Statistical Manual of Mental Disorders*. (DSM-IV), 4th Edition. Washington, DC: American Psychiatric Association.
American Psychiatric Association (2013) *Diagnostic and Statistical Manual of Mental Disorders*. (DSM 5), 4th Edition. Washington, DC: American Psychiatric Association.
American Society of Addiction Medicine (2016) 'Public Policy Statement: Definition of Addiction'. At: www.asam.org/quality-practice/definition-of-addiction (accessed 9 October 2016).

Andreassen, C.S., Griffiths, M.D., Pallesen, S., Bilder, R.M., Torsheim, T. and Aboujaoude, E. (2015) 'The bergen shopping addiction scale: Reliability and validity of a brief screening test'. *Frontiers in Psychology* 6: 1374.

Appadurai, A. (ed.) (1986) *The Social Life of Things: Commodities in Cultural Perspective*. New York: Cambridge University Press.

Appleby, J. (1993) 'Consumption in early modern social thought'. In Brewer, J. and Porter, R. (eds.) *Consumption and the World of Goods*. London: Routledge, 162–173.

Arcview (2016) *The State of Legal Marijuana Markets*, 4th Edition. Executive Summary. At: https://www.arcviewmarketresearch.com/4th-edition-legal-marijuana-market

Aristotle (2004 [350 BCE]) *Nicomachean Ethics*, 2004 Edition. Trans. J.A.K. Thomson. Harmondsworth: Penguin Classics.

Auge, M. (1995) *Non-Places: An Introduction to Supermodernity*. London: Verso.

Balzac, H. (1977) *The Wild Ass's Skin*. Harmondsworth: Penguin Classics.

Bancroft, A. (2009) *Drugs, Intoxication and Society*. London: Polity Press.

Barbeau, E., Leavy-Spernoius, E. and Balbach, E. (2004) 'Smoking, social class and gender: What can public health learn from the tobacco industry about disparities in smoking?'. *Tobacco Control* 13: 115–120.

Barry, A., Osborne, T. and Rose, N. (eds.) (1996) *Foucault and Political Reason: Liberalism, Neoliberalism and Rationalities of Government*. Chicago: University of Chicago Press.

Bartlett, W. (2001) *First Annual Review of the Global Betting and Gaming Market 2000–2001*. West Bromwich, UK: Global Betting and Gaming Consultants.

Bataille, G. (1985) *Visions of Excess*. Trans. A. Stoekl. Minneapolis: University of Minnesota Press.

Bataille, G. (1991) *The Impossible*. Trans. R. Hurley. San Francisco: City Lights Publishers.

Baudrillard, J. (1983) *Simulations*. Trans. P. Beitchman. New York: Semiotext(e).

Baudrillard, J. (1998) *The Consumer Society: Myths and Structures*. London: Sage Publications.

Bauman, Z. (1998a) *Freedom*. Milton Keynes: Open University Press.

Bauman, Z. (1998b) *Work, Consumerism and the New Poor*. Buckingham: Open University Press.

Bauman, Z. (2005) *Liquid Life*. Cambridge: Polity Press.

Bauman, Z. (2007) *Consuming Life*. Cambridge: Polity Press.

BBC News (2015) 'Obese could lose payments if they refuse treatment'. 14 February 2015. At: www.bbc.co.uk/news/uk-31464897

Beard, P. (2017) 'Hoarder stole £370,000: And blew it on TV shopping channels'. *The Birmingham Mail*. 10 January 2017. At: www.birminghammail.co.uk/news/midlands-news/hoarder-stole-370000-blew-tv-12430816

Beardsworth, A. (1997) *Sociology on the Menu: An Invitation to the Study of Food and Society*. London: Routledge.

Bechara, A. (2003) 'Risky business: Emotion, decision making and addiction'. *Journal of Gambling Studies* 19(1): 23–51.

Beck, U. (1992) *Risk Society: Towards a New Modernity*. London: Sage Publications.

Becker, H. (1973) *Outsiders: Studies in the Sociology of Deviance*. New York: The Free Press.

Becker, P. (2000) *The Self Help Umbrella: Clearinghouse of Self Help Groups in Maricopa County*. Phoenix, AZ: The Self Help Umbrella.

Belk, R. (1988) 'Possessions and the extended self'. *Journal of Consumer Research* 15(2): 139–168.

Bell, D. (1976) *The Cultural Contradictions of Capitalism*. London: Heinemann.

Bell, K. (2011) 'Legislating abjection? Second hand smoke, tobacco control polity, and the public's health'. In Bell, K., McNaughton, D. and Salmon, A. (eds.) *Alcohol, Tobacco and Obesity: Morality, Mortality and the New Public Health*. London: Routledge.

Bell, K., McNaughton, D. and Salmon, A. (eds.) (2011) 'Introduction'. In *Alcohol, Tobacco and Obesity: Morality, Mortality and the New Public Health*. London: Routledge.

Berg, M. (2005) *Luxury and Pleasure in Eighteenth-Century Britain*. Oxford: Oxford University Press.

Berg, M. and Eger, E. (eds.) (2003) *Luxury in the Eighteenth Century: Debates, Desires and Delectable Goods*. Basingstoke: Palgrave MacMillan.

Bermingham, A. (2014) 'My twitter crush on @Paddy Power'. *Utter Digital*. 10 August 2014. At: http://utterdigital.com/digital-marketing/social-media-digital-marketing/my-twitter-crush-on-paddypower/

Bernays, E.L. (1947) 'The Engineering of Consent'. *Annals of the American Academy of Political and Social Science* 250(1): 113–120.

Berridge, V. (2013) *Demons: Our Changing Attitudes to Alcohol, Tobacco and Drugs*. Oxford: Oxford University Press.

Berridge, V. and Edwards, G. (1987) *Opium and the People: Opiate Use in Nineteenth Century England*. London: Allen Lane.

Berry, C. (1994) *The Idea of Luxury: A Conceptual and Historical Investigation*. Cambridge: Cambridge University Press.

Bevilacqua, L. and Goldman, D. (2009) 'Genes and addictions'. *Clinical Pharmacological Therapy* April; 85(4): 359–361.

Bey, H. (1991) *T.A.Z: The Temporary Autonomous Zone: Ontological Anarchy, Poetic Terrorism*. New York: Autonomedia.

Birkmeyer, N.J. and Gu, N. (2012) 'Race, socioeconomic status, and the use of bariatric surgery in Michigan'. *Obesity Surgery*. February; 22(2): 259–265.

Blackman, S. (2004) *Chilling Out: The Cultural Politics of Substance Consumption, Youth and Drug Policy*. Maidenhead: Open University Press.

BMA (2009) *Under the Influence: The Damaging Effect of Alcohol Marketing on Young People*. London: British Medical Association. At: https://www.drugsandalcohol.ie/12380/

Bordo, S. (1993) *Unbearable Weight: Feminism, Western Culture and the Body*. Berkeley: University of California Press.

Borg, M., Mason, P. and Shapiro, S. (1991) 'The incidence of taxes on casino gambling: Exploiting the tired and poor'. *American Journal of Economics and Sociology* 50(4): 323–332.

Bourdieu, P. (1984) *Distinction: A Social Critique of the Judgment of Taste*. London: Routledge and Kegan Paul.

Bourgois, P. (2000) 'Disciplining addictions: The bio-politics of methadone and heroin in the United States'. *Culture, Medicine, and Psychiatry* 24(2): 165–195.

boyd, d. (2011) 'Social network sites as networked publics affordances, dynamics, and implications'. In Papacharissi, Z. (ed.) *Networked Self: Identity, Community and Culture on Social Network Sites*. New York: Routledge, 39–58.

Brain, K.J. (2000) 'Youth, alcohol and the emergence of the postmodern alcohol order'. Occasional Paper No 1. London: Institute of Alcohol Studies. At: www.ias.org.uk/uploads/pdf/IAS%20reports/brainpaper.pdf

Brandt, A. (2009) *The Cigarette Century: The Rise, Fall and Deadly Persistence of the That Defined America*. New York: Basic Books.

Braudel, F. (1979) *Civilization and Capitalism, 15th–18th Centuries*, 3 vols. Vol. 1: *The Structures of Everyday Life*. Trans. S. Reynolds. New York: Harper and Row.

Breiter, H.C., Aharon, I., Kahneman, D., Dale, A. and Shizgal, P. (2001) 'Functional imaging of neural responses to expectancy and experience of monetary gains and losses'. *Neuron* 30: 619–639.

Brewer, J. and Porter, R. (eds.) (1993) *Consumption and the World of Goods*. London: Routledge.

British Crime Survey (2004) *2004–5 British Crime Survey (England and Wales): Technical Report Volume 1*. London: Home Office. At: www.esds.ac.uk/doc/5347/mrdoc/pdf/5347userguide1.pdf

Brownell, K.D. (2004) *Food Fight: The Inside Story of the Food Industry, America's Obesity Crisis and What We Can Do about It*. New York: McGraw-Hill.

Bullet Business (2013) *Marketing for and on Mobile: New Tactics and Best Practice*. At: www.bulletbusiness.com/mobilegambling/pdf/MobileMarketingWhitepaper.pdf

Bunton, R. (2011) 'Permissible pleasures and alcohol consumption'. In Bell, K., McNaughton, D. and Salmon, A. (eds.) *Alcohol, Tobacco and Obesity: Morality, Mortality and the New Public Health*. London: Routledge.

Burroughs, W. (1977) *Junky*. New York: Penguin Classics.

Campbell, C. (1987) *The Romantic Ethic and the Spirit of Modern Consumerism*. Oxford: Basil Blackwell.

Campos, P. (2004) *The Obesity Myth: Why America's Obsession with Weight Is Hazardous to Your Health*. New York: Gotham Books.

#CandyCrushAddiction (2014). Twitter thread. Accessed 22 January 2014.

Canguilhem, G. (1978) *On the Normal and the Pathological*. Trans. C. Fawcett. Dordrecht, Holland: D. Reidel Publishing Company.

Cao, F. and Su, L. (2006) 'Internet addiction among Chinese adolescents: Prevalence and psychological features'. *Child: Care, Health and Development* 33(3): 275–281.

Carmody, B. (2016) 'When silicon valley takes on the Marijuana industry: Growth like the industry has never seen'. *Inc.com*. 18 May 2016. At: www.inc.com/bill-carmody/when-silicon-valley-takes-on-the-marijuana-industry-growth-like-the-industry-has.html

Cassidy, R. (2009) 'Casino capitalism and the financial crisis'. *Anthropology Today* 25(4): 10–13.

Castel, R. (1991) 'From dangerousness to risk'. In Burchell, G., Gordon, C. and Miller, P. (eds.) *The Foucault Effect: Studies in Governmentality*. Chicago: University of Chicago Press.

Castellani, B. (2000) *Pathological Gambling: The Making of a Medical Problem*. New York: State University of New York Press.

Castells, M. (1996) *The Rise of the Network Society, Volume 1: The Information Age: Economy, Society and Culture*. Oxford: Basil Blackwell.

Cedertrom, C. and Spicer, A (2015) *The Wellness Syndrome*. London: Polity.

Cerni, P. (2007) 'The age of consumer capitalism'. *Cultural Logic*. At: http://clogic.eserver.org/2007/Cerni.pdf (accessed 7 October 2016).

Charles, R. (1675) *A Proclamation for the Suppression of the Coffee-Houses*. Digital Version: Janet Clarkson (Australia), Thomas Gloning (Germany). 13 July 2003. At: www.staff.uni-giessen.de/gloning/tx/suppress.htm

Cheney-Lippold, J. (2011) 'A new algorithmic identity: Soft biopolitics and the modulation of control'. *Theory, Culture and Society* 28(6): 164–181.

Chernin, K. (2009) *The Obsession: Reflections on the Tyranny of Slenderness*. London: HarperCollins.

Cheyne, G. (1733) *The English Malady: Or, a Treatise of Nervous Diseases of All Kinds*. London: Strahan.

Chomsky, N. (1991) *Deterring Democracy*. London: Vintage Books.

Clark, L., Lawrence, A. J., Astley-Jones, F. and Gray, N. (2009) 'Gambling near-misses enhance motivation to gamble and recruit win-related brain circuity'. *Neuron* 61: 481–490.

Clark, L., Studer, B., Bruss, J., Tranel, D. and Bechara, A. (2014) 'Damage to insula abolishes cognitive distortions during simulated gambling'. *Proceedings of the National Academy of Sciences of the United States of America*. April 22. 111 (16): 6098–6103.

Clayton, R., Leshner, G. and Almond, A. (2015) 'The extended iSelf: The impact of iPhone separation on cognition, emotion and physiology'. *Journal of Computer Mediated Communication* 20(2): 119–135.

Clotfelter, C.T. and Cook, O. J. (1989) *Selling Hope: State Lotteries in America*. Cambridge, MA: Harvard University Press.

Coffield, F. and Goften, L. (1994) *Drugs and Young People*. London: Institute for Public Policy Research.

Cohen, S. and Taylor, L. (1992) *Escape Attempts: The Theory and Practice of Resistance to Everyday Life*, 2nd Edition. London: Routledge.

Coleman, B. (2011) *Hello Avatar: Rise of the Networked Generation*. Cambridge, MA: MIT Press.

Collin, M. (1996) 'Medicated followers of fashion'. *Time Out*. 12–14 November.

Collin, M. (1997) *Altered State: The Story of Ecstasy Culture and Acid House*. Chatham: Serpent's Tail.

Collins, A.F. (1996) 'The pathological gambler and the government of gambling'. *History of the Human Sciences* 9(3): 69–100.

Comings, D.E. (1998) 'The molecular genetics of pathological gambling'. *CNS Spectrums* 3(6): 20–37.

Conrad, P. and Schneider, J. (1992) *Deviance and Medicalisation: From Badness to Sickness*. Philadelphia, PA: Temple University Press.

Contagious Marketing (2014) 'Where next?' At: www.contagious.com/blogs/news-and-views/14849861-where-next

Costello, T (2017) *ABC News*. 'Crown Casino, pokies maker Aristocrat sued after woman's 14-year gambling addiction'. Reported by Florance, L. and Percy, K. 12 September 2017. At: www.abc.net.au/news/2017-09-12/maurice-blackburn-legal-action-crown-casino-aristocrat-pokies/8895018

Coulombe, A., Ladouceur, R., Desharnais, R. and Jobin, J. (1992) 'Erroneous perceptions and arousal among regular and occasional video poker players'. *Journal of Gambling Studies* 8(3): 235–244.

Coupland, D. (1991) *Generation X: Tales for an Accelerated Culture*. New York: St Martin's Press.

Courtwright, D.T. (2001) *Forces of Habit: Drugs and the Making of the Modern World*. Cambridge, MA: Harvard University Press.

Crawford, R. (1984) 'A cultural account of "health": Control, release and the social body'. In McKinlay, J.B. (ed.) *Issues in the Political Economy of Health Care*. New York: Tavistock.

Cruickshank, B. (1996) 'Revolutions within: Self government and self esteem'. In Barry, A., Osborne, T. and Rose, N. (eds.) *Foucault and Political Reason: Liberalism, Neoliberalism and Rationalities of Government*. Chicago: University of Chicago Press.

Csikszentmihályi, M. (1990) *Flow: The Psychology of Optimal Experience*. New York: Harper and Row.

Cummins, S. and Macintyre, S. (2006) 'Food environments and obesity: Neighbourhood or nation?'. *International Journal of Epidemiology* 35: 100–104.

The Daily Mail (2016) 'Mum addicted to Coke drinks six litres'. 24 January. At: www.dailymail.co.uk/femail/article-3414263/Mum-addicted-Coke-drinks-SIX-LITRES.html#ixzz3yvVEnDuR

Damasio, A. (1995) 'Structure and function of the human prefrontal cortex'. In Holyoak, E.A. (ed.) *Annals of the New York Academy of Sciences*, Vol. 769. New York: New York Academy of Sciences, 241–251.

Davey, M. (2015) 'Pokies operators could face legal action under Australian consumer laws'. *The Guardian*. 22 October. At: www.theguardian.com/society/2015/oct/22/pokies-operators-could-face-legal-action-under-australian-consumer-laws

Davey, S. and Davey, A. (2014) 'Assessment of smartphone addiction in Indian adolescents: A mixed method study by systematic-review and meta-analysis approach'. *International Journal of Preventive Medicine* December; 5(12): 1500–1511.

Dean, M. (1999) *Governmentality: Power and Rule in Modern Society*. London: Sage Publications.

De Andrade, M., Hastings, G. and Angus, K. (2013) 'Promotion of electronic cigarettes: Tobacco marketing reinvented?'. *BMJ* 347.

DeCaria, C.M., Bergaz, T. and Hollander, E. (1998) 'Serotonegenic and noradrenegenic function in pathological gambling'. *CNS Spectrums* 3(6): 38–47.

De Graf, J., Wann, D. and Naylor, T. (2001) *Affluenza: The All Consuming Epidemic*. Oakland, CA: Berrett-Koehler Publishers.

Deleuze, G. (1992) 'Postscript on the societies of control'. *October* 59: 3–7.

Deleuze, G. (1995) *Negotiations*. New York: Columbia University Press.

De Lillo, D. (1985) *White Noise*. New York: Picador.

Department of Culture, Media and Sport (DCMS) (2001) *Gambling Review Report*. London: HMSO Stationary Office.

Department for Education and Employment (1998) *Protecting Young People-Good Practice in Drug Education in Schools and the Youth Service*. London: Author.

Department of Health (2002) *Models of Care for Substance Misuse Treatment: Promoting Equality, Efficiency and Effectiveness in Drug Misuse Treatment Services*. London: Author.

Department of Health (2015) *2010 to 2015: Government Policy: Obesity and Healthy Eating*. Policy Paper: Department of Health. At: www.gov.uk/government/publications/2010-to-2015-government-policy-obesity-and-healthy-eating/2010-to-2015-government-policy-obesity-and-healthy-eating

Department of Health (2016) *Alcohol Guidelines Review: Report from the Guidelines Development Group to the Chief Medical Officers*. Crown Copyright 2015. At: www.gov.uk/government/uploads/system/uploads/attachment_data/file/545739/GDG_report-Jan2016.pdf

De Quincey, T. (1982) *Confessions of an English Opium Eater*. Harmondsworth: Penguin Classics.

Derrida, J. (1981a) *Difference*. Trans. B. Johnson. Chicago: University of Chicago Press.

Derrida, J. (1981b) 'Plato's Pharmacy'. In *Dissemination*. Trans. B. Johnson. London: Athlone Press.

Derrida, J. (1993) 'The rhetoric of drugs'. *Differences: A Journal of Feminist Cultural Studies* 5(1): 1–25.

Discussion #CandyCrushAnonymous (22 January 2014).

Dixon, D. (1991) *From Prohibition to Regulation: Bookmaking, Anti-Gambling and the Law*. Oxford: Clarendon Press.

Bibliography

Dixon, M., Harrigan, K., Sandhu, R., Collins, K. and Fegelsang, J. (2010) 'Losses disguised as wins in modern multi-line video slot machines'. *Addiction* 105: 1819–1824.

Dobbs, R., Sawers, C., Thompson, F., Manyika, J., Woetzel, J., Child, P. et al. (2014) *Overcoming Obesity: An Initial Economic Analysis*. McKinsey Global Institute. November. At: www.mckinsey.com/~/media/McKinsey/Business%20Functions/Economic%20Studies%20TEMP/Our%20Insights/How%20the%20world%20could%20better%20fight%20obesity/MGI_Overcoming_obesity_Full_report.ashx

Doran, B. and Young, M. (2010) 'Predicting the spatial distribution of gambling vulnerability: An application of gravity modelling using ABS mesh blocks'. *Applied Geography* 30: 141–152.

Dostoevsky, F. (1914) *Letters*. Trans. E.C. Mayne. London: Chatto and Windus.

Dostoevsky, F. (1972) *The Gambler*. Trans. V. Terras, Ed. E. Wasiolek. Chicago and London: University of Chicago Press.

Drug Sense (2005) At: www.drugsense.org/wodclock.htm

Dumit, J. (2004) *Picturing Personhood: Brain Scans and Biomedical Identity*. Princeton, NJ: Princeton University Press.

Durkheim, E. (1970 [1897]) *Suicide: A Study in Sociology*. Trans. J.A. Spaulding and G. Simpson. London: Routledge and Kegan Paul.

Durkheim, E. (1984 [1893]) *The Division of Labour in Society*. Trans W.D. Halls. Basingstoke: MacMillan,

Duvall, C. (2015) *Cannabis*. London and New York: Reaktion Books.

The Economist (2004) 'Inside the mind of the consumer'. *Technology Quarterly* Q2. 10 June 2004. At: www.economist.com/node/2724481 (accessed 9 October 2016).

Elias, N. (2000 [1939]) *The Civilizing Process*. Trans. E. Jephcott. London: Blackwell Publishing.

Elias, N. and Dunning, E. (1986) *Quest for Excitement: Sport and Leisure in the Civilizing Process*. Oxford: Basil Blackwell.

European College of Neuropsychopharmacology (ECNP) (2015) 'Food may be addictive: Food craving may be "hard-wired" in the brain'. *ScienceDaily*. 31 August 2015. At: www.sciencedaily.com/releases/2015/08/150831001121.htm

Ewen, S. and Ewen, E. (1982) *Channels of Desire*. New York: McGraw-Hill.

Eyal, N. (2014) *Hooked: How to Build Habit-Forming Products*. London: Penguin Portfolio.

Fahrenkopf, F. (2004) 'Evidence to select committee on draft gambling bill, 2004'. At: www.publications.parliament.uk/pa/jt200304/jtselect/jtgamb/63/40127a05.htm

Falk, P. (1994) *The Consuming Body*. London: Sage Publications.

Federal Trade Commission (2008) *Marketing Food to Children and Adolescents: A Review of Industry Expenditures, Activities, and Self-Regulations*. Washington, DC: Federal Trade Commission. At: www.ftc.gov/os/2008/07/P064504foodmktingreport.pdf

Felski, R. (1995) *The Gender of Modernity*. Cambridge, MA: Harvard University Press.

Fifield, A. (2016) 'Meet the Internet addicted tens forced into rehab'. *Sydney Morning Herald*. 26 January 2016. At: www.smh.com.au/technology/technology-news/meet-the-internetaddicted-teens-forced-into-rehab-20160125-gmdxxh.html#ixzz3yvOnfsb8

Food Marketing Institute (2014) At: www.fmi.org (accessed 7 October 2016).

Forbes, D. (1744) *Some Considerations on the Present State of Scotland*. Edinburgh: Sands, Murray and Cochran.

Foucault, M. (1975) *The Birth of the Clinic*. New York: Vintage Books.

Foucault, M. (1976) *The History of Sexuality*, Vol. 1. Trans. R. Hurley. Harmondsworth: Penguin Classics.

Foucault, M. (1977) *Discipline and Punish: The Birth of the Prison*. London: Allen Lane.

Foucault, M. (1991) 'Governmentality'. In Burchell, G., Gordon, C. and Miller, P. (eds.) *The Foucault Effect: Studies in Governmentality*. Chicago: University of Chicago Press.

Frank, G.K.W., Reynolds, J.R., Shott, M.E., Jappe, L., Yang, T.T., Tregellas, J.R. and O'Reilly, R.C. (2012) 'Anorexia nervosa and obesity are associated with opposite brain reward response'. *Neuropsychopharmacology* 37(9): 2031–2046.

Fraser, S. (2015) 'A thousand contradictory ways: Addiction, neuroscience and expert autobiography'. *Contemporary Drug Problems* 42(1): 38–59.

Fraser, S., Moore, D. and Keane, H. (2014) *Habits: Re-Making Addiction*. Basingstoke: Palgrave MacMillan.

Freeman, B., Kelly, B., Baur, L., Chapman, K., Chapman, S., Gill, T. and King, L. (2014) 'Digital junk: Food and beverage marketing on Facebook'. *American Journal of Public Health* December; 104(12): e56–e64.

Freud, S. (1985 [1930]) 'Civilisation and its Discontents'. In Dickson, A. (ed.) *Civilisation, Society and Religion*. Trans. J. Strachey. Harmondsworth: Penguin Classics.

Friedman, M. (1980) *Free to Choose*. London: Secker and Warburg.

Gadboury, A. and Ladouceur, R. (1989) 'Erroneous perceptions and gambling'. *Journal of Social Behavior and Personality* 4: 411–420.

Gamblers Anonymous (n.d.) At: www.gamblersanonymous.org

Gambling Commission (2016) *Key Facts about Gambling*. At: www.gamblingcommission.gov.uk/news-action-and-statistics/Statistics-and-research/Statistics/Gambling-key-facts.aspx

Geertz, C. (1973) 'Notes on the Balinese Cockfight'. In *The Interpretation of Cultures*. London: Basic Books.

Gever, J. (2010) 'APA: Obesity Rejected as Psychiatric Diagnosis in DSM-5'. *Medpage Today*. 29 May 2010. At: www.medpagetoday.com/MeetingCoverage/APA/20381

Giddens, A. (1991) *Modernity and Self-Identity*. Cambridge: Polity Press.

Giddens, A. (2000) *Runaway World: How Globalisation is Reshaping our Lives*. London: Profile Books.

Gilman, S. (2008) *Fat: A Cultural History of Obesity*. Cambridge: Polity Press.

Gilovich, T. (1983) 'Biased evaluation and persistence in gambling'. *Journal of Personality and Social Psychology* 44: 1110–1126.

Global Gaming Business Magazine (2012) 11(8). At: http://ggbmagazine.com/issue/vol-11-no-8-august-2012/article/windows-on-the-world

Goffman, E. (1972) 'Where the action is'. In *Interaction Ritual: Essays in Face to Face Behavior*. London: Penguin Classics.

Goggin, G. (2006) *Cell Phone Culture: Mobile Technology in Everyday Life*. London: Routledge.

Goggin, G. (2010) *Global Mobile Media*. London: Routledge.

Goodman, J. (1993) *Tobacco in History: The Cultures of Dependence*. London: Routledge.

Goodman, J. (2007) 'Excitantia: Or, How enlightenment Europe took to soft drugs'. In Goodman, J., Lovejoy, P.E. and Sherratt, A. (eds.) *Consuming Habits: Global and Historical Perspectives in How Cultures Define Drugs*. London: Routledge.

Goodman, R. (1995) *The Luck Business: The Devastating Consequences and Broken Promises of America's Gambling Explosion*. New York: Free Press.

The Government's Alcohol Strategy (2012) *Introduction to Government's Alcohol Strategy*. HM The Stationery Office Limited. At: www.gov.uk/government/policies/reducing-harmful-drinking

Granfield, R. and Reinarman, C. (2014) *Expanding Addiction: Critical Essays*. New York: Routledge.

Grant, J. and Kim, S. (2006) 'Medication management of pathological gambling'. *Minnesota Medicine*. September; 89(9): 44–48.

Grier, S. and Kumanyika, S. (2008) 'The context for choice: Health implications of targeted food and beverage marketing to African Americans'. *American Journal of Public Health* September; 98(9): 1616–1629.

Griffin, C., Bengry-Howell, A., Hackley, C., Mistral, W. and Szmigin, I. (2009) 'Every time I do it I absolutely annihilate myself'. *Sociology* 43(3): 457–476.

Griffiths, J. (2011) *Tea: A History of the Drink That Changed the World*. London: Andre Deutsch.

Griffiths, R. and Casswell, S. (2011) 'Intoxigenic digital spaces: Youth, social networking sites and alcohol marketing'. *Drug and Alcohol Review* 29(5): 525–530.

Grittner, U., Kuntsche, S., Gmel, G. and Bloomfield, K. (2013) 'Alcohol consumption and social inequality at the individual and country levels: Results from an international study'. *European Journal of Public Health* 23(2): 332–339.

Gusfield, J. (1963) *Symbolic Crusade: Status Politics and the American Temperance Movement*. Urbana, IL: University of Illinois Press.

Guthman, J. (2011) *Weighing In: Obesity, Food Justice and the Limits of Capitalism*. Berkeley: University of California Press.

Guthman, J. and DuPois, M. (2006) 'Embodying neoliberalism: Economy, culture and the politics of fat'. *Environment and Planning D: Society and Space* 24: 427–448.

Hacking, I. (1986) 'Making up people'. In Heller, T., Sosna, M. and Wellbery, D. (eds.) *Reconstructing Individualism: Autonomy, Individuality and the Self in Western Thought*. Stanford: Stanford University Press.

Hamilton, C. and Dennis, R. (2005) *Affluenza: When Too Much Is Never Enough*. London: Allen and Unwin.
Hanway, J. (1756) *An Essay on Tea*. London: Printed by H. Woodfell M.DCC.LVI.
Hardt, M. and Negri, A. (2000) *Empire*. Cambridge: MA: Harvard University Press.
Harkin, J. (2003) *Mobilisation: The Growing Public Interest in Mobile Technology*. London: Demos.
Harley, N. (2016) 'Sugar addiction like drug abuse, study reveals'. *The Telegraph*. 13 April 2016. At: www.telegraph.co.uk/news/2016/04/13/sugar-addiction-like-drug-abuse-study-reveals/
Harman, H. (2011) 'The problem of betting shops blighting our high street'. At: www.harrietharman.org/uploads/d2535bc1-c54e-6114-a910-cce7a3eff966.pdf (accessed 25 January 2012).
Harris, J.G. (1998) *Foreign Bodies and the Body Politic: Discourses of Social Pathology in Early Modern England*. Cambridge: Cambridge University Press.
Harris, J.L., Schwartz, M.B., Brownell, K.D., Javidizadeh, J., Weinberg, M. et al. (2011) 'Fast food facts: Evaluating sugary drink nutrition and marketing to youth: Rudd center for food policy and obesity'. In *Yale Rudd Centre for Food Policy and Obesity*. Yale University Press. At: www.fastfoodmarketing.org/media/FastFoodFACTS_Report.pdf
Harvey, D. (2006) *Spaces of Global Capitalism: Towards a Theory of Uneven Geographical Development*. London: Verso.
Harvey, D. (2011) *The Enigma of Capital and the Crises of Capitalism*. London: Profile Books.
Hearne, T. (1698) *Remarks and Collections Volume III*. Oxford, England: The Oxford Historical Society, Clarendon Press.
The Heineken Company (2014) 'Heineken launches @wherenext an innovative digital compass to inspire discovery in cities of the world'. 24 July 2014. At: www.theheinekencompany.com/media/media-releases/press-releases/2014/07/1822551
Helm, B. (2010) 'Ethnic marketing: McDonald's is lovin' it'. *Bloomberg Business*. 8 July 2010.
Hewig, J., Kretschmer, N., Trippe, R. et al. (2010) 'Hypersensitivity to reward in problem gambling'. *Biological Psychiatry* 67: 781–783.
Hickman, T. (2007) *The Secret Leprosy of Modern Days: Narcotic Addiction and Cultural Crisis in the United States 1870–1920*. Amherst, MA: University of Massachusetts Press.
Hickman, T. (2014) 'Target America: Visual culture, neuroimaging, and the "hijacked brain" theory of addiction'. *Past and Present* 9: 207–226.
Hilferding, R. (1981) *Finance Capital*. London: Routledge and Kegan Paul.
Hobhouse, H. (2006) *Seeds of Change: Six Plants That Transformed Mankind*. Emeryville: Shoemaker and Hoard.
Hodgins, D.C. and el-Guebaly, N. (2003) 'Natural and treatment-assisted recovery from gambling problems: A comparison of resolved and active gamblers'. *Addiction* 95: 777–789.
Holehouse, M. (2015) 'Cost of obesity, drug abuse and alcoholism to be revealed'. *The Telegraph*. 28 July 2015. At: www.telegraph.co.uk/news/health/news/11769531/Cost-of-obesity-drug-abuse-and-alcoholism-to-be-revealed.html
Hunt, A. (1996) *Governance of the Consuming Passions: A History of Sumptuary Law*. Basingstoke: Palgrave MacMillan.
Inciardi, J. and Cicero, T. (2009) 'Black beauties, gorilla pills, footballs, and hillbilly heroin: Some reflections on prescription drug abuse and diversion research over the past 40 years'. *Journal of Drug Issues* January; 39: 101–114.
Institute of Alcohol Studies (2005) 'Binge Drinking: Nature, Prevalence and Causes'. At: www.ias.org.uk/factsheets/binge-drinking.pdf
Jahiel, R. and Babor, T. (2007) 'Industrial epidemics, public health advocacy and the alcohol industry: Lessons from other fields'. *Addiction* 102(9): 1335–1339.
James, K.I. (1604) *Counterblaste to Tobacco*. G. Putnam and Sons. At: www.laits.utexas.edu/poltheory/james/blaste/
James, W. (1902 [2012]). *The Varieties of Religious Experience: A Study in Human Nature*. Oxford: Oxford World's Classics.
James, W.P., Jackson-Leach, R. and Rigby, N. (2010) 'An international perspective on obesity and obesogenic environments'. In Lake, A., Townshend, T. and Alvanides, S. (eds.) *Obesogenic Environments: Complexities, Perceptions and Objective Measures*. Hoboken, NJ: Wiley Blackwell.

Jameson, F. (1991) *Postmodernism, or the Cultural Logic of Late Capitalism*. Durham, NC: Duke University Press.
Jameson, F. (1997) 'Culture and finance capital'. *Critical Inquiry* 24: 246–265.
Jameson, F. (2004) 'The politics of utopia'. *New Left Review* 25: 35–54.
Järvinen, M. (2012) 'A will to health? Drinking, risk and social class'. *Health, Risk and Society* 14(3): 241–256.
Jernigan, D. and O'Hara, J. (2004) 'Alcohol advertising and promotion'. In O'Connell, B. (ed.) *Reducing Underage Drinking*. Washington, DC: National Academy Press.
Johnson, S. (1775) *A Dictionary of the English Language . . . Volumes I and II*, 4th Edition. Longmans: London.
Jones, A., Bentham, G., Foster, C., Hillsdon, M, and Panter, J. (2007) *Tackling Obesities: Future Choices – Obesogenic Environments. Evidence Review*. Foresight, The Government Office for Science. At: https://assets.publishing.service.gov.uk/government/uploads/system/uploads/attachment_data/file/295681/07-735-obesogenic-environments-review.pdf
Juniper Research (2014) *Mobile Gambling: A Smart Bet, Whitepaper*. Basingstoke: Juniper Research.
Kacen, J. and Lee, J. (2002) 'The influence of culture on consumer impulsive buying behaviour'. *Journal of Consumer Psychology* 12(2): 163–176.
Keane, H. (2002) *What's Wrong with Addiction?* Melbourne: Melbourne University Press.
Kellett, S. and Bolton, J.V. (2009) 'Compulsive buying: A cognitive-behavioural model'. *Clinical Psychology and Psychotherapy* 16: 83–99.
Kindt, J. (2001) 'The costs of addicted gamblers: Should the states initiate mega-lawsuits similar to the tobacco cases?'. *Managerial and Decision Economics* 22: 17–63.
King, A.L.S., Valença, A.M., Silva, A.C.O., Baczynski, T., Carvalho, M.R. and Nardi, A.E. (2013) 'Nomophobia: Dependency on virtual environments or social phobia?'. *Computers in Human Behavior* 29(1): 140–144.
Klein, K. (1999) *No Logo: Taking Aim at the Brand Bullies*. New York: Picador.
Klein, M. (1932) *The Psychoanalysis of Children*. London: Hogarth Press.
Klein, R. (1994) *Cigarettes are Sublime*. Durham, NC: Duke University Press.
Kohn, M. (1987) *Narcomania: On Heroin*. London: Faber and Faber.
Kopytoff, I. (1986) 'The cultural biography of things: Commoditization as process'. In Appadurai, A. (ed.) *The Social Life of Things: Commodities in Cultural Perspective*. New York: Cambridge University Press.
Korn, D. and Shaffer, H. (1999) 'Gambling and the health of the public'. *Journal of Gambling Studies* 15: 289–365.
Lambos, C. and Delfabbro, P. (2007) 'Numerical reasoning ability and irrational beliefs in problem gambling'. *International Gambling Studies* 7(2): 157–171.
Langer, E. (1975) 'The illusion of control'. *Journal of Personality and Social Psychology* 32: 311–328.
Lasch, C. (1979) *Culture of Narcissism: American Life in an Age of Diminishing Expectations*. New York: Norton.
Lears, J. (2003) *Something for Nothing: Luck in America*. New York: Viking, Penguin.
Lee, H., Ahn, H., Choi, S. and Choi, W. (2014) 'The SAMS: Smartphone Addiction Management System and verification'. *Journal of Medical Systems* 38(1): 1.
Leiseur, H. and Blume, S. (1987) 'The South Oaks Gambling Screen (SOGS): A new instrument for the identification of pathological gamblers'. *American Journal of Psychiatry* 144(9): 1184–1188.
Lenoir, M., Serre, F., Cantin, L. and Ahmed, S.H. (2007) 'Intense sweetness surpasses cocaine reward'. *PLoS One* 2(8): 698.
Leshner, A. (1997) 'Addiction is a brain disease, and it matters'. *Science* October 3; 278(5335): 45–47.
Levenstein, H. (1993) *Paradox of Plenty: A Social History of Eating in Modern America*. Berkeley: University of California Press.
Levine, H. (1978) 'The discovery of addiction: Changing conceptions of habitual drunkenness in America'. *Journal of Studies on Alcohol* 39(1): 143–174.
Livingstone, C. (2001) 'The social economy of poker machines'. *International Gambling Studies* 1: 12–45.

Livingstone, C. (2005) 'Desire and the consumption of danger: Electronic gaming machines and the commodification of interiority'. *Addiction Research and Theory* 13(6): 523–534.

Livingstone, C. and Adams, P. (2010) 'Harm promotion: Observations on the symbiosis between government and private industries in Australasia for the development of highly accessible gambling markets'. *Addiction* 106(1): 3–8.

Livingstone, C. and Woolley, R. (2007) 'Risky business: A few provocations on the regulation of electronic gaming machines'. *International Gambling Studies* 7(3): 361–376.

Lovell, A.M. (2007) 'Addiction markets: The case of high-dose buprenorphine in France'. In Petryna, A., Lakoff, A. and Kleinman, A. (eds.) *Global Pharmaceuticals: Ethics, Markets, Practices*. Durham, NC: Duke University Press, 136–170.

Lupton, D. (1995) *The Imperative of Health: Public Health and the Regulated Body*. London: Sage Publications.

Lustig, R. (2012) *Fat Chance: The Bitter Truth about Sugar*. London: Fourth Estate.

Lyng, S. (1990) 'Edgework: A social psychological analysis of voluntary risk taking'. *American Journal of Sociology* 95(4): 851–886.

MacIntyre, S., McIver, S. and Sooman, A. (1993) 'Area, class and health: Should we be focusing on people or places?'. *Journal of Social Policy* 22: 213–234.

MacSween, M. (1993) *Anorexic Bodies: Feminist and Sociological Perspective on Anorexia Nervosa*. London: Routledge.

Malaby, T. (2003) *Gambling Life: Dealing in Contingency in a Greek City*. Urbana, IL: University of Illinois Press.

Mandeville (1714) *Fable of the Bees, or Private Vices, Publick Benefits*, 2 vols, Vol. 1. With a Commentary Critical, Historical, and Explanatory by F.B. Kaye. Indianapolis: Liberty Fund, 1988. 4 October 2016. At: http://oll.libertyfund.org/titles/846

Markham, F. and Young, M. (2015) 'Big gambling: The rise of the global state-industrial gambling complex'. *Addiction Research and Theory* 23(1): 1–4.

Marsh, A. and McKay, S. (1994) *Poor Smokers*. London: Policy Studies Institute.

Marshall, D. and Baker, R. (2001) 'Clubs, spades, diamonds and disadvantage: The geography of electronic gaming machines in Melbourne'. *Australian Geographical Studies* 39: 17–33.

Marx, K. (1972 [1844]) *Economic and Philosophic Manuscripts of 1844*. Trans. M. Milligan. New York: International Publishers.

Marx, K. (1976 [1867]) *Capital*, Vol. 1. Trans. B. Fowkes. London: Penguin Classics.

Marx, K. (1977 [1867]) *Capital*, Vol. 3. Trans. D. Fernbach. New York: Vintage Books.

Marx, K. (1979 [1867]) *Capital*, Vol. 1. Trans. B. Fowkes. London: Penguin Classics.

Matthee, R. (1995) 'Exotic substances: Introduction and global spread of tobacco, coffee, coca, tea, and distilled liquor'. In Porter, R. and Teich, M. (eds.) *Drugs and Narcotics in History*. Cambridge: Cambridge University Press.

May, C. (2001) 'Pathology, Identity and the Social Construction of Alcohol Dependence'. *Sociology* 35(2): 385–401.

McClure, S.M., Li, J., Tomlin, D., Cypert, K.S., Montague, L.M. and Montague, P.R. (2004) 'Neural correlates of behavioral preference for culturally familiar drinks'. *Neuron* October 14; 44(2): 379–387.

McCracken, G. (1988) *Culture and Consumption: New Approaches to the Symbolic Character of Consumer Goods and Activities*. Minneapolis: Indiana University Press.

McKendrick, N., Brewer, J. and Plumb, J.H. (1982) *The Birth of a Consumer Society: The Commercialization of Eighteenth-Century England*. London: Europa Publications.

Measham, F. (2004) 'Play space: Historical and socio-cultural reflections on drugs, licensed leisure locations, commercialization and control'. *International Journal of Drug Policy* 15: 337–345.

Measham, F. and Brain, K. (2005) 'Binge drinking, British alcohol policy and the new culture of intoxication'. *Crime, Media, Culture* 1(3): 262–283.

Mennell, S. (1993) *The Sociology of Food: Eating, Diet and Culture*. London: Sage Publications.

Meredith, S.E., Juliano, L.M., Hughes, J.R. and Griffiths, R.R. (2013) 'Caffeine use disorder: A comprehensive review and research agenda'. *Journal of Caffeine Research* 3(3): 114–130.

Metcalf, A. (1993) 'Living in a clinic: The power of public health promotions'. *Anthropological Journal of Australia* 4(1): 31–44.

Bibliography

Meyer, E. (2014) 'Gambling with America's health: The public health costs of legal gambling'. *The 2x2 Project*. 10 September 2014. At: http://the2x2project.org/gambling-public-health/

Miller, D. (2008) *Stuff*. London: Polity Press.

Millward, D. (2015) 'Cheese as addictive as drugs study finds'. *The Telegraph*. 23 October 2015. At: www.telegraph.co.uk/news/worldnews/northamerica/usa/11949643/Cheese-is-addictive-as-drugs-study-finds.html

Mintz, S. (1985) *Sweetness and Power: The Place of Sugar in Modern History*. New York: Viking.

Moss, M. (2014) *Salt, Sugar, Fat: How the Food Giants Hooked Us*. London: WH Allen.

Mukerji, C. (1983) *From Graven Images: Patterns of Modern Materialism*. New York: Columbia University Press.

Munting, R. (1996) *An Economic and Social History of Gambling in Britain and the U.S.A.* Manchester and New York: Manchester University Press.

Murray, S. (2008) *The (Fat) Female Body*. New York: Palgrave MacMillan.

Nadelmann, E. (1989) 'Drug prohibition in the United States: Costs, consequences and alternatives'. *Science* September 1.

National Conference of State Legislatures (2016) *Drug Testing for Welfare Recipients and Public Assistance*. 28 March 2016. At: www.ncsl.org/research/human-services/drug-testing-and-public-assistance.aspx

The National Institute on Drug Abuse Blog Team (2016) 'Peering into the teen brain: What does risky behavior look like?'. At: https://teens.drugabuse.gov/blog/post/peering-teen-brain-what-does-risky-behavior-look (accessed 8 November 2016).

The National Institute of Health (2008) *Alcohol: A Women's Health Issue*. U.S Department of Health and Human Services: National Institutes of Health. At: https://pubs.niaaa.nih.gov/publications/brochurewomen/Woman_English.pdf

National Research Council (NRC) (1999) *Pathological Gambling: A Critical Review*. Washington, DC: National Academy Press.

Nealon, J. (2002) 'Empire of the intensities: A random walk down Las Vegas Boulevard'. *Parallax* 8(1): 78–91.

Nestle, M. (2002) *Food Politics: How the Food Industry Influences Nutrition and Health*. Berkeley: University of California Press.

Netherland, J. (ed.) (2012) *Critical Perspectives on Addiction*. Advances in Medical Sociology Vol. 14. Bingely: Emerald Group Publishing.

NGISC (National Gambling Impact Study Commission) (1999). *Final Report*. Washington, DC: Government Printing Office. Available at http://govinfo.library.unt.edu/ngisc/index.html

Nicholls, J. (2006) 'Liberties and licenses: Alcohol in liberal thought'. *International Journal of Cultural Studies* 9(2): 131–151.

Nicholls, J. (2012) 'Everyday, everywhere: Alcohol marketing and social media-current trends'. *Alcohol and Alcoholism* 47(4): 486–493.

Nichter, M. (2015) *Lighting Up: The Rise of Social Smoking on College Campuses*. New York: State University of New York Press.

Nicotine Anonymous (2015) At: www.nicotineanonymous.org/publications_content.php?pub_id=456

Nietzsche, F. (1987) *The Will to Power*. Trans. W. Kaufman and R.J. Hollingdale. New York: Random House, 124.

Nutt, D. (2009) 'Equasy: An overlooked addiction with implications for the current debate on drugs harms'. *Journal of Psychopharmacology* 23(1): 3–5.

Ofcom (2013) *Trends in Advertising Activity*. At: www.ofcom.org.uk/__data/assets/pdf_file/0026/53387/trends_in_ad_activity_gambling.pdf

The Office of National Drug Control Policy (2005) *National Drug Control Strategy Budget Summary 2005*. Washington, DC. At: www.whitehousedrugpolicy.gov/

O'Malley, P. (1996) 'Risk and responsibility'. In Barry, A., Osborne, T. and Rose, N. (eds.) *Foucault and Political Reason: Liberalism, Neo-Liberalism and Rationalities of Government*. London: UCL Press.

O'Malley, P. (1999) 'Consuming risks: Harm minimization and the government of "drug users"'. In Smandych, R. (ed.) *Governable Places: Readings in Governmentality and Crime Control*. Ashgate and Dartsmouth.

O'Malley, P. and Mugford, S. (1992) 'The demand for intoxicating commodities: Implications for the "war on drugs"'. *Social Justice* 18(4): 49–75.

O'Malley, P. and Valverde, M. (2004) 'Pleasure, freedom and drugs: The uses of pleasure in liberal governance of drug and alcohol consumption'. *Sociology* 38(1): 25–42.

Orford, J. (2011) *An Unsafe Bet? The Dangerous Rise of Gambling and the Debate We Should Be Having*. London: John Wiley and Sons.

Oxford Economics (2014) 'When Gaming Grows, America Gains'. At: https://www.oxfordeconomics.com/my-oxford/projects/283075

Oxford English Dictionary (2003) *The Oxford English Dictionary*, 2nd Edition. Oxford: Oxford University Press.

Oxford Latin Dictionary (2012) *The Oxford Latin Dictionary*, 2nd Edition. Ed. P.G.W. Glare. Oxford: Oxford University Press.

Parker, H., Aldridge, J. and Measham, F. (1998) *Illegal Leisure: The Normalisation of Adolescent Recreational Drug Use*. London: Routledge.

Parker, H. and Measham, F. (1994) 'Pick "n" mix: Changing patterns of illicit drug use among 1990s adolescents'. *Drugs: Education, Prevention and Policy* 1(1): 5–13.

Parker, H., Measham, F. and Aldridge, J. (1995) *Drugs Futures: Changing Patterns of Drug Use Amongst English Youth*. London: Institute for the Study of Drug Dependence.

Paules, X. (2010) 'Gambling in China reconsidered: Fantan in South china during the early twentieth century'. *International Journal of Asian Studies* 7: 179–200.

Peele, S. (1985) *The Meaning of Addiction*. San Francisco: Jossey Bass.

Peretti, J. (2013) 'Fat profits: How the food industry cashed in on obesity'. *The Guardian*. Wednesday 7 August 2013. At: www.theguardian.com/lifeandstyle/2013/aug/07/fat-profits-food-industry-obesity

Peterson, A. and Lupton, D. (1996) *The New Public Health: Health and Self in the Age of Risk*. London: Sage Publications.

PHAI (2016) *PHAI Files Amicus Brief Comparing Tobacco and Gambling Industries*. Public Health Advocacy Institute. 16 April 2014. At: www.phaionline.org/2014/04/16/phai-files-amicus-brief-comparing-gambling-and-tobacco-industries/

Pine, J. and Gilmore, J. (1999) *The Experience Economy*. Boston: Harvard Business School Press.

Pitts Taylor, V. (2010) 'The plastic brain: Neoliberalism and the neuronal self'. *Health (London)* November; 14(6): 635–652.

Porter, R. (1992) 'Addicted to modernity: Nervousness in the early consumer society'. In Melling, J. and Barry, J. (eds.) *Culture in History: Production, Consumption and Values in Historical Perspective*. Exeter: University of Exeter Press.

Porter, R. (1993a) 'Introduction'. In Brewer, J. and Porter, R. (eds.) *Consumption and the World of Goods*. London: Routledge, 1–18.

Porter, R. (1993b) 'Consumption: Disease of the consumer society?'. In Brewer, J. and Porter, R. (eds.) *Consumption and the World of Goods*. London: Routledge, 58–84.

Potenza, M., Steinberg, M., Skudlarsky, P., Fulbright, R., Lacadie, C., Wilbur, C., Rounsaville, B., Gore, J. and Wexler, B. (2003) 'Gambling urges in pathological gambling: A functional magnetic resonance imaging study'. *Archive of General Psychiatry* 60(8): 828–836.

Powell, L.M., Auld, M.C., Chaloupka, F.J., O'Malley, P.M. and Johnston, L.D. (2007) 'Associations between access to food stores and adolescent body mass index'. *American Journal of Preventative Medicine* 33: S301–S307.

Power, M. (2013) *Drugs 2.0: The Web Revolution That's Changing How the World Gets High*. London: Portobello Books.

Productivity Commission (1999) *Australia's Gambling Industries. Report No. 10*. Canberra: AusInfo. At: http://www.pc.gov.au/

Productivity Commission (2010) *Gambling. Report No 50*. Canberra: AusInfo. At: http://www.pc.gov.au/projects/inquiry/gambling-2009

Public Health England (2015) *Sugar Reduction: The Evidence for Action*. October 2015. At: www.gov.uk/government/publications/sugar-reduction-from-evidence-into-action

Reid, R. (1986) 'The psychology of the near miss'. *Journal of Gambling Behavior* 2: 32–39.
Reinarman, C. (2005) 'Addiction as accomplishment: The discursive construction of disease'. *Addiction Research and Theory* 13(4): 307–320.
Reinarman, C. and Levine, H. (1989) 'Crack in context: Politics and media in the making of a drug scare'. *Contemporary Drug Problems* Winter: 535–573.
Reith, G. (1999) *The Age of Chance: Gambling in Western Culture*. London: Routledge.
Reith, G. (2004) 'Consumption and its discontents: Addiction, identity and the problems of freedom'. *British Journal of Sociology* 55(2): 283–300.
Reith, G. (2005) 'On the edge: Drugs and the consumption of risk in late modernity'. In Lyng, S. (ed.) *Edgework: The Sociology of Risk Taking*. New York: Routledge.
Reith, G. (2007) 'Gambling and the contradictions of consumption: A genealogy of the pathological subject'. *American Behavioral Scientist* 51(1): 33–56.
Reith, G. (2013) 'From the back street to the high street: Commercial gambling and the commodification of chance'. In Blackshaw, T. (ed.) *The Routledge Handbook of Leisure Studies*. Oxon: Routledge.
Reith, G. (2014) 'Techno economic systems and excessive consumption: A political economy of "pathological" gambling'. *British Journal of Sociology* 64(4): 717–738.
Reith, G. and Dobbie, F. (2012) 'Lost in the game: Narratives of addiction and identity in recovery from problem gambling'. *Addiction Research and Theory* 20(6): 511–521.
Responsible Gambling Council (2004a) *BetCheck: Your Responsible Gambling Safety Check*. At: www.responsiblegambling.org/safer-play/betcheck
Responsible Gambling Council (2004b) *Within Limits: Problem Gambling Prevention Month in Ontario*. Tornoto, Ontario: Ontario Responsible Gambling Council.
Ribot, T (1896) *The Diseases of the Will*. Chicago: Open Court Publishing Company.
Richardson, B. (2015) *Sugar*. Cambridge: Polity Press.
Rintoul, A., Livingstone, C., Mellor, A. and Jolley, D. (2012) 'Modelling vulnerability to gambling related harm: How disadvantage predicts gambling losses'. *Addiction Research and Theory* 20: 145–152.
Ritzer, G. (1993) *The McDonaldisation of Society*. Thousand Oaks, CA: Pine Forge Press.
Ritzer, G. (1999) *Enchanting a Disenchanted World: Revolutionizing the Means of Consumption*. Thousand Oaks, CA: Pine Forge Press.
Ronell, A. (1992) *Crack Wars: Literature, Addiction, Mania*. Lincoln and London: University of Nebraska Press.
Room, R. (1969) 'The cultural framing of addiction'. *Janus Head* 6(2): 221–234.
Room, R. (1998) 'Alcohol and drug disorders in the International Classification of Diseases: A shifting kaleidoscope'. *Drug and Alcohol Review* 17(3): 305–317.
Room, R. (2011) 'Addiction and personal responsibility as solutions to the contradictions of neoliberal consumerism'. In Bell, K., McNaughton, D. and Salmon, A. (eds.) *Alcohol, Tobacco and Obesity: Morality, Mortality and the New Public Health*. London: Routledge.
Rose, N. (1999) *Governing the Soul: The Shaping of the Private Self*, 2nd Edition. London: Free Association Books.
Rose, N. (2004) 'Becoming neurochemical selves'. In Stehr, N. (ed.) *Biotechnology, Commerce and Civil Society*. Somerset: Transaction Publishers, 89–128.
Rose, N. and Novas, C. (2005) 'Biological citizenship'. In Ong, A. and Collier, S. (eds.) *Global Assemblages: Technology, Politics and Ethics as Anthropological Problems*. Malden, MA: Blackwell Publishing, 439–463.
Rosenthal, R. and Faris, S. (2016) 'The etymology and early history of "addiction": In the beginning there was gambling'. Paper presented to the 16th International Conference on Gambling and Risk Taking. Las Vegas, Nevada. 7-6-16.
Rush, B. (1785) *Medical Inquiries and Observations upon the Diseases of the Mind*. Philadephia, PA: Grigg and Elliot.
Santry, H., Gilen D., and Lauderdale, D. (2005) 'Trends in bariatric surgical procedures'. *Journal of the American Medical Association* October 19, 294(15): 1909–1917.
Saunders, N. (1997) *Ecstasy Reconsidered*. Saunders: Turnaround.

Savage, M. (2003) 'A new class paradigm? Review essay'. *British Journal of Sociology of Education* 24(4): 535–541.

Schama, S. (1987) *The Embarrassment of Riches: An Interpretation of Dutch Culture in the Golden Age*. New York: Alfred A. Knopf.

Schellinck, T. and Schrans, T. (2008) 'Inside the black box: Using player tracking data to manage risk'. Paper presented at the Conference of the European Association for the Study of Gambling. Nova Gorica. [Cited November 2009]. At: www.easg.org/media/file/conferences/novagorica2008/thursday/1610-ses1/schrans_tracy.pdf

Schivelbusch, W. (1992) *Tastes of Paradise: A Social History of Spices, Stimulants and Intoxicants*. New York: Pantheon Books.

Schlosser, E. (2001) *Fast Food Nation: The Dark Side of the American Meal*. Boston: Houghton Mifflin.

Schor, J. (1999) *The Overspent American: Upscaling, Downshifting and the New Consumer*. New York: HarperCollins.

Schor, J. (2008) 'Tackling turbo consumption'. *Cultural Studies* 22(5): 588–598.

Schrecker, T. and Bambra, C. (2015) *How Politics Makes Us Sick: Neoliberal Epidemics*. Basingstoke: Palgrave MacMillan.

Schull, N.D. (2005) 'Digital gambling: The coincidence of desire and design'. *Annals of the American Academy of Political and Social Sciences* 579: 65–81.

Schull, N.D. (2012) *Addiction by Design: Machine Gambling in Las Vegas*. Princeton, NJ: Princeton University Press.

Schull, N.D. (2015) 'Interview in Pokie nation: How gamblers get hooked, hijacked and hypnotized by Australia's electronic morphine'. *ABC News*. 21 October 2015. At: http://mobile.abc.net.au/news/2015-10-20/pokie-nation-documentary-highlights-australia-gambling-addiction/6856878

Schulte, E.M., Avena, N.M. and Gearhardt, A.N. (2015) 'Which foods may be addictive? The roles of processing, fat content, and glycemic load'. *PLoS One* 10(2).

Schwartz, B. (2009) *The Paradox of Choice: Why More is Less*. London: HarperCollins.

Schwartz, H. (1986) *Never Satisfied: A Social History of Diets, Fantasies and Fat*. New York: Palgrave MacMillan.

Seddon, T. (2009) *A History of Drugs: Drugs and Freedom in the Liberal Age*. London: Routledge-Cavendish.

Sedgewick, E. (1993) *Tendencies*. Durham, NC: Duke University Press.

Sekora, J. (1977) *Luxury: The Concept in Western Thought, Eden to Smollett*. Baltimore and London: John Hopkins University Press.

Shaffer, H.J. (2003) 'A public health perspective on gambling: Four principles'. *AGA Responsible Gaming Lecture Series* 2(1): 1–27.

Shaffer, H.J., Vander Bilt, J. and Hall, M.N. (1999) 'Estimating the prevalence of disordered gambling behavior in the United States and Canada: A research synthesis'. *American Journal of Public Health* 89(9): 1369–1376.

Shammas, C. (1990) *The Pre-Industrial Consumer in England and America*. New York: Oxford University Press.

Shariff, M., Quik, M., Holgate, J., Morgan, M., Patkar, O., Tam, V., Belmer, A. and Bartlett, S. (2016) 'Neuronal nicotinic acetylcholine receptor modulators reduce sugar intake'. *PLoS One* 11(3).

Sheron, N. and Gilmore, I. (2016) 'Fiscal policy, economic factors and the changing alcohol marketplace: Impacts on alcohol-related deaths in England and Wales'. *BMJ* 353: 1–7.

Sherratt, A. (2007) 'Peculiar substances'. In Goodman, J., Lovejoy, P.E. and Sherratt, A. (eds.) *Consuming Habits: Global and Historical Perspectives in How Cultures Define Drugs*, 2nd Edition. London: Routledge.

Shewan, D., Dalgarno, P. and Reith, G. (2000) 'Perceived risk and risk reduction among ecstasy users: The role of drug, set and setting'. *The International Journal of Drug Policy* 10: 431–453.

Shiner, M. and Newburn, T. (1997) 'Definitely, maybe not? The normalization of recreational drug use amongst young people'. *Sociology* 31(3): 511–529.

Shiner, M. and Newburn, T. (1999) 'Taking tea with Noel: The place and meaning of drug use in everyday life'. In South, N. (ed.) *Drugs: Cultures, Controls and Everyday Life*. London: Sage Publications.

Bibliography

Shortt, A. (2013) 'Marketing for and on mobile: New tactics and best practice'. *Bullet Business*. At: www.bulletbusiness.com/mobilegambling. © FC Business Intelligence ® 2012.

Shortt, A. (2014) 'Bringing gambling to the "always on" consumer'. The Mobile and Tablet Gambling Summit. Atlantic City, U.S.A. 28–29 October.

Showalter, E. (1985) *The Female Malady: Women, Madness and English Culture 1830–1980*. London: Virago.

Shulgin, A. (1991) *PIHKAL: Phenethylamines I Have Known and Loved: A Chemical Love Story*. Berkeley, CA: Transform Press.

Singer, S. (2008) *Drugging the Poor: Legal and Illegal Drugs and Social Inequality*. Long Grove, IL: Waveland Press.

Skeggs, B. (1997) *Formations of Class and Gender: Becoming Respectable*. London: Sage Publications.

Skinner, B.F. (2004) *Science and Human Behaviour*. New York: Free Press.

Slater, D (1997) *Consumer Culture and Modernity*. London: Sage.

Smith, A. (1776) *An Inquiry into the Nature and Causes of The Wealth of Nations*, 5th Edition. London: Methuen and Co.

Smith, L.P., Ng, S.W. and Popkin, B.M. (2013) 'Trends in U.S. home food preparation and consumption: Analysis of national nutrition surveys and time use studies from 1965–1966 to 2007–2008'. *Nutrition Journal* 12: 45.

Smith, W.D. (1992) *Consumption and the Making of Respectability, 1600–1800*. London: Routledge.

Smith, W.D. (2007) 'From coffeehouse to parlour: The consumption of coffee, tea, and sugar in North-Western Europe in the seventeenth and eighteenth centuries'. In Goodman, J., Lovejoy, P.E. and Sherratt, A. (eds.) *Consuming Habits: Global and Historical Perspectives in How Cultures Define Drugs*. London: Routledge, 154–155.

Smith, W.D. (2014) 'This is what Candy Crush Saga does to your brain'. *The Guardian*; Neuroscience: Notes and Theories. Tuesday 1 April 2014. At: www.theguardian.com/science/blog/2014/apr/01/candy-crush-saga-app-brain

Sobal, D. and Maurer, D. (1999) *Weighty Issues: Fatness and Thinness as Social Problems*. New York: Aldine de Gruyter.

Sombart, W. (1913 [1922]) *Luxury and Capitalism*. München: Duncker and Humblot. Ann Arbor: University of Michigan Press.

Sontag, S. (1978) *Illness as Metaphor*. New York: Farrar, Straus and Giroux.

SOOMLA. Yaniv Nizan (2014) 'Addictive games: Getting users to dream about virtual goods'. Paper presented at Casual Connect Conference. Amsterdam. 11–13–14. At: www.slideshare.net/yanivnizan/addictive-games-final

Sours, J. (1980) *Starving to Death in a Sea of Objects*. New York: Jason Aronson.

South, N. (ed.) (1999) *Drugs: Cultures, Controls and Everyday Life*. London: Sage Publications.

Spanier, D. (1992) *All Right, O.K, You Win: Inside Las Vegas*. London: Mandarin.

Standage, T. (2007) *A History of the World in Six Glasses*. New York: Atlantic Books.

Standing, G. (2011) *The Precariat: The New, Dangerous Class*. London: Bloomsbury.

Stanley, C. (1996) *Urban Excess and the Law*. London: Cavendish.

The Star (2015) 'Local care home manager stole 42,000 from vulnerable residents'. 14 August. At: www.thestar.co.uk/news/local/care-home-manager-stole-42-000-from-vulnerable-residents-to-fund-out-of-control-shopping-addiction-1-7409354

The State Journal (2014) 'Gambling addict's widow claims WV casino exploited her husband's out-of-control behavior'. 8 August 2014. At: www.statejournal.com/story/26236710/gambling-addicts-widow-claims-casino-exploited-her-husbands-out-of-control-behavior

Strange, S. (1986) *Casino Capitalism*. Manchester: Manchester University Press.

Swinburn, B. and Figger, G. (2002) 'Preventive strategies against weight gain and obesity'. *Obesity Reviews* 3: 289–301.

Talbot, M. (2009) 'Brain gain: The underground world of "neuroenhancing" drugs'. *New Yorker*. 27 April 2009.

Tallis, R. (2011) *Aping Mankind: Neuromania, Darwinitis and the Misrepresentation of Humanity*. Slough, Buckinghamshire: Acumen Publishing.

Tanabe, J., Thompson, L., Claus, E. et al. (2007) 'Prefrorotal cortex activity is reduced in gambling and nongambling substance abuse use during decision-making'. *Human Brain Mapping* 28: 1276–1286.

Thomas, S., Lewis, S., McLeod, C. and Haycock, J. (2011) '"They are working every angle": A qualitative study of Australian adults' attitudes towards, and interactions with, gambling industry marketing strategies'. *International Journal of Mental Health and Addiction* 12(1): 111–127.

Thompson, H.S. (1972) *Fear and Loathing in Las Vegas*. London: Paladin.

Torres, C.A. and Goggin, G. (2014) 'Mobile social gambling: Poker's next frontier'. *Mobile Media & Communication* 2(2): 94–109.

Toynbee, P. (2004) '700,000 reasons to ditch those Las Vegas dreams'. *The Guardian*. 21 April 2004. At: www.theguardian.com/politics/2004/apr/21/society.politicalcolumnists

Triggle, N. (2014) 'Obesity is the new smoking, says NHS boss in England'. *BBC News*. 18 September 2014. At: www.bbc.co.uk/news/health-29253071

Trocchi, A. (1992) *Cain's Book*. London: Calder.

Trocki, C. (1999) *Opium, Empire and the Global Political Economy*. London: Routledge.

Tsai, G. (2000) 'Eating disorders in the Far East'. *Eating and Weight Disorders: Studies on Anorexia, Bulimia and Obesity* 5(4): 183–197.

Tuggle, J. and Holmes, J. (1997) 'Blowing smoke: Status politics and the Shasta County smoking ban'. *Journal of Deviant Behaviour* 18(1): 77–93.

Turner, B. (2008) *The Body in Society: Explorations in Social Theory*, 3rd Edition. London: Sage Publications.

The U.S. Weight Loss Market (2015) *Status Report and Forecast*. Marketdata Enterprises. At: www.bharatbook.com/healthcare-market-research-reports-467678/healthcare-industry-healthcare-market-research-reports-healthcare-industry-analysis-healthcare-sector1.html

Vale, A. (2015) 'Please tweet responsibly: The future of alcohol brands on twitter'. At: www.audiense.com/please-tweet-responsibly-the-future-of-alcohol-brands-on-twitter-marketing-tips-strategy/

Valverde, M. (1997) 'Slavery from within: The invention of alcoholism and the question of Free Will'. *Social History* 22(3): 251–268.

Valverde, M. (1998) *Diseases of the Will: Alcohol and the Dilemmas of Freedom*. Cambridge: Cambridge University Press.

van Dijk, J. (2012) *The Network Society*, 3rd Edition. London, Thousand Oaks CA, New Delhi, and Singapore: Sage Publications.

Van Holst, R., van der Brink, W., Veltman, D. and Goudriaan, A. (2010) 'Brain imaging studies in pathological gambling'. *Current Psychiatry Reports* 12(5): 418–425.

Van Ree, E. (1997) 'Fear of drugs'. *International Journal of Drug Policy* 8(2): 93–100.

Varghese, J. (2015) 'Landmark pokies legal challenge on the cards'. *The Age*. 22 October 2015. At: www.theage.com.au/victoria/landmark-pokies-legal-challenge-on-the-cards-20151021-gketox.html

Veblen, T. (1899) *The Theory of the Leisure Class*. London: Allen and Unwin.

Victorian Gaming Machine Industry (2004) *Gamblers Help*. Victoria, Australia: Author.

Virilio, P. (1977) *Speed and Politics: An Essay on Dromology*. New York: Semiotext(e).

Volberg, R. A. (2001) *When the Chips Are Down: Problem Gambling in America*. New York: The Century Foundation Press.

Volkow, N. and Li, T (2004) 'Drug addiction: the neurobiology of behavior gone awry'. *National Review of Neuroscience* 5(12): 963–970.

Vrecko, S. (2010) 'Global and everyday matters of consumption: On the productive assemblage of pharmaceuticals and obesity'. *Theory and Society* 39: 555–573.

Wagenaar, W. (1988) *Paradoxes of Gambling Behaviour*. Hove and London: Lawrence Erlbaum Associates.

Wallman, J. (2014) *Stuffication: Living More with Less*. London: Penguin Classics.

Walton, S. (2003) *Out of It: A Cultural History of Intoxication*. New York: Three Rivers Press; Reprint edition. October.

Wardle, W., Keily, R., Astbury, G. and Reith, G. (2012) 'Risky places? Mapping gambling machine density and socio-economic deprivation'. *Journal of Gambling Studies* 30: 201–212.

Weber, M. (1985 [1930]) *The Protestant Ethic and the Spirit of Capitalism*. London: Counterpoint.

Weinberg, D. (2005) *Of Others Inside: Insanity, Addiction, and Belonging in America*. Philadelphia, PA: Temple University Press.

Welsh, I. (1993) *Trainspotting*. Edinburgh: Vintage Books.

Welte, J., Wieczorek, W., Barnes, G.M., Tidwell, M.-C. and Hoffman, J.H. (2004) 'The relationship of ecological and geographic factors to gambling behavior and pathology'. *Journal of Gambling Studies* 20: 405–423.

Wheeler, B., Rigby, J. and Huriwai, T. (2006) 'Pokies and poverty: Problem gambling risk factor geography in New Zealand'. *Health and Place* 12: 86–96.

WHO (2007) *The Challenge of Obesity in the WHO European Region and the Strategies for Response*. Branca, F., Hikogsian, H. and Lobstein, T. (eds). At: http://www.euro.who.int/__data/assets/pdf_file/0008/98243/E89858.pdf

WHO (2014) *The Economic and Health Benefits of Tobacco Taxation*. At: http://www.who.int/fctc/mediacentre/news/2015/WHOTobaccoReport.pdf

Wild, A. (2005) *Black Gold: A Dark History of Coffee*. London: Harper Perennial.

Wilde, O (1891) *The Picture of Dorian Gray*. London: Ward, Locke and Co.

Williams, R. (1982) *Dream Worlds: Mass Consumerism in Nineteenth Century France*. Berkeley: University of California Press.

Williams, R. and Wood, R. (2004) *The Demographic Sources of Ontario Gaming Revenue*. Report Prepared for the Ontario Problem Gambling Research Centre. At: http://stoppredatorygambling.org/wp-content/uploads/2012/12/The-Demographic-Sources-of-Ontario-Gaming-Revenue.pdf

Williams, S. (2015) 'Thirty stone at thirteen: Meet the obese teenagers going under the knife'. *The Guardian*. 19 September 2015. At: www.theguardian.com/society/2015/sep/19/obese-teenagers-gastric-surgery-sally-williams

Withington, P. (2011) 'Intoxicants and society in early modern England'. *The Historical Journal* 54(3): 631–657.

Withington, P. (2014) 'Introduction: Cultures of intoxication'. *Past and Present* 9: 9–33.

Withington, P. (2017) 'Alcohol and consumption in the early modern era'. In Tlusty, A. (ed.) *A Cultural History of Alcohol: Early Modern World*. London: Bloomsbury.

Woolley, R. and Livingstone, C. (2010) 'Into the zone: Innovating the Australian poker machine industry'. In Kingma, S.F. (ed.) *Global Gambling: Cultural Perspectives on Gambling Organisations*. London: Routledge, 38–63.

Wordsworth, W. (1807) *The World Is Too Much with Us*. Chicago: Poetry Foundation.

World Drug Report (2014) *World Drug Report*. Vienna: United Nations office on Drugs and Crime.

Wynn, S. (2016) Keynote presented to the 16th International Conference on Gambling and Risk Taking. Las Vegas, Nevada. 7–6–16.

Yeomans, H. and Critcher, C. (2013) 'The demon drink: Alcohol and moral regulation, past and present'. In Blackshaw, T. (ed.) *Routledge Handbook of Leisure Studies*. Oxon: Routledge.

Young, M. (2011) 'Towards a critical geography of gambling spaces: The Australian experience'. *Human Geography*: 33–47.

Young, M., Lamb, D. and Doran, B. (2011) 'Gambling, resources and racial economy: An analysis of EGM expenditure patterns in three remote Australian towns'. *Geographical Research* 49: 59–71.

Yudkin, J. (1972) *Pure, White and Deadly: How Sugar Is Killing Us and What We Can Do about It*. London: Penguin Classics.

Zangeneh, M. and Haydon, E. (2004) 'Psycho-structural cybernetic model, feedback and problem gambling: A new theoretical approach'. *International Journal of Mental Health and Addiction* 1(2).

Zelizer, V. (2011) *Economic Lives: How Culture Shapes the Economy*. Princeton, NJ: Princeton University Press.

Zola, E. (2008) *The Ladies Paradise*. Trans. B. Nelson. Oxford: Oxford University Press.

INDEX

addiction: commodities and 7; definition of 6, 33, 69, 149; as a 'disease of the will' 38–42; disordered identities and the proliferation of 71–73; expanding landscape of 63–74; as form of enslavement/surrender 33–34; gambling 1, 135–144; heroin 73; making up 67; as metaphor 70–71; modernity and 36–38; neuroscientific explanations 63–66, 82; psychological explanations 63, 67–73; quasi-medical ideas about 41–42; risk and 73–74, 138–140; socio-economic status and 42; term of medical pathology 6
addicts 50–52
advertising 56–57, 84–87
African Americans 47–48, 106
alcohol 13, 16–20, 24, 26–27, 31, 39–40, 54, 84, 89–91, 151
Alcohol-Free Zones 99
Alcohol Harm Reduction Strategy 97–99
Alcoholics Anonymous (AA) 71–72
ale 26
aleatory environments 129–131
algorithmic identity 56
Alliance for Gambling Reform 140
American Psychiatric Association 67
American Society of Addiction Medicine (ASAM) 67–68
amphetamines 89
anorexia 121–122
Appadurai, Arpan 18
Apple, Inc. 1
aqua vitae ('water of life') 15, 26
Aristotle 17
Armstrong-Jones, Ronald 42
'autonomous imaginative hedonism' 58

Balzac, Honore 127
Bambra, Clare 108
Bancroft, Angus 24, 92
barbiturates 89
Bataille, George 5, 20, 81, 93, 100
Bauman, Zygmunt 3, 55–58, 60, 62, 72, 123, 149
beer 26
Belk, Russell 56
Bell, Daniel 5
Bell, Kristen 95, 152
Bernays, Edward 56–57
Berridge, Virginia 44, 45, 54
Beware of Luxury ['In Weelde Siet Toe'] (Steen) 20, 21
Big Food: manufacture of desire 105–106; marketing junk 106–108; medical-industrial complex and 114; producing excess 104–105
Big Pharma 114
Big Sugar 105
binge drinkers 97–99
'binge eating disorder' (BED) 109
biopolitical control 42–43, 83, 109, 113, 123
biopolitical economy 114
Blackman, Shane 93
bliss 105–106
body image 113–114
Bordo, Susan 113–114, 120, 121
Bourdieu, Pierre 113
Bourgois, Philippe 83
Brain, Kevin 90, 92
Brandt, Allan 93
brandy 16
Braudel, Fernand 15, 108
Brownell, Julie 112
bulimia 122–123

caffeine 40, 116
'caffeine use disorder' 112
Cameron, David 98, 119
Campaign for Fairer Gambling 140
Campbell, Colin 2, 57–58, 69, 122, 154
Canguilhem, Georges 71
cannabis 87–88
capitalism 7, 14, 43, 55, 57, 104–105, 126–127, 149–151
Capital (Marx) 7
Casswell, Sally 90
Castells, Manuel 55
Cheney-Lippold, John 56
Chernin, Kim 117
Cheyne, George 27, 118, 120
Chinese opium addicts 46–47, 81
Chomsky, Noam 81, 83
Civilization and Capitalism (Braudel) 15
Civilization and Its Discontents (Freud) 5
Clifford, Denise 1, 155
Coca-Cola 1, 107, 112, 118, 152, 155
cocaine 47–48
coca leaf 16
coffee 15–19, 24–25, 28–30, 40, 54, 151
cognitive deficiency 142–143
Coleridge, Samuel 42, 81
colonialism 14–15
commodities: addiction and 7; critical discourses on 19–20; economic impact of global 17–18; 'fetishism' of 7; psychoactive 14–19; read as 'social hieroglyphics' 7, 18, 34; shifting trajectories of 151–153; trajectories of 54–55
Confessions of an English Opium-Eater (De Quincey) 42, 81
consumption: biomedical governance 42–43; conspicuous 14, 20, 33–34, 37; 'contagious' aspects of 48; contradictions of consumer capitalism 149–151; definition of 5, 28, 149; desire and 55–60; disciplinary practices to regulate 48–49; discontents 3–6; disorders of chance and dematerialised 141–144; drivers of 55–60, 69; dualism of 18–31, 62; emergence of a new vocabulary of 41–42; etymology of word 5, 72–73; hyper 57; legislation to outlaw/regulate forms of working class 49; medicalisation of ideas about 27–28, 44, 63, 67–73, 147; negative associations of 6–7; neuroscientific explanations 74–75; obesity and 108–109, 120–121; pathologised notion of 27; political-economic system as driver for global expansion of 55–60, 84, 148, 150; problematic pleasures 153–155; psychological explanations 75; relations between smuggling/contraband and 33; responsible 54; risky types of 73–74, 93–97, 100, 108–109, 120–121; role in social hierarchy 20–21, 37; self-realisation through 2–3; shifting problem of 146–149; taxation 32–33; tensions embodied in
5–6; term of medical pathology 33; therapeutic interventions 49–50; 'turbo' 57
contagion 27–28, 37, 43, 44, 47, 96
contraband 33
Costello, Tim 141
Counterblaste to Tobacco (King James I of England) 25, 96
Coupland, Douglas 55
Courtwright, David 15, 24, 54, 96–97, 115, 153
craving 105–106
Criminal Justice and Police Act of 2001 99
Cultural Contradictions of Capitalism, The (Bell) 5
Czikszentmihalyi, Mihaly 130

dark net 88
Defoe, Daniel 31
de Lillo, Don 3
department stores 36
De Quincey, Thomas 42, 81
Derrida, Jacques 7, 79
designer drinks 90
desire 17–18, 39, 54–60
Diagnostic and Statistical Manual of Mental Disorders (DSM-5) 67–69, 109, 137–138
diatetick management 27, 118, 120
Dickens, Charles 47
dipsomania 40–41
discipline 82–83, 117–118
Diseases of the Will, The (Ribot) 40
Diseases of the Will (Valverde) 41
disease theory 42
distilled spirits 15, 16, 26
Division of Labour in Society, The (Durkheim) 37
Doyle, Arthur Conan 47
drug foods 14–15, 115, 152
drugs: alcohol 13, 16–20, 24, 26–27, 31, 39–40, 54, 84, 89–91; cannabis 87–88; commodification and normalisation 83–91; denormalisation and new forms of governance 91–99; Ecstasy 84–87, 88, 89, 100, 152; intoxication and governance 80–83; legal highs 88–89; opium 15–16, 23–24, 26, 42–46, 54, 81; pharmaceutical 88–89; tobacco 15–18, 24–25, 28, 30, 32, 40, 54, 93–97
'drug scares' 81
drug trades 15
Dunning, Eric 92
Dupuis, E. Melanie 119, 150
Durkheim, Émile 37–38, 44, 70, 72, 96

East India Company 16, 21, 23
eating disorders 2, 108–113, 119–123
Economic and Philosophic Manuscripts (Marx) 37
Ecstasy 84–87, 88, 89, 100, 152
Edwards, Griffith 44, 45
electronic gaming machines (EGMs) 129–131, 133, 134

Electronic Nicotine Delivery Systems (ENDS) 96
Elias, Norbert 92
England's Treasure by Forreign Trade (Mun) 21–22
English Malady, The (Cheyne) 27
Ephedra 114–115
epidemics of the will 73
Esquirol, J.E.D. 40
Essay on Tea (Hanway) 22
eudaimonia (desire) 17–18
Ewen, Elizabeth 3, 60
Ewen, Stuart 3, 60
excess 5, 20, 37, 104–105, 151–153
Eyal, Nir 57

Fable of the Bees (Mandeville) 31
Facebook 1, 56, 90, 106, 131–132
fast food 107
Fat Chance (Lustig) 112
(Fat) Female Body, The (Murray) 121
Felski, Rita 40–41
'fetishism' 7
Fielding, Henry 26
foetal alcohol syndrome 26, 98–99
food: body image and 113–114; commercial strategies of Big Food 104–108; eating disorders 108–113, 119–123; hidden despotism of 118–119; neurochemical selfhood and 109–110; 'techno products' 115
Foucault, Michel 42, 48, 50–51, 61
Fraser, Suzanne 64, 67
freedom 54, 60–63
Freud, Sigmund 5
Friedman, Milton 60
functional Magnetic Resonance Imaging (fMRI) 64

gambling: addiction 1; community based and political forms of resistance to 140–141; dematerialised consumption and the disorders of chance 141–144; emergence of global industry 126–129; governing risk 138–140; intensified consumption and the spread of aleatory environments 129–135; neuroscientific explanations for addiction 136–137, 141; poor gamblers 134–135; Protestant critique of 25; psychological explanations for addiction 135, 137–138; regulation 128–129; risky technologies and addiction 135–141; social/mobile technologies 131–134
Gambling Act of 2005 129
Gaming Act of 1845 49
General Foods 115–116
Giddens, Anthony 3, 60, 62, 71
gin 19, 26
Gin Act of 1736 26
Gin Lane 26, 98–99
'Gin Lane' (Hogarth) 26

Global North 54–55, 62, 105
Global South 54, 105
global trading 14–15
Goggin, Gerard 56, 131
Goodman, Jordan 18, 30–31
Goodman, Robert 128
governance: biopolitical 42–43, 83, 109, 123; of consuming bodies 113–119; denormalisation and new forms of 91–99, 150; freedom and 60–63; intoxication and 80–83; risk 138–140; of space and the mobilisation of morality 93–99
Governance of the Consuming Passions (Hunt) 20
Griffiths, Richard 90
Gusfield, Joseph 87
Guthman, Julie 119, 150

habit-forming products 57–58, 69
Hacking, Ian 50
Hanway, Jonas 22–23, 27
Hardt, Antonio 57
Harvey, David 127
healthism 118
Hearne, Thomas 6
Heineken Company 90–91
heroin 73
Hickman, Timothy 43, 46, 48
History of Sexuality (Foucault) 50–51
Hobbes, Thomas 27
Hogarth, William 26
Holmes, Malcolm 96
Hooked (Eyal) 57
Hume, David 31–32
Hunt, Alan 20, 22

identity 55–57
idleness 25
Illness as Metaphor (Sontag) 70
Inebriates Act of 1879 49
Inebriates Act of 1898 49
inebriety 41
informational capitalism 55
insatiability 57–58
International Statistical Classification of Diseases and Related Health Problems (ICD-10) 112
Internet addiction 1, 2
intoxication: disciplinary and biopolitical control 82–83; drug use and 81–82; governance and 80–83

James I, King of England 25, 96, 152
Jameson, Fredric 125
James, William 81
Jarvinen, Margaretha 92

Keane, Helen 69, 122
Klein, Naomi 55

176 Index

Klein, Richard 97
kleptomania 40–41
Kohn, Mark 42, 44
Kopytoff, Igor 18, 45
Kraepelin, Emil 40
Kruger, Barbara 122
Kubla Khan (Coleridge) 81

Ladies' Paradise, The (Zola) 36
Lasch, Christopher 73, 146
legal highs 88–89
Leshner, Adam 69
Leshner, Alan 64
Levenstein, Harvey 113
Leviathan (Hobbes) 27
Levine, Harry 81–82
Levinstein, E. 46
Licensing Act of 2003 89
Lustig, Robert 112
luxury: associations with women 22; association with 'foreignness' 21; consumption and 19–22; contagion of 27–28; critical discourses on 19–21, 25, 27–28; democratisation of 36; dualism of 22; presented as 'the Other' 28; reinterpretation of 32; relationship between affluence and health 27–28; role in social hierarchy 20–21, 37; transformation of 31–33
Lyng, Steve 92

MacSween, Morag 122
Mandeville, Bernard 31–32
marketing 56–57, 106–108
Markham, Francis 128
Marx, Karl 7, 18, 34, 37, 51, 69, 126–127, 152
Maudsley, Henry 44
McCracken, Grant 58, 69
McGlone, Francis 111
Measham, Fiona 90, 92
mental disorder 109–110
mephedrone 88
mercantilism 15–16, 28, 75
methadone 83
Mill, John Stuart 5
Ministry of Sound 84–85
Mintz, Sidney 17, 18
mobile technologies 55–57, 90, 131–134
monomania 40–41
More, Hannah 39
morphine 46
morphinism 46
Moskowitz, Howard 106
Moss, Michael 105–106, 111
Mun, Thomas 21–22
Murray, Samantha 121

Narcomania (Kohn) 44
National Anti-Gambling League 49

National Institute on Drug Abuse (NIDA) 64
Negri, Michael 57
neoliberalism 3, 60–61, 147–148, 150
Nestle, Marion 104, 115
neuroenhancers 89
neuroscience 63–66, 82, 136–137, 141
Nicholls, James 91
Nicomachean Ethics (Aristotle) 17
nicotine 40
Nietzsche, Friedrich 5, 20
No Logo (Klein) 55

obesity 108–109, 120–121, 152
O'Malley, Pat 60
oniomania 40
opiates 39–40
Opioid Use Disorder 68–70
opium 15–16, 23–24, 26, 42–46, 54, 81
Opium and the People (Berridge and Edwards) 45
O'Sullivan, Kathy 1, 155
'the Other' 28
Out of It (Walton) 81
OxyContin 89

Paradox of Choice (Schwartz) 62
Pareto Principle 107
pharmaceutical drugs 88–89
Pharmacy Act of 1868 45, 49
pharmakon 79–80, 83–84, 123, 150
Philip Morris 115–116
Picture of Dorian Gray, The (Wilde) 47
Pitt, William 33
Plato 6
Plato's Pharmacy (Derrida) 79
'The Politics of Utopia' (Jameson) 125
Porter, Roy 33–34, 38
Positron Emission Tomography (PET) 64
Pring, Christopher 114
Protestant work ethic 25
'psychoactive revolution' 15
public health 116–117, 152
punishment 82–83
Pure, White and Deadly (Yudkin) 112

racialised discourses 46–48
Reinarman, Craig 81–82
Ribot, Theodule 40
risk 73–74, 93–97, 100, 108–109, 138–140
Ritzer, George 57
Romantic ethic 57–58, 84
Romantic Ethic and the Spirit of Modern Consumerism, The (Campbell) 2, 57
Ronnel, Avital 46
Room, Robin 7, 84
Rose, Nikolas 63
rum 16
Rush, Benjamin 39

Salt, Sugar, Fat (Moss) 105–106
Savage, Mike 69
Schlosser, Eric 107
Schor, Juliet 57
Schrecker, Ted 108
Schwartz, Barry 62
Schwartz, Hillel 116, 117
Sedgewick, Eve 73, 150
Sekora, John 20, 28
self-control 54
self-fulfilment 2–3, 6, 84
self-governance 117–118
self-realisation 2–3, 6, 17
Shariff, Masroor 112
Shewan, David 92–93
'Silk Road' 88
Slater, Don 154
slavery 15–16, 21, 28
smartphones 1, 2
Smith, Adam 31–32
Smith, Goldwin 47
Smoking Opium Exclusion Act of 1908 49
Smollett, Tobias 26
smuggling 33
Snapchat 106
'social gaming' 132
social influence marketing 56–57
social media 2, 56–57, 90–91, 106, 131–134
social technologies 55–57, 90, 131–134
Society for the Suppression of the Opium Trade (SSOT) 47, 48
Sontag, Susan 70
Sours, John 121
Standage, Tom 16
Steen, Jan 20
Stevens, Scott 1, 155
Stevens, Simon 108
Street Betting Act of 1853 49
Street Betting Act of 1874 49
Street Betting Act of 1906 49
'substance use disorder' (SUD) 67
sugar 15–18, 28, 30–31, 54, 105, 110–113, 152
Suicide (Durkheim) 37–38
sumptuary law 19–20

Talbot, Mary 89
taxation 32
tea 15–19, 22–24, 28–31, 33, 54, 151
technology: neuroscience 64–66; social/mobile 55–57, 90, 131–134
'techno products' 115
television shopping addiction 1
Theory of the Leisure Class, The (Veblen) 37
tobacco 15–18, 24–25, 28, 30, 32, 40, 54, 93–97, 151, 152

Torres, Albarres 56, 131
Trainspotting (Welsh) 73
Trotter, Thomas 40
Tuggle, Justin 96
Turner, Bryan 57
Twitter 56, 90, 106, 131–132

Unbearable Weight (Bordo) 113

Vale, Andy 90
Valium 46
Valverde, Mariana 41, 61, 69, 93
van Dijk, Jan 55
Van Ree, Erik 100
vaping 96
Varghese, Jacob 140
Veblen, Thorstein 37
Vice Society 49, 152
Vicodin 89
Victorian morality 48
Visions of Excess (Bataille) 81
Vrecko, Scott 64, 149

'Walmart capitalism' 104
Walton, Stuart 81
War on Drugs 54, 64, 80, 82–83, 94, 100, 152
Wealth of Nations, The (Smith) 32
Weber, Max 5
weight reduction industry 115
Weinberg, Darin 41–42
Welsh, Irvine 73, 122
Wesley, John 23
White Noise (de Lillo) 3
Wilde, Oscar 47
will 38–42, 71
Williams, Rosalind 5, 36
wine 26
Withington, Phil 5, 27, 32, 80
women: consumption of opiates by 46; gin consumption 26; shopping 32; suffering disease of kleptomania 40–41; tea drinking 22–23, 29–30; treatments for various forms of addictive consumption 50; use of opium-based medicines for children 45
Wordsworth, William 37
'World Is Too Much With Us, The' (Wordsworth) 37
Wynn, Steve 130

Xenophon, Nick 140

Young, Martin 128
Yudkin, John 112

Zola, Emile 36